IN MY FATHER'S FOOTSTEPS

WITH THE 53RD WELSH DIVISION
FROM NORMANDY TO HAMBURG

IN MY FATHER'S FOOTSTEPS

WITH THE 53RD WELSH DIVISION FROM NORMANDY TO HAMBURG

GWILYM DAVIES

Pen & Sword
MILITARY

This edition published in 2015 by

Pen & Sword Military
An imprint of
Pen & Sword Books Ltd.
47 Church Street
Barnsley
South Yorkshire
S70 2AS

Copyright © Coda Publishing Ltd. 2015.
Published under licence by Pen & Sword Books Ltd.

ISBN: 9781473833548

A CIP catalogue record for this book is available from the British Library.

Printed and bound in England
By CPI Group (UK) Ltd., Croydon, CR0 4YY

Pen & Sword Books Ltd. incorporates the imprints of Pen & Sword Aviation, Pen & Sword Family History, Pen & Sword Maritime, Pen & Sword Military, Pen & Sword Discovery, Pen & Sword Politics, Pen & Sword Atlas, Pen & Sword Archaeology, Wharncliffe Local History, Wharncliffe True Crime, Wharncliffe Transport, Pen & Sword Select, Pen & Sword Military Classics, Leo Cooper, The Praetorian Press, Claymore Press, Remember When, Seaforth Publishing and Frontline Publishing

For a complete list of Pen & Sword titles please contact
PEN & SWORD BOOKS LIMITED
47 Church Street, Barnsley, South Yorkshire, S70 2AS, England
E-mail: enquiries@pen-and-sword.co.uk
Website: www.pen-and-sword.co.uk

CONTENTS

INTRODUCTION

*M*y father was called up for service in August 1941. His twentieth birthday was still a couple of weeks away, and he had to put his study for a degree in metallurgy at Swansea University on hold. His first three years in the army were spent training or on active service in various parts of the UK, including a spell with 117 Heavy Anti-aircraft Regiment serving on 4.5 inch anti-aircraft guns deployed in defence of Scapa Flow. In 1942, he attended a War Office Selection Board and was passed fit for Officer training. He went on to eventually serve as a Captain in the Royal Artillery as part of the 53rd (Welsh) Division. He was Troop Leader of F Troop, 497 Battery of 133 Field Regiment. Their weaponry consisted of the famed 25-pounder, possibly the most important artillery piece of the Allied Forces in World War II. From late June 1944, to the eventual surrender of the German Armed Forces at Luneberg in May 1945, the 53rd Welsh saw almost continual action as they fought their way through Northern France, Belgium and Holland, before entering Germany in the spring of 1945. In the course of just ten months, as they criss-crossed France, Belgium, Holland and Germany, the Division covered over 1,900 miles, and went through more than 1.3 million rounds of 25-pounder shells. The 53rd suffered 9,849 casualties, officers and men, killed, wounded and missing. On the plus side, they captured 35,000 enemy troops along the way, and a further 40,000 at the end of the war in Hamburg.

Shortly before he passed away in 2005, I discovered among his papers, a manuscript of my father's war diaries recounting his memories of the Second World War. They run from the time he was called up in 1941 through to the end of the war, which in his case was near Hamburg. I believe they were written towards the end of the 1990s. I'm pleased to say his decision to put pen to paper was inspired by a book I gave him entitled 'The History of the 53rd Welsh Division in the Second World War', by Brigadier C N Barclay, C.B.E., D.S.O.

Like many World War II veterans, he spoke little of his active service, although in later years, he did confide in me about certain memories. His brother, who served as a Captain in the Royal Navy told me that my father's war action had been brutal at times, and having spent many months researching the role of the 53rd Welsh Division and the 133rd Field Regiment in particular, I can now understand what he meant.

When I was much younger, my father took the family on a journey around Europe, and we visited many of the towns and cities you will read of in this book. As a small boy, I could not really understand the significance some of these places held in my father's memory, although I very much can now. I can still picture certain of the places we visited such as the beaches at Arromanches, the streets of Antwerp, the mountains and forests of the Ardennes and the row upon row of gleaming white tombstones at the military cemeteries at Arnhem and Nijmegen. My journey back through these places this year, with my knowledge of the role of the 53rd (Welsh) Division in 1944-45 has brought my father's diaries into sobering context.

I am fortunate that my father also left us a photograph album, which I have used to help illustrate this book, and which gives us an invaluable vision of life at the front. Copies of these images have been passed to the museums of the Royal Artillery and the Royal Welsh Regiment. Included in this album are a few photographs from the camera of a deceased SS Officer he came across.

My research persuaded me that the time had come to do him the honour of preparing his memoirs for publication. After all, he had clearly written the diaries with the intention that they would be read by others. The book you now hold is the result of that pledge and I am deeply grateful to Charles Hewitt at Pen and Sword for showing the faith in me to allow the manuscript to reach the printed page.

Like many of his contemporaries he attended regimental reunions up until a few years before his death and was privileged to be invited by the people of 's-Hertogenbosch to celebrate the anniversary of the town's liberation by the 53rd. Indeed my mother and father forged strong friendships with a few families from Den Bosch, and visited the town regularly until they were no longer able to travel. I was fortunate to be able to meet up with Jan de Wit and Pierre Kisters when we visited Den Bosch in 2014. The spirit of friendship and appreciation is still very strong in Den Bosch and these two men went out of their way to show us the town's memorials to the 53rd Welsh and invited us back there to join in the 70th Anniversary Celebrations of their liberation from years of German occupation. I was privileged to be able to read the Book of Remembrance listing the details of the 146 men of the 53rd (Welsh Division) who gave their lives in the liberation of Den Bosch. Pierre also recounted to us his memories of those days back in 1944 when he was just four years old.

As I read his memoirs once more, it is strange to read that as a twenty-three year old he had never visited London, a trip I make regularly in the line of work. His first footsteps in France would have been as he disembarked in June 1944. We take travel very much for granted these days, but if we stop to think for a moment, it is because of the men such as my father that we are able to travel across Europe without a second thought.

In order to present the diary in its proper context I have added some of the history of the 53rd from books and archives. In order to round out the picture I also felt it was worthwhile to add some information from the German perspective. As I began to work on the diary I felt that there was also the possibility of a film for television. I'm pleased to say that this idea found favour with my colleagues at the Visions of War Channel and the film has now been completed and will be available on DVD. It is very much a personal journey but I am proud of the result we achieved on screen.

With the 70th Anniversary of the D-Day landings on the horizon I decided that the book would benefit from a return to the battlefields. It was an idea I had toyed with for a long time, but with the last of the old veterans slipping away I knew the final opportunity had come and it was now time for me to undertake a journey back to France and to trace my father's footsteps onwards through Belgium and France to Holland and Germany.

The journey began at the East India Docks in London where he boarded the American Liberty Vessel, USS William Phips at the start of his journey to do his part in the great fight to liberate Europe. He was not a *"hero"* in the truest sense of that all too often used word, in that he won medals for valour; but he certainly was a hero to people of the farm outside Bethune whom he helped to liberate in October 1944. In common with thousands of men just like him, he made the ultimate sacrifice and gave up some of the "best" years of his life to protect the future of people yet to be born. He wore his campaign medals with pride every Armistice Day and the hairs on the back of my neck still rise whenever I hear the words of Laurence Binyon's poem, "For the Fallen" which my grandmother recited every day at our village Armistice Day Service.

"They shall grow not old, as we that are left grow old:
Age shall not weary them, nor the years condemn.
At the going down of the sun and in the morning,
We will remember them."

I am indebted to the many sources I consulted in the writing of this book and I have included them in a list of acknowledgements later in this book, but I feel I must mention the following now, The Royal Artillery Association, The Royal Welsh Regiment Museum and the National Archives. The help they have given me has been unstinting and given freely and I thank them for their time and help. I have also read other contemporary accounts of the role of the 53rd Welsh and in particular 497 Battery. These include:

'The History of the 53rd Welsh Division in the Second World War' by Brigadier C. N. Barclay, C.B.E., D.S.O.

'Sheldrake' by Major Dick Hughes, M.C., a man I was fortunate enough to meet when we stayed at his hotel in Falmouth in the late 1960s and who was my father's Commanding Officer. I must also thank Dick's son Paul, who has shared with me many of his father's photographs and maps and allowed me to use these and quote from his father's book.

'For Gunners Sake' by L. J. Hughes, a Gunner from Lancashire who served in 497 Battery.

'Red Crown and Dragon' by Patrick Delaforce.

'Team Spirit' by Major A. D. Bolland, M.B.E..

While I have undertaken extensive research in the writing of this book, and the making of the film, I am not a trained historian and I would ask that you therefore forgive any factual inaccuracies. This is history, but history from the heart.

GWILYM DAVIES
STRATFORD-UPON-AVON
SEPTEMBER 2014

- CHAPTER I -
IN MY FATHER'S FOOTSTEPS

*M*y father served in 497 Battery, part of the 133rd Field Regiment of the Royal Artillery. A regiment consisted of twenty-four 25-pounders split into three batteries of eight guns. Each infantry battalion when in action generally had an artillery regiment assigned to it; throughout the war in Europe, 497 Battery frequently supported the 2nd Battalion of the Monmouthshire Regiment, an infantry battalion of the 53rd Welsh Division. "The Mons" as they were known, comprised some 1,200 officers and men. They were assigned to one of four Infantry Companies, A, B, C and D Companies, each of around 300 men. Each Company consisted of three Platoons, of around 100 men. From time to time, the gunners of 497 Battery also found themselves acting in concert with the 1/5th Welsh. 497 Battery comprised two troops, E and F troops, each composed of four of these highly effective field guns. It was these guns which would fire over the infantry as they advanced towards the enemy. It's important to note that the guns were also the cause of the vast majority of enemy casualties. Something like eighty per cent of the casualties on both sides resulted from artillery fire.

The 25-pounder was probably the most important artillery piece of the Second World War. They were versatile, mobile and deadly effective in combat. The guns had a calibre of 3.45 inches and a range of seven miles. They were capable of firing a wide range of ordnance, at rates of up to eight shells per minute. The guns were handled by a crew of six men known as the gun detachment. The full complement comprised the following: No. 1 – the detachment commander was always a sergeant, No. 2 – operated the breech and rammed the shell, No. 3 – was the gun layer, No. 4 – was the loader, No. 5 – passed the ammunition, No. 6 – also handled the ammunition and was also known as the 'coverer', he was also second in command and responsible for ammunition preparation and operating the fuse indicator. The official 'reduced detachment' was four men. A total battery complement was some 200 men.

The 25-pounder was the main field artillery weapon used by British Commonwealth and colonial infantry and armoured divisions of all types during the Second World War. Throughout the war each British-pattern infantry division such as the 53rd (Welsh) Division was established with a complement of seventy-two 25-pounders, organised into three field artillery regiments (sometimes referred to as battalions). Regiments were further organised into batteries of eight guns.

Many different companies manufactured the guns and component parts in the UK. Vickers Armstrong in Scotswood, Baker Perkins in Peterborough and Weirs in Glasgow were some of the most significant. The various Royal Ordnance factories produced most of the ordnance components. In all, over 13,000 25-pounders were manufactured worldwide. The rate of fire, coupled with the speed at which it could be deployed caused devastation, and the German troops were in awe of it.

The artillery targets were under the control of the Battery Tactical HQ (Tac), who would be based in a Halftrack for ease of movement through the battlefield. They would move in conjunction with the Infantry tactical command vehicle, Battalion HQ, at or near the front line of battle. The Battery Commander would designate an Observation Post (OP) typically within the battle front line, either in another halftrack or a high vantage point such as a building. The OP, manned by a Battery Forward Observation Officer (FOO) would radio back the target coordinates and direct the gunfire.

Occasionally, heavier artillery was required and the Medium and Heavy batteries would be called into action. These had larger guns and specialised ammunition but were not as mobile as the Light Artillery.

The radio of WWII vintage was still relatively primitive, but was an essential means of communication at the battle front. Code words were used to improve communication, ensuring vital orders got through to the gun crews. The wireless code for a call to action for the guns was

"Sheldrake" which would be called through together with the target coordinates.

My story starts on August 13th 1941. This was the day that my father left his home in the village of Clydach in the Swansea valley to take his place in the fight for Europe. He was just shy of his twentieth birthday, and had to forego his studies in metallurgy at Swansea University. At the end of World War II he took a two year commission in the Indian Army, returning to the UK in 1947, when he returned to University, but did not conclude his studies, but went on to work in the tinplate industry in South Wales until his retirement in 1981. For the first three years of his service, he spent his time in the UK undergoing training in the various weapons of the Royal Artillery, which included a spell on anti-aircraft duties in Scapa Flow.

The main theme of this book is to follow his journey, and that of the 53rd (Welsh) Division in which he served, from June 1944, when he left the East India Docks in London to join the combined Allied Forces in Normandy, to the unconditional surrender of the German Army at Luneburg Heath in May 1945. This was a ten month journey through Northern Europe, witnessing some of the heaviest action of this campaign, and the liberation of a multitude of grateful civilians who had seen their homelands occupied by the Germans for four terrible years. One of the principal towns to be the liberated, in October 1944, was 's-Hertogenbosch. The citizens of this particular Dutch town forged a strong link with the men of the 53rd in October 1944, and he was honoured to revisit many years later to join in the celebration of their liberation. Following this he forged lifelong friendships with a number of families from the town.

I will start by including an excerpt from my father's wartime diaries, covering the period from his call up to the time just before he boarded the USS William Phips for the start of the fight in Normandy. This gives a valuable insight into the life of these young men, for whom life had changed out of all recognition following their call up. For those who survived, the next ten months would see their lives changed forever.

"I awoke to a bright and sunny morning on Monday, 13th August 1941. It was to be the start of a new life. I ate a substantial breakfast, because it was to be my last at home for some time. Picking up my bag I bade farewell to my mother and Sal. Poor Sal was openly weeping because it was her birthday on which we were actually saying goodbye. My mother worked virtually fulltime with my father in the family shop; Sal was a housemaid who had been with us since the day I was born. In so many respects she was a second mother to me, and was considered one of the family. I jumped into the car with Dad and we were soon at High Street railway station in Swansea, where I would join a troop train bound for Towyn in Mid Wales. There, I would join the H.A.A. Training Regiment. I was simply one of a very mixed mob of nineteen and thirty-nine year olds who were being called up together, and who would be joining the train at all stations en route east to Newport, then up to Pontypool Road, and Shrewsbury, and finally west to Towyn. It was a thirsty and hungry mob that finally arrived late that evening.

Although I knew of Towyn as a seaside resort I had never actually visited there before. The road from the town to the beach arrived at the very north end of a nice long promenade. The camp was an assembly of Nissen huts on the landward side of the southern end of the prom. There was a triple roll of barbed wire across the prom about half way up, so the northern end was still open to the holidaying public. But all the houses along the prom had been commandeered. Various offices such as the M.O. and the regimental barber were situated in this 'civilian' zone. Our parade ground was at the southern end of the prom where all our marching and rifle drill was carried out.

Our troop sergeant was Sgt. Blewitt who was a first class instructor and a real gent. Our pay was two shillings a day (10p). From that the army kept back one shilling a week for 'sport' and the same for the regimental barber. That left us a net weekly pay of twelve shillings (60p). Fortunately the army had used its noodle, so that all in our hut were nineteen, and the 'old men' were in a separate hut. So we were a completely happy and cheerful crowd. For the first three weeks we were not allowed to leave camp because we were not considered capable of deporting ourselves in a military manner! The only recreation in the evening was the NAAFI. The only edible refreshment served here was a Lyons fruit pie. A square pie packed in a little square cardboard box, priced at three pence (1p) each. There were a number of different fruits available in the complete range, but the NAAFI manager was an absolute genius of organisation. There was only ever one type of pie available on any given night. Each hungry soldier having consumed three or four of the same flavour each night, the end of the three weeks confinement was waited with boundless anticipation. We had all heard of Jones's caff, and the very thought of being allowed there one day made us literally drool.

Eventually, the great night arrived and every one of us made absolutely sure that we would pass inspection and be allowed out into the town. We had asked others the way to Jones's caff so often that each of us could have found his way there blindfold. Down the High Street, turn right then left, and there before you on the left pavement was an external wooden staircase. We dashed upstairs and entered a large rectangular hall. It was full to capacity with plain wooden trestle tables. Each table had a four-seat bench on each side – eight to a table. Immediately we sat down and filled a table. We waited for the action.

No menu was ever published, but the promise was – 'All you can eat for one and six' this translated to one shilling and six pence (7 ½ p). We knew that chips would be the main ingredient, but the rest was decided by what was available. It could be bacon, bacon and egg, sausage, sausage and egg, or on very rare nights of good fortune it could be all three! That's when you thought it must be your birthday! The filler up of course was bread and scrape. The poor waitress would approach the table with a large plate holding eight equally large chunks of bread. Now the competition really started. As the waitress bent forward to plonk the plate in the centre of the table, eight prehensile hands darted forward to grab a slice each. As soon as the plate was empty we were allowed to shout 'more bread please miss'.

The question always was, did the waitress win, by landing the plate before it was empty, or did we win, by emptying it before it was fairly grounded. The fight went on until our appetites were sated.

Haven't we done well so far? We've been in the army for three weeks, and we haven't seriously mentioned training. But it has taken place, and we had surprisingly coped well with it. Marching and rifle drill took place for at least a part of the morning and afternoon sessions. This was coupled with learning to strip and assemble the Lewis machine gun. But our main training was meant to be that we would learn all the duties necessary to operate and fire a 3.7" heavy anti-aircraft gun. There were separate duties to be learnt for each member of a team of ten. We were a complete team of Davies's, and as my army number was 1817810, I was known as Davies 810. The only drawback to our training was that we only had two 3.7" guns to learn on. One was a wooden copy which had a couple of handles which turned, but controlled nothing; the other had been a genuine article, but was absolutely rock solid with rust. So we had perforce to stretch our imaginations appreciably!

It was amazing how quickly and quietly our bodies really toughened up and were soon doing thirty-mile route marches whilst carrying full kit. It was on the physical side of things that the age differences began to show themselves. Not so much in the physical toughness side of things, but in the agility and dexterity. The older lads had so much more difficulty in carrying out some of the more intricate movements. This remark certainly applied generally, but by no means were the older lads the only ones with 'two left feet'.

Of course there were lots of humorous moments to look back on. PT as we called it was carried out on a small field behind the row of houses. When PT was finished we had to go for a swim. Very few of the older lads had costumes so the army lent them some. These were trunks, which had one leg open. The waist and the leg were secured by tying up tapes, which were an integral part of the costume. If the costume was slightly oversize, or if the thighs were a little undersize, then the whole things tended to be rather immodest to say the least.

From the field we doubled under orders across the civilian end of the prom. The young holiday making females were fully aware of the situation, and aligned themselves along our route so that they would not miss any example of visual immodesty. We used to split our sides at the efforts of some of the lads to keep their dignity!

I've already mentioned that the M.O.'s surgery was at the 'open' end of the prom. One day we had to fall in outside the surgery, forming a queue. We had to strip off our shirts, drop our braces and open our 'flies'. We stood in the queue, left hand on hip, right hand holding the top of our trousers ready to receive an inoculation and to be inspected by the M.O. We stood there in the blazing heat, idly watching through the uncurtained window, as the line slowly progressed, each man in turn receiving his jab from what seemed to be a gigantic needle, before passing to the M.O. without delay. It was suddenly realised that one of the lads was feeling distinctly queasy. His eyes were virtually shut, his left arm had dropped and he was gently swaying. Those around him immediately stepped back so that he was fully exposed to public view. Yes it did happen. It was now the turn of his right hand to drop, closely followed by his trousers. The young ladies enjoyed themselves, and before he dropped into a complete faint, his loyal friends jumped in and caught him.

The regimental barber was a corporal who had three underlings actually doing the hair cutting. He simply controlled the queue and told the next man where to go. Our Troop Officer inspected us on the first parade of the morning, and also on the first parade in the afternoon. On one particular morning, as he passed behind me, he tapped me on the shoulder with his cane and shouted "Haircut". I immediately fell out and went for my haircut. In the afternoon as the same officer passed behind me, he again tapped with his cane and said "Haircut". From the side of my mouth I said "Had one this morning Sir". There was an immediate and loud response in my left ear. "Speak when you're spoken to, son. Now fall out." So again I went. Would you believe me if I said that the next morning the same thing happened again. Off I went for my third haircut in twenty-

four hours. The corporal recognised me and queried my presence. He believed my story and signalled me to a chair. He shouted to my barber, "This is the third time. If you can find any bloody hair, cut it off." I felt that I'd had my shilling's worth that week!

So, the end of our six week training period arrived. We were inspected by some anonymous general and posted out to operational units. I was one of eight or ten posted out to 369 Battery, 117 Heavy Anti-Aircraft (HAA) Regiment which was actually situated on Bootle Golf Course in Liverpool. So we went by train to Lime Street station, where a sergeant in a three-tonner picked us up and took us to camp. We were given a hot meal for which we were extremely grateful, and a palliasse which we ourselves filled with straw. We were then allocated to our various huts. It was apparently a permanent site with nice brick built huts. Because we arrived in the dark, we saw little else. We had wooden beds which were quite comfortable.

The next morning we were immediately put on 'fatigues'. As the day wore on we gradually found out more about our surroundings. We could see the guns about three hundred yards away across the golf course. Each gun was virtually surrounded by a wall which appeared to be about six feet high. Inside the walls were concrete storage cells for the ammunition. The guns, we were told, were 4.5"s and not 3.7"s. As a matter of fact, I never saw a live 3.7" throughout my active service. They were extremely short of manpower, so the lads were delighted to see us, even though we were such rookies. Liverpool was still suffering from air raids so the guns had to be manned permanently. Each man was only allowed six hours out of camp every third week. That was between the hours of 5 and 11 P.M. So that very evening we were told by our sergeant that we were "standing in". Not to worry, if the alarm went we would simply run with our mates to the guns, which we hadn't even seen yet. Sod's Law, sometime in the night the alarm went, so off we trotted on this three hundred yard dash in the dark. Around the gun it was black as night. We were two rookies on this gun. In the dark, we could just discern a heavy steel protective shield which virtually surrounded the gun. The only illumination was from a small bicycle-type torch that the sergeant carried, and which he only switched on at intervals. He showed us a wooden tray about waist high onto which we should load six shells from the cell behind us. When we had filled the tray, one of us would have to stand there with a shell in his arms ready to replace one on the tray and so keep the latter full at all times. I drew the short straw, and so stood there in the dark with the shell in my arms. All eighty-four pounds of it! Time dragged on, we heard lots of noises and orders which we didn't understand, but we couldn't see a thing and certainly had no idea of what was happening. Suddenly the world erupted, and there was a blinding flash and an almighty roar. We were standing directly under the barrel when the gun fired. Our heads vibrated and rang for days afterward. When our senses returned, I nobly stepped forward to put my shell on the tray. It was only then we realised the tray was a part of the gun-shield and had been turning with the gun throughout our wasted vigil.

From here on we quickly familiarised ourselves with the camp and the equipment. In the Command Post were a range-finder and a predictor, both of which could be used to follow targets in daylight. We also had a fairly new radar machine which could, of course, follow targets by night. Allied to this was a new plotting and prediction system. Our O.C. was a Major Caffin who in peacetime had been some kind of BBC executive. He had interviewed us all soon after arrival, and now he asked me if I was prepared to learn this new system. If I was able to cope, he promised me a stripe. This would increase my pay to four shillings and three pence a day (21p). My immediate response was "yes please Sir" so I soon became a TCOA (Technical Control Officer's Assistant).

One of the more pleasant fatigues was to go out in a three-tonner to pick up our laundry from a civilian firm. The locals could identify our vehicles, and very often some old dear, out shopping would throw a packet of cigarettes into the back of the lorry and shout a greeting. There was one housing estate within about one hundred yards from our guns. They had a charming and unique way of showing their appreciation. The army had lent them the buckets which enabled them to carry out their good deeds. As soon as an air raid alarm sounded, the appointed persons immediately put these large buckets of water onto their fires or stoves. As soon as the All Clear sounded, the appointed team came staggering across the golf course with the necessary to boil out the guns. Once this job was completed the guns were ready for action once more, but not before. Then out came the second team with buckets of hot cocoa. I thought that this was a wonderful example of the appreciation of, and the cooperation with the civilian population.

There wasn't a great deal to amuse us in camp. There was a little canteen which served a very few items, and mostly someone played a piano and we had a singsong. But all were happy. On our six hour night out we could walk to a nice little club in Litherland run by a band of volunteers, and there was a cinema in Seaforth. I fell in lucky too in so much as I became quite friendly with a Lance Bombardier Cyril Jones from Chester. He was an insurance actuary in civilian life and was a great mathematician. His party piece was that if he was given the cube of any number between one and a hundred, he could respond with the cube root. He assured me that this was a mental calculation which he had devised. I eventually solved it, but he had a certain way with people and had struck up a friendship with the manager of a local golf club and his wife, with whom he took coffee most mornings. They subsequently extended the invitation to me, which I found a most pleasant interlude.

It was about this time that the Germans started bombing the cathedral cities. Anti-aircraft guns nationally were in very short supply so the authorities had to resort to subterfuge in order to maintain morale. In Aigburgh Park was a battery of 3.7s (mobile), and guns were needed badly for places such as Canterbury. There really was none spare. So very quickly dummy guns were made which would fit into the emplacements in Aigburgh when the real guns were shipped out. The whole battery slipped out in the early hours of darkness and about fifteen of us moved into the accommodation to take their place. Fortunately the camp was of a Hore Belisha design. This was rather like a spider's web with huts radiating from a central point. Marching in to one hut and then, in different clothes, marching out from another, we kept up the pretence that one battery had moved out and another moved in.

In June 1942 we were ready to move to the Orkneys to participate in the defence of Scapa Flow. We were to be replaced on the site by a mixed battery. The majority of the technical jobs were to be carried out by ATS girls. About eight or ten of us had to stay behind for a few weeks to pass on necessary information when the rest of the battery moved out in mid-June. When we followed on, we caught a train to Aberdeen, and then went by boat to Stromness. The battery was situated in a little place named Orphir on the edge of Scapa Flow and on the mainland, which was also called Pomona (Goddess of Plenty). The town of Stromness was about ten miles to the west and the capital Kirkwall was about fourteen miles to the east.

Again the guns were 4.5s. Accommodation was in Nissen huts which would be quite comfortable in the winter because each had its own round coal-fired cast-iron stove. Because there were no signs of civilisation in the immediate surroundings, we now had a reasonably palatial NAAFI, which served reasonably priced meals in the evenings. We soon found that there was a little general store, just over a mile away which sold virtually everything, and to our surprise, and great joy, there was no rationing in the Orkneys! This was going to solve all our evening snack problems once we began to have our fire going. We immediately began the acquisition of a few pots and pans so as to be well prepared. Although no transport was laid on for personnel given some time off duty, the main road passed within about four hundred yards of the camp and it was normally possible to hitch a lift with some service transport.

On my twenty-first birthday I managed to have the whole day off. At mid-morning I set off along the way, confidently waiting for the first passing vehicle to come and pick me up. Some hours later I was really despondent and still walking. Yes, I had to walk the *whole fourteen miles because no vehicles came along that morning. There was a first class Church of Scotland canteen in Kirkwall which served good hot meals. I was soon tucking in to Scotch egg and chips, with bread and butter, followed by a range of oatcakes. Then came a few leisurely cups of tea. After this, I was sufficiently refreshed to go and explore Kirkwall. The cathedral, dedicated to St Magnus, was very interesting and his bones were supposedly interred in one of the pillars. The only tree I ever saw in the Orkneys was in its churchyard. About all we could do on short leisure breaks was to go for walks up in the hills or along the road. On one of the latter I bumped into Mr Frisken, a local crofter, who invited me home for some refreshment and a chat. He and his wife had three lovely children at home and a daughter who was down in Scotland nursing. She was the only member of the family who had seen a train! But they were all intelligent, well-read individuals, and we had many a good long chat, which we all enjoyed. There were also a son and daughter in the shop. These were really my only outside contacts in the nine months or so I spent there.*

One of the main air-defence features over Scapa Flow was that every gun in the area had a series of points at which to shoot. This meant that by issuing one given code word a complete umbrella of fire would cover the Flow at any given height. No aircraft would have been able to survive in such conditions. We were well trained in this little operation. As the months changed, so did the weather. Summer days were pleasant and long, winter days became exceedingly short and conditions severe. Northern lights appeared frequently, and were really bright and beautiful. The winds were unbelievable, one hundred mile an hour gales were commonplace. The strength of these winds was such that if you were walking against them, your entire body had to be inclined forward at forty-five degrees, with the reverse applying when the wind was in the opposite direction. Quite often one could lose control and be blown forward until you could grab hold of something to stabilise yourself. There was no lighting or hot water in the ablutions (toilet block), so in the winter we washed and shaved by feel. We would have had breakfast and be on parade for inspection whilst it was completely dark. By the light of a small torch the officer was normally able to examine us. That was until we had an outbreak of some skin trouble, and the M.O. insisted that we had our heads completely covered in gentian violet. Even with the benefit of his torch he couldn't identify us.

The weather worsened as winter deepened. Gales and snow became commonplace. There was a door at each end of the hut, but if someone wanted to visit the toilet late at night he might have to wake up a friend and then check to see which door they might be able to open by combined effort. On one very stormy night, there were dreadful noises for ages. When we went out we couldn't believe our eyes. A destroyer had dragged its anchor, and was now lying alongside the hut, not more than ten or twelve yards away. It took over a day to refloat it.

One night two of us were on rota to go up the shop to buy bacon, eggs, bread and butter for our evening snack. As we left the hut the snow started falling, quite gently at first. We plodded on and reached our destination. We gave our order, then stayed for a while chatting and smoking with the son and daughter. Time passed. When we opened the shop door to leave, the weather was unbelievable. The snow was now lying a couple of feet deep, and was being blown horizontally by the force of the wind. When we went forth, we met the full force of the gale and the snow felt more like ice. It was so solid and sharp we could not tolerate it on our faces. The only solution was to walk backwards. We fought for over two and a half hours to reach the shelter of our little hut. We were greeted by shouts of "Where have you been?" or something similar.

Although I had only spoken with Major Caffin on a very few occasions, I knew that he had something of reputation as a leg puller. He sent for me and queried whether I had ever studied physics. I said yes, at least to some extent. He then asked if I had ever been on any courses since I joined the army. I told him that, no I hadn't. He then announced that I had been selected to go on a three day Signals

Course. "Do your best lad, don't let me down." I quite enjoyed the course which concerned telephones, line repairs etc. At the end we had a written test. When I returned to the battery I was sent for once more. I was then given the basic facts. The major could not stand the Signals CO, who was forever demanding that he send junior NCOs on Signals Courses. I had managed to fluke a one hundred per cent result in my test which caused the Signals CO to complain to the Brigadier that Major Caffin was wasting army time by sending people on the same course more than once. This enabled Major Caffin to go to town and explain that he could guarantee absolutely that I had never been on any army course. I was simply typical of all the junior NCOs in the Royal Artillery, and it just verified the major's contention that his men needed no instruction from any Signals personnel.

Probably the worst part of our Orkneys service was the poor food we had to endure. Our main meals appeared to be an unending parade of tinned stews in various guises, Irish, oxtail and others. Thank goodness for our evening snacks. There had been a large Naval Store on Orkney since the 1914-18 war. Now things began to emerge. We suddenly had Roughriders as our cigarette ration, and then we were issued with hard tack biscuits as our midday meal on Wednesdays with corned beef or something. We had to make our own fires and boil these biscuits on our dixies in an attempt to soften them. It was a good man who was able to scoff a complete one.

The battery was composed of ten Welshmen, thirty English and two hundred and sixty Scots and Hogmanay was approaching. A middle-aged captain whose name I forget gathered us together secretly. We were honour bound to keep all our meetings secret. He worked on us with all the tricks in the book, until we could render four or five Welsh airs, and the Old Rugged Cross. The night arrived and we were all in the NAAFI eating, drinking and enjoying ourselves. Then the Welsh Glee Party was introduced. Those who knew us well when they saw who it was that composed the Party. Then we burst into song. The laughter quickly stopped as it was replaced by admiration.

They were no more surprised than we had been. It made me realise what one clever musician could do with a completely useless bunch of non-performers. We weren't allowed off the stage until we had gone through our complete repertoire three times.

I had one leave from Orphir and it was a terrible journey. We were picked up from our camp by truck and taken to the port of Stromness. Here we faced a sea crossing of at least two and a half hours to Scrabster, near Thurso in the north of Scotland. The Pentland Firth was reputed to be one of the roughest crossings that exists. We spent the night in Thurso, and then caught the train to Carlisle, Liverpool, Crewe, and Cardiff and eventually to home. Very often in winter the Pentland Firth was so rough that the journey could not be undertaken. When that happened, everybody's leave would be put back one day. How those "one-days" built up. Many a time a man who was supposed to be home to see his family for Christmas, wouldn't even be home in time for New Year.

In February 1942 I was sent on a three day WOSB (War Office Selection Board) to see if I would be suitable Officer Material. A week or two later, I was informed that I had passed and would be posted south. I had spent eighteen months with the same crowd and had made some wonderful friends. Parting would not be easy.

The only action the army had taken to help us survive the severe weather conditions that prevailed in the Orkneys was to issue each of us with a fourth blanket and a set of thick woollen vests and "long johns". As soon as my orders came to proceed south to "Pre-octu" in Wrotham in Kent, I confidently went to the stores to hand in all this surplus equipment. Imagine my consternation when I was told that it could not be handed in while I was still in Orkney. I was given my orders to proceed to London, report to the RTO (Railway Transport Officer) at a certain station, who would allocate me a bed for the night, then I would carry on the next day to Maidstone where I would be picked up by an army vehicle and delivered to the camp. All this for a young lad who had only ever seen London in the newsreels. The train journey south was boring and extremely exhausting. But crossing London by tube in the rush hour was both a revelation and an ordeal. I was wearing my thick army greatcoat, carrying a massive, fully laden kit bag, steel helmet, gas mask, large back pack and a small side pack. To manoeuvre myself through the mad crowds and the turnstiles without knocking someone over seemed an almost impossible task, but despite all the scowls, I managed to survive. I just couldn't describe my feelings throughout that forty-eight hour ordeal, I was thrilled just to survive, and be able to clock in at my destination. I was to spend about ten weeks before having leave and then proceeding to Octu proper.

I was now what was officially known as a cadet. We were differentiated by wearing a little white tape on our epaulettes, as well as on our caps. I would no longer be a HAA Gunner, but would be trained on 25-pounders, so as to be a field gunner.'

It was now that my father was to become familiar with the famous 25-pounder. It was a comparatively new innovation which had replaced the 18-pounder field gun which had served the British forces so well in the Great War. In the years following the Great War, the British Army had begun the process of seeking a replacement for its two standard types of guns, the 18-pounder and the 4.5-inch howitzer. In previous years the field guns, which possessed a relatively low arc of fire, were mainly used to engage direct targets while howitzers with their high arc of fire could be used to lob shells over intervening obstacles to reach targets obscured by hills and ridges. This did lead to supply difficulties with differing calibres of ammunition required for each gun and led to a proliferation of the types of equipment and ammunition which were needed on the battlefield.

Rather than design two new guns for post-war service, it was decided to explore the possibility of designing a single weapon that combined the high-angle fire capability of the howitzer with the direct fire ability of the 18-pounder. After assessing their options, the British Army decided that a gun of approximately 3.7 inches in calibre with a range of 15,000 yards was needed.

In 1933, experiments began using 18-pounder, 22-pounder, and 25-pounder guns. Following careful study of the results, the General Staff made the wise conclusion that the 25-pounder should be adopted as the standard field gun for the British Army in the post-war era.

Initially the programme did not progress smoothly however, after ordering a prototype in 1934 budget restrictions forced a change in the development programme. There were insufficient funds to do the job of re-equipping the whole of the artillery service. An uneasy compromise was reached and it was decided that, rather than design and build new guns, the existing Mark 4 18-pounders would be converted to 25-pounders. This change of plan necessitated reducing the calibre of the gun to 3.45 inches and with it the range. The first of the new breed of guns began testing in 1935, and as a result of its hybrid origins the Mark 1 version of 25-pounder was also known as the 18/25-pounder.

It was necessary to make a series of adaptations to the split trail 18-pounder carriage. Compromises had to be made and as a result of those compromises came a further reduction in range as the 18/25-pounder proved incapable of taking a charge strong enough to fire a shell 15,000 yards without displacing the relatively flimsy carriage. As a result, the initial 25-pouders could only fire to a maximum range of 11,800 yards.

However, in 1938 with Hitler in power and re-armament in full swing the funds began to flow again and it was decreed that a field gun with a range of 15,000 yards would be required immediately and that funding would be available. As a result hastily convened experiments were resumed with the goal of designing a purpose-built 25-pounder with the necessary range. When these tests were concluded, the Royal Artillery opted to place the new 25-pounder on a box trail carriage which was fitted with a firing platform rather like the old 18-pounder carriage with its split trail. This combination was designated the 25-pounder Mark II on a Mark I carriage. It acted as both a field gun, a howitzer and at a pinch an anti-tank gun. It soon became the standard British field gun during the Second World War. The secret of its success lay partially in the adoption of late model 18-pounder carriages. These models incorporated an innovative element in the form of a circular firing platform and this novel idea contributed to the efficiency of the new guns. The firing platform was attached to the gun and when lowered the gun was pulled onto it. This platform transferred most of the recoil forces to the ground, instead of relying upon the spade at the end of the trail. This made the gun very stable when firing. It also provided a flat smooth surface for the carriage to rotate on using the road wheels; this enabled the gunners to quickly traverse the carriage in any direction.

In British terminology the 25-pounder was called "Quick Firing" (QF), originally because the cartridge case provided rapid loading compared to bag charges, and the cartridge case was automatically released when the breech was opened. The use of separate shell and charge allowed the charge to be changed for different ranges. For the Mk 1 Ordnance on 18-pounder carriage there were three "charges", Charge 1, 2 and 3, all of which could be used in the common cartridge design. The Mk 2 Ordnance on Mk 1 Carriage added a "Super" charge in a different cartridge. In 1943 a separately bagged "increment" charge was added; used with the Super it provided higher velocity for anti-tank use. The introduction of the increment to Super was only possible following the addition of the muzzle-brake in the previous year. Subsequently another type of increment was introduced to be added to charges 1 and 2 to provide additional combinations for use in high angle fire. However, this fire required a dial sight adaptor, removal of the platform and some excavation of the ground.

The gun was remarkably versatile and due to the fact that it was able to fire with a flat trajectory and high velocity it was also suitable for anti-tank use. Although it was never the equal of the 18-pounder anti-tank gun it was nonetheless a welcome option in a close corner. For that reason the 25-pounder was also supplied with a limited amount of 20-pound solid armour-piercing (AP) shot, later replaced with a more potent version with a ballistic cap (APBC). As a high muzzle velocity was critical in direct fire for penetration of armour, the AP shot was fired with maximum charge, Charge No. 3, Super, or Super with Super Increment depending on the ordnance mark.

By World War II standards, the 25-pounder had a smaller calibre and lower shell-weight than many other field-artillery weapons, although importantly it had longer range than most. Most forces had entered the war with even smaller 75 mm (3-in.) designs but had quickly moved to 105 mm (4.1-in.) and larger weapons. The 25-pounder was designed to support for the British artillery doctrine of suppressive (neutralising) fire, not the destructive fire that had proved impossible to achieve in the early years of World War I. Nevertheless the 25-pounder was considered by all to be one of the best artillery pieces in use. The effects caused by the gun (and the speed at which the British artillery control system could respond) in the North-West Europe Campaign of 1944–1945 made many German soldiers believe that the British had secretly deployed an automatic 25-pounder.

The complex lessons which were required for gunnery officers meant that it would be some time before my father was able to come to grips with this unfamiliar new weapon. Firstly it was necessary to become familiar with the towing vehicles.

The early 18 and 25-pounders had been towed in the field by the Light Dragon, a tracked vehicle derived from a light tank, and on occasion by the Morris CDSW. Throughout most of the Second World War the 25-pounder was normally towed, with its limber, behind a 4x4 Field Artillery Tractor called a "Quad". These were manufactured by Morris, Guy and Karrier in England, and, in greater numbers, by Ford and Chevrolet in Canada.

An important accessory for the gun was the ammunition trailer ("Trailer, Artillery, No. 27"). The gun was hooked to the trailer and the trailer was in turn hooked to the tractor for towing. The gun did not need a limber and could be hooked directly to a tractor. The trailer provided the brakes as only a hand-brake was fitted to the gun carriage. The trailer carried ammunition; thirty-two rounds in trays (two rounds per tray) which was stored in the trailer and protected by two doors. Ammunition was also carried in the gun tractor along with the detachment and various gun stores. Some stores, such as sights, were carried cased on the gun. Each section of two guns had a third tractor that carried ammunition and towed two ammunition trailers. Various other vehicles were required including motorbikes with which my father had a great deal of fun.

'We would be having no gunnery instruction here, but would spend time learning army rules and regulations. We would also be made proficient in driving various army vehicles and riding motor bikes. Vehicle maintenance and testing was also given us. Bike riding was taught to me by a Corporal Pinder, RASC, who showed us, then made us do them, tricks that we never thought a bike could do. The word had flashed around early to say that you could not drive, otherwise you would spend long hours on maintenance. Driving lessons consisted of as many as seven of you being loaded into the back of a truck, chatting and smoking while one took his turn to learn to drive. About every thirty minutes the driver would change. Touring around Kent in glorious sunny weather was infinitely better than stripping down dirty engines. We also managed to stop at the odd café for a quick break. My first day, I didn't even get a chance to drive. When my turn eventually came, I made sure that I steered badly, made the truck jump and crashed the gears. The sergeant then gave me a certain manoeuvre to execute and stop the vehicle. When I stopped I could not believe my ears. "OK" he said, "stop fooling around and drive back to camp – properly, you've passed your test". I hadn't realised that in carrying out the last manoeuvre I had changed gear with an immaculate "double declutch". On I went to maintenance.

All this had been interspersed with marching and rifle drill, physical training and unarmed combat. With the glorious weather as an extra bonus, this was certainly better than the cold north. Most evenings and weekends were free, so we could visit places like Canterbury and Maidstone. This is where for a bet, I saw a man drink a pint in three seconds. One of my thirty-nine-year-old pals from Towyn had been a farm labourer with five children. His home was in a little hamlet situated almost beneath our camp. I was able to visit his family and assure them that their dad was OK. At the end of this course we all went home for ten days leave before having to report to Catterick Camp near Richmond in Yorkshire, for our next and final period of training.'

It was now that the serious lessons of the craft of the artilleryman had to be assimilated. It was just as well my father was a scientist with a good grounding in physics, mathematics and chemistry. Command of a troop of 25-pounders required a practical aptitude for range finding, map reading and dealing with the appropriate charges for each fire mission. Initially it must have proved a bewildering experience as in common with all British guns of the period the indirect fire sight of the 25-pounder was "calibrating". This meant that the range, not elevation angle, was set on the sight. The sight compensated for the difference in the gun's muzzle velocities from standard. The gun was also fitted with a direct-fire telescope for use with armour-piercing shot. It also used "one-man laying" in accordance with normal British practice.

The QF 25-pounder fired "separate" or two-part ammunition – the projectile and the propelling charge in its (usually brass) cartridge case with its integral primer were loaded separately. Typically for a quick-firing gun, the cartridge case provided obturation.

There were two types of cartridge. The "Normal" cartridge contained three cloth charge bags (coloured red, white and blue). White and/or blue bags would be removed from the cartridge to give "Charge 1" or "Charge 2", leaving all three bags in the cartridge case gave "Charge 3". The cartridge case was closed at the top with a leatherboard cup. The second type of cartridge was "Super", which provided one charge only. The cup could not be removed from the cartridge case. In 1943, an Incremental Charge of 5.5 oz (160 g) of cordite ("Super-plus") was introduced to raise the muzzle velocity when firing AP shot with charge Super; this required a muzzlebrake to be fitted. Adoption of "upper-register" (high-angle) fire needed more charges to improve the range overlap. This led to the development of the "Intermediate Increment" of 4 oz cordite, which was introduced in 1944. The bags inside the cartridges were striped red and white to indicate that they should only be used with Charges 1 and 2. When one bag was used with Charge 1 it provided Charge 1 1/2. When one was added to Charge 2 it provided Charge 2 1/3, and two bags, Charge 2 2/3. This allowed a maximum of seven charges instead of four.

There were many marks of cartridge, mostly differentiated by propellant type. Double-base propellant (nitrocellulose/nitro-glycerine) was the UK standard but one mark used U.S. single-base (nitrocellulose only). However, triple-base nitrocellulose/nitro-glycerine/picrite was used throughout the war and eventually replaced all others.

The 25-pounder's main ammunition was the high-explosive (HE) streamlined shell with a 5/10 CRH ogive and boat tail. It was also provided with base ejection smoke (white and coloured), star shells, and chemical shells. The UK did not develop a WP smoke shell for the 25-pounder smoke shells were sometimes reloaded with propaganda leaflets or metal foil "window". There was all of this and a great deal more besides to take in for the new intake. Learning such complicated lessons was not helped by the generally unpleasant atmosphere which prevailed at Catterick.

'Wrotham had certainly been the most pleasant time that I had experienced in the army. I had certainly never been unhappy, but to have time off and somewhere to go was a complete revelation. But Catterick was something else again. Its reputation was such that the NCOs who were your instructors would call you "Sir" and treat you like dirt. The accommodation was beautiful two storey brick buildings. In the middle of a block of buildings would be the Parade Ground, a large sacrosanct rectangular area which all mortal souls were forbidden to cross.

All of us cadets had to proceed around the perimeter – AT THE DOUBLE. We soon found out that we were now a squad or troop of forty-three individuals who would be in the direct control of a senior officer and two sergeants. I have a terrible memory for names, and always have had, but I will never forget the name of that major because he was the worst example of the human race I have ever had *the misfortune to meet. He was Irish, and on our very first parade, he asked if there were any Welsh present. Five of us acknowledged our nationality, whereupon he told us how much he hated Welshmen. Life now became really hard. The main part of our being was to learn every single aspect of every single occupation concerned with the firing of a twenty-five pound field gun. That wasn't easy. They also went out of their way to test us to the limits of our mental and physical endurance, and to make sure that we were really made to suffer for any mistake we might make. For example, we were taken many miles on our bikes and then made to ride across or through shallow streams. If you allowed your engine to stall under these conditions, you had to push your bike all the way back to camp. Every military driver in the whole county knew that he dare not offer a lift to a cadet.*

We were transported to the Lake District for two weeks of Battle School. We lived in bell tents in the freezing cold. Every morning at six thirty we fell in, washed and shaved, in our denims with our rifles. We then doubled about half a mile down the hillside to a particularly flat field. Then, we formed a single line along the length of one side, whereupon we would be ordered to "leopard crawl" across the field. This meant lying full length on the ground, holding rifle in both hands and working elbows and toes to creep forward. The field was permanently covered with an inch or two or ice cold water, so we would be trying to hold our middles out of the water. This was OK until an instructor came along and stood on your back with a sadistic grin on his face. We were constantly sent on forced marches, assault courses, running up and down small mountains. When we were fording rivers they would detonate submerged charges, which were sufficient to blow you off your feet. This was very unnerving for any non-swimmer. The worst words that could be spoken to any cadet were RTU – returned to unit. This was the dire punishment that was dished out when you were thought to be lacking in some respect or other. On top of Hellvelyn one cadet was found to be afraid of heights – RTU and no appeal.

Back at camp, we spent long periods out on the hills practising our gun drill. Going through every single motion except the actual firing. Once they thought it time we were proficient, the punishment for any error whatsoever would be to run back to camp, and woe betide the fellow who was not in the office awaiting the major's return.

By this time we had really become extremely proficient and understood how vital so much of our training had been. But that didn't make it any more acceptable! We had been considerably hardened both mentally and physically. It was also amazing what we could perform as a team. We could transport our gun, physically, over the most fantastic obstacles, but this honing had sadly depleted our ranks. At least eight of out squad had been given the terrible order – RTU, and this had included the other four Welshmen.

We had already had a short leave during which we had followed orders and ordered our uniforms, for which we were allowed a £30 grant. We were only a few days short of the end of our training, and our passing out parade, when we were on the hills, still doing gun drill. I was acting as the "officer in charge" of the troop, and I made a small but definite mistake in giving an order to the fellow acting as the gun sergeant. The major pounced on this and told me to apologise to the fellow. This I did. The major then shouted, "Go on your knees and apologise." Once again I apologised, most profusely, but I remained standing. He was now almost hysterical and repeated the order. I repeated the apology, but remained upright. He screamed, "Run back to camp and wait for me in the CO's office." I don't know how long I was there, sitting down in the CO's office but it was the worst period of my life. I thought that I had probably lost all that I had worked for and wondered if the tailor would insist upon me paying for my uniform. Quaking in my boots, I was summoned into the CO's office. I was asked why I had not obeyed the order. I apologised to the CO for not having done so, but explained that I had apologised as requested, but as a Christian, I did not consider it right to have to go down on my knees to any other man. I was told to leave the room for a while before being recalled. I had a talking to from the CO, but he accepted my reasoning but with reservations. I nearly dropped with gratitude, and I didn't breathe easily until I had gone through my passing out parade and caught my train out of Catterick on my way to London, and then home for fourteen days leave.

It was quicker to take the train to London, then to go to Paddington to catch the train home. About eight of us had our farewell dinner at Veeraswamy's Indian restaurant. There was wartime control and the maximum permitted price was five shillings. Seemed like very good value.

My leave was not a very happy one because I found out that my father was quite a sick man, and was having to face up to the fact that if he survived his heart trouble, he would still not be able to carry on in his business. He was in the process of looking for a buyer.

After my leave I was to report to 497 Battery, 133 Field Regiment in Battle near Hastings. This was of course, the site of William the Conqueror's defeat of Harold. After about two days we moved to Herne Bay, a very pleasant little spot on the coast of Kent. We had very comfortable billets in a nice house in the centre of the town, situated on a small square with a small park in the centre with enough space therein to keep the guns. The CO was a Colonel Gibson, an ex-governor of Dartmoor. The OC was Major Dick Hughes from the South West somewhere. I was appointed Troop Leader F Troop which meant that my troop commander was Captain David Thomson and my GPO was Lieutenant Hugh Drummond. They were a very friendly crowd and I soon settled in. The troops had very nice billets, which were also on the sea front. The days passed with endless gun drill, and various exercises. I had the task of maintaining the daily records of all the vehicles, ensure that they had their monthly maintenance and then road test them to make sure that they were road worthy. After dinner we might go out for a quiet drink, or to a dance, if there was one, or just stay in the mess chatting. This latter was where Dick Gadd of Liverpool came into his own. He had the biggest repertoire of jokes that I have ever come across in my life. As he was able to tell them in the appropriate accent he was an absolute joy to listen to. His family owned a small chain of cold meat shops.

Time passed on. We went down to the South Downs a few times to practise firing the guns. It was usually wet and the subsoil was almost pure chalk. A combination that made for very uncomfortable digging and living conditions. In each position of course, we had to dig in our guns, command post and our slit trenches. All very laborious and time consuming, but nevertheless absolutely essential.

About this time we received our first Jeeps, which were extremely welcome. They really were marvellous little machines. We also went through a period of liaison with Americans. A few came to stay with us, and some of our lads went to visit them. Without going into petty detail, in many ways they worked in the complete reverse of us.

I arrived home on leave during the evening of December 31st 1943. I had arranged to meet Ruth in the dance, because I had no idea what my time of arrival would be. Yes the inevitable happened. Ruth went to the Mond, while I went to the Rink. But there were far worse things to worry about. My father had deteriorated badly and was seriously ill. The handing over of the business was virtually complete and I was able to sell the car.

In a way I really enjoyed the evenings of my leave, but naturally there was a great air of sadness about the house. My father did not have long to live, and we were all aware of it. On my return to Herne Bay there was plenty to keep me occupied.

Then, in mid-February a telegram arrived granting me a few days compassionate leave because my father was dying. In the few weeks since my previous leave there had been a terrible deterioration in my father. Now, he could do very little for himself, and his voice was very weak. We all felt so helpless and could do nothing except sit by his bedside. He was too tired to speak much. My compassionate leave had been granted, as my father had been very demanding to my mother and our doctor, Harvard Jones that he wanted to see his boys once more. Harvard knew the score and initiated the necessary proceedings. Arranging my leave had been easy as my lodgings were *known, things were very different for my brother however, as he was a young Naval officer serving overseas. We were convinced he was on convoy working the North Atlantic, but all the Navy could say was that his whereabouts were not definitely known. My father was given this news, but he was adamant, "We know where he is, he's in Madagascar!" It was years later when my brother came home that he was able to confirm that indeed, at the time of my father's death he was in Madagascar.*

My short leave ended and I caught the train back to London and thence to Herne Bay. It was tea time when I arrived back so I just dumped my kitbag in my room and joined the rest of the lads. I was still on my first cup of tea when a telegram arrived informing me that my father had passed away. I picked up my bag and retraced the saddest journey of my life. I was home for the funeral and then straight back to my unit. I was so glad that I had been able to see my father before he died, and yet I felt cheated that for the sake of a few hours I had not been there when he actually died. He passed away on the 20th February 1944.'

Once my father was back with his regiment, the really serious business of training for action had begun. The lessons which were now being learned were the most vital aspects of gunnery. This was the knowledge which would prove essential during the forthcoming campaign in Europe. Like so many others in the army my father always enjoyed the business of firing the guns, but there was one duty which was always a much hated task. At every new location the guns had to be dug in for protection against counter-battery fire. It was a task which would be undertaken hundreds of times in the months ahead. He wrote:

'We now had to complete our preparations for a massive exercise. The entire regiment, which would consist of more than seventy vehicles, was to travel north to Otterburn some way further north than York. To minimise disruption of normal road traffic, we would travel only at night. Our CO was Lt. Col. Gibson, and he would

be leading the convoy. He always insisted that a squad of young subalterns and sergeant-majors would ride motor bikes and travel immediately behind his vehicle. The nation's signposts had all been removed, so at a signal from the CO a pair of riders would stop and wave the convoy across that particular junction and count the vehicles to make sure that none had dropped out. As soon as all had passed, this pair would have to hare past the entire convoy and report to the CO. This kind of effort certainly cut out the boredom of just riding behind the vehicle in front.

So we duly progressed northward, stopping near dawn at some predetermined bivouac area for a day's rest. After some three hundred miles or so we arrived at Newcastle on Tyne. One officer actually came from Newcastle so he was given the job of leading the convoy through the complicated streets of the town. Everything appeared to be OK until it was realised that the front of the convoy had caught up with its own tail. Fortunately a couple of "bobbies" were spotted and they kindly put us back on the road to Otterburn. The actual "firing" part of the firing camp was always pleasurable, but the other duties such as digging in at every firing position were a shocking but very necessary chore. We had to learn that it was a really lifesaving operation.

At the last bivouac area on our return journey some distance north of London, I was detailed to stay behind with a fatigue party to clean up the complete area. This meant quite a few hours' work. Followed by a journey through London to reach Herne Bay. As I had never seen London before joining up, and my map was certainly of no help in finding my way through a large city, I was not particularly pleased with my predicament. I would have to find my way south, steering by the sun! My driver was a lad named Benny Halpern. I knew his family were Jewish and that they had escaped from Germany pre-war. Benny now told me that he lived in the East End of London and that he would be able to find his way north to south if he were to be allowed to travel via his home! A nod was as good as a wink. So we were in Benny's capable hands, and when we arrived at his home the whole street came to welcome us. After a suitable pause for refreshments, and to give Benny time to collect his thoughts re his future route south, we carried on our way and safely returned to camp. Benny was to prove his worth again at a much later date.

The regiment later travelled to Builth Wells where we undertook more firing practice at the Sennybridge ranges. This time I was responsible for taking all the regiment's carriers to and fro by train. At the end of May I was detailed to report to a camp on Hayling Island near Portsmouth with two of our signallers. There were tents already erected to accommodate us. The next day all was revealed. We were given very large scripts, extremely detailed, with times alongside. We spent a couple of days practising without actually broadcasting, on our radio sets. The whole thing was a sham. We were going to pretend that whole masses of troops were practising a large scale sea landing. But there wouldn't be any troops and we would be on land anyway. When all was completed we just upped sticks and returned to Herne Bay. We were now on standby for immediate movement. One evening we were told that we were moving out the next morning to travel by road to the Epping Forest area in north London. The regiment would move by road, and once again I would be responsible for taking all the tracked vehicles (Bren carriers) by train. Perhaps I should explain that these carriers looked a little like small topless tanks. The people travelling in them are plainly visible. Sometime, quite early, we heard that the big day had arrived. The first wave of troops had actually landed in Normandy that morning. I got all the carriers offloaded, and we were to be led to our destination by two military policemen on motorcycles. The population had gone mad. It seemed that everyone had come out to see what was happening. They were cheering us like mad as if we had actually taken part in the LANDING. People were thrusting refreshments at us – which we were literally forced to accept. Never before or since have I consumed such a motley, ill-assorted mixture of foods. Fish paste, meat and jam sandwiches interspersed with little cakes, drinks of lemonade, tea and coffee, all consumed at double quick time in order to hand the container back to the kind donor who was running alongside.

We were completely confined to the camp at Epping Forest and were surrounded by high wire fencing. Looking through the wire one day I was amazed to see some friends from my old HAA Regiment 117 passing. A quick shout brought them over. They were now stationed just a few hundred yards away, part of the anti-aircraft defence of the City. We were held here for some time because of the bad weather in France. Eventually we were given the opportunity of having Communion, and then down to the East India docks, where we boarded our American Liberty ship, the USS William Phips. The Captain seemed very young, with a well-trimmed Imperial beard. We set sail, and got well out into the estuary before we had to heave to and await orders. Apparently it was because of the continuing bad weather, which had created a massive build-up in the reinforcements waiting to land.'

- CHAPTER II -
LANDING IN NORMANDY

*I*n June 1944, my father's battalion was to join the Normandy battles; they arrived around two to three weeks after the first wave had departed to commence the liberation of France. After a short period waiting for their call in Epping Forest, they made the short journey to the East India Docks in London where they boarded the U.S. Liberty Ship the USS William Phips. With the turn in the weather slowing down the transportation of the second wave of troops to Normandy, they had to wait off the coast for some time before heading to the beaches of Normandy.

Having made what I believe was a much easier journey to Normandy than they did in 1944, we arrived at Le Havre, before travelling to Caen, Bayeux, where we attended the Franco-British Ceremony commemorating the 70th Anniversary of the Allied D-Day landings at Arromanches. Whereas they arrived prior to the construction of Mulberry Harbour, but with a few elements of it already evident in the bay, some seventy years later, the ruins of this incredible feat of engineering survive as a lasting memory of the success of this operation. Doubtless his landing was much easier than that of those that lead the assault a few weeks earlier, and having disembarked, they made their way off the beach to commence the journey that would see horrific battles as they fought their way first through France, across Belgium to Arnhem. Following the successful liberation of 's-Hertogenbosch they were diverted to the Ardennes to support the U.S. push in the battle of the Bulge, before joining in Operation Veritable and the gruelling fight in the Reichswald Forest. After this they crossed the Rhine and finally ended their war in Hamburg. I begin with an excerpt from my father's diary, giving an insight into the build up to his part in the Normandy landings.

'Eventually our turn came and I think it was the morning of the 27th of June that saw us land at Arromanches. Mulberry Harbour did not yet exist, there were a couple of elements only in the bay. Our vehicles were being offloaded by crane to LCTs (Landing Craft Tanks) which were positioned alongside. We would have to scramble down large nets, which had been draped down the ship's side. Although things were pretty quiet, I know that we had a peculiar gut feeling, knowing that at long last we were actually landing in enemy held territory, and that we were about to put all our training into practice as we really came up against the enemy. As my truck, a fifteen hundredweight had been the last to be loaded on the ship; it was the first to be offloaded. I would be leading the charge! A couple of hundred yards away, a sister battery was going through the same motions. I was the Troop Leader of F Troop, which was the junior troop of the junior battery in the regiment. And I was its junior officer. My troop commander was Captain David Thompson, as good a man as you could ever wish to meet. We were all proud of our units, and always keen to accept a challenge. David had been able to assess the general situation and could see that it would be a close thing as to who would land first. He shouted to me, and my driver Gunner Bell, to get a move on. The LCT left the ship's side and headed for the shore. We were still quite a way out from the shore when we grounded, the front of the LCT dropped and old Bell gave her the works. We were actually in a few feet of water, but ploughed inshore rapidly to arrive first, to a loud cheer from those left on board the William Phips.

We roared up the beach and were guided off by several beach-masters. Then to an open area where we had to remove all our waterproofing. To drive too far with that on would seriously damage the engine. When we had all assembled and finished our de-waterproofing, we were led to action positions. There would be no great time to pass before we were to engage the enemy.

Perhaps I should digress a little here and explain how life in action would differ from that life we had become accustomed to in training. The active components of a battery become split. The OC

(Officer Commanding) is a major, and under him, he has two Troop Commanders who are captains. These three people spend virtually all their time with their opposite numbers in the particular infantry units they are supporting. Each troop position of four guns is in charge of a subaltern (lieutenant) called a GPO (Gun Position Officer). The GPO has as his assistant a TL (Troop Leader). The eight guns of the battery are synchronised by the CPO (Command Post Officer) who is the senior subaltern. So the infantry liaison team and the gun position team can now spend months apart, the only lines of communication being by radio or telephone. The troop commanders simply identify the target by one means or another and the gun teams are given the necessary information to respond. Each GPO is responsible for correctly locating his guns by means of a map reference, while the CPO and others in the division check and, if necessary, correct this information. All this action has to take place each time a gun position is changed. This means that if necessary, all seventy-two guns in the division could engage the same target. This ability was used, very successfully, on a number of occasions in northwest Europe.

All this means that the gunners are in so many ways kept in the dark as to what is happening. They never see their targets and have to be informed as to what success has been achieved. So the actual training was so important in building up complete confidence between these entities. There also needs to be a complete rapport between the Troop Commander and his infantry counterpart. Quite obviously, the sooner the gunner can bring fire to bear, exactly where the infantryman wants it and in the quantity required, the sooner does this mutual trust develop."

The waterproofing for the vehicles consisted of wrapping plasticine around the various engine parts that they needed to keep dry. Apparently a few tons of plasticine was delivered to the troops prior to their departure for Normandy to enable them to carry out the waterproofing.

- CHAPTER III -
THE NORMANDY BATTLES

*H*aving secured the beachhead, General Montgomery's plan of campaign was as follows:

1. Utilising deceptive measures from back home in England to lead the enemy to believe that other Allied forces were concentrated in Kent and Sussex with the intention of carrying out a second landing across the Straits of Dover. This was designed to lead to the retention of strong enemy forces in the Pas de Calais, which proved to be the case.

2. By maintaining pressure from British forces on the left around Caen, to attract the bulk of the German forces, particularly the armour to that area.

3. Depending on the success of 2, this would allow the U.S. forces easier conditions to break out on the right and sweep east towards Paris and the Seine. The U.S. Third Army, under the command of Lieut.-General George S. Patton, consisting of three Corps each with an Armoured Division as it spearhead, had been specially organised for this purpose.

The battalion were brought together in Subles on 29th June, elements having arrived in Normandy over the preceding two weeks. The training and waiting were things of the past and though they did not know it at the time, they would spend the next ten months in virtually continuous action. The fierce fighting on the left flank was in full swing, but it was to be some weeks before the U.S. forces were able to eventually break out on the right. While they gathered their strength for the break out, British and Canadian troops were involved in heavy and costly engagements in the vicinity of Caen.

Out of the combined enemy forces in North-West Europe on D-Day, only one Panzer and nine Infantry Divisions were in the vicinity of the Normandy coast, with the bulk of the ten Panzer and fifty Infantry Divisions being located in the Pas de Calais. In the West the Supreme Commander of these forces was Field Marshal Karl Gerd von Rundstedt, regarded as one of the most able German Generals of World War II. The Commander of Army Group B was Field Marshal Erwin Rommel, who had suffered defeat at the hands of General Montgomery in North Africa.

By the end of June, the ten German Divisions had been substantially reinforced, but with the reinforcements arriving piecemeal the German command could not mount an effective counterattack. This was blamed on the German High Command, including Hitler, being reluctant to deplete the troop concentration in the Pas de Calais, where they still expected a second landing. In addition to this, the intense action from the British and American air forces, causing long delays and heavy casualties to both men and vehicles which meant that German troops were only really safe to move in the hours of darkness. It is interesting to note that as the war to liberate Europe from the German forces rolled out the 53rd Welsh were to find themselves in conflict with the 9th SS Panzer-Division, *Hohenstaufen* and the 10th SS Panzer-Division, *Frundsberg*, on numerous occasions. Together these two divisions formed the II SS Panzer Korps. These were two of the elite Divisions of the Waffen-SS. They were well supplied with the latest equipment and they proved highly effective opposition as the 53rd Divisions crossed paths with the II SS Panzer Korps at various points in the months ahead.

The II SS Panzer Korps came into being when 9th SS-Panzer Division *Hohenstaufen* was formed, along with its sister formation 10th SS-Panzer Division *Frundsberg*. They were raised in February 1943 and initially stationed in France. The 9th was the senior division and was mainly formed from Reichsarbeitdienst (RAD) conscripts. Originally, *Hohenstaufen* was designated as a *Panzergrenadier* division, but in October 1943 it was promoted to full Panzer Division status. At its formation, *Hohenstaufen* was commanded by *SS-Obergruppenführer* Wilhelm Bittrich. The title

Hohenstaufen came from the Hohenstaufen dynasty, a Germanic noble family who produced a number of kings and emperors in the 12th and 13th centuries AD. It is believed that the division was named specifically after Friedrich II, who lived from 1194-1250.

After the encirclement of Generaloberst Hans-Valentin Hube's 1st Panzer Army near Kamenets Podolsky in Ukraine, *Generalfeldmarschall* Erich von Manstein requested that the *Hohenstaufen* and *Frundsberg* divisions be sent to attempt to link up with the trapped force. Arriving in the east in late March 1944, the divisions were formed into the II SS-Panzer Korps and were sent into the attack near the town of Tarnopol. After heavy fighting in the horrifying conditions caused by the rasputitsa ("mud season"), the division effected a link-up with Hube's forces near the town of Buczacz. During these battles, *Hohenstaufen* had suffered heavy casualties, and in late April was pulled out of the line to refit. The II SS Panzer Korps was to act as reserve for Army Group North Ukraine, performing "fire brigade" duties for the Army Group. After the Allied invasion of northern France on 6th June 1944, the II SS Panzer Korps, including the *Hohenstaufen* and *Frundsberg*, was sent west on 12th June to defend Caen in Normandy. *Hohenstaufen* suffered losses from Allied fighter bombers during its move to Normandy, delaying its arrival until 26th June 1944. The original plan for *Hohenstaufen* to attack towards the Allied beachhead was made impossible by a British offensive to take Caen. The II SS Panzer Korps was instead put into the line to support the weakened forces defending Caen. *Hohenstaufen* was involved in ferocious fighting until early July, suffering 1,200 casualties. On 10th July, the division was so weakened it was pulled back into reserve, to be replaced by the 277th Infantry Division. After the launching of another British offensive aimed at taking Caen, *Hohenstaufen* was again put back into the line, this time defending Hill 112, taking over the positions of the battered *Frundsberg*. After more heavy fighting, *Hohenstaufen* was again pulled out of the line on 15th July. Their paths would cross once more with the 53rd at Falaise, Arnhem and the Ardennes.

Like its sister division the 10th SS-Panzer Division *Frundsberg* was a German Waffen-SS-Panzer Division. The division was formed at the beginning of 1943 as a reserve for the expected Allied invasion of France. However, their first campaign was in the Ukraine in April 1944. Highly motivated after combat success in the Ukraine, the unit was then transported back to the west, where it fought the Allies in France and later at Arnhem and in the Ardennes. Initially, the name Karl der Große (Charlemagne) was used for the Division for some time in 1943. However, French volunteers in the *Wehrmacht* and the Waffen-SS used the name Charlemagne (33rd Waffen Grenadier Division of the SS Charlemagne (1st French)), so instead the title *Frundsberg* was chosen, which refers to the 16th century German landsknecht commander Georg von Frundsberg. The *Frundsberg* division differed from *Hohenstaufen* and was mainly formed from conscripts. It first saw action at Ternopol in April 1944 and later took part in the rescue of German troops cut off in the Kamianets-Podilskyi pocket. It was then sent to Normandy to counter the Allied landings. Together its "twin" Division, the 9th SS Panzer-Division *Hohenstaufen*, this hard fighting unit played an important part in holding the British Forces back in Normandy, particularly during Operation Epsom.

One of the reasons why the II SS Panzer Korps proved so successful lay in the fact that it was equipped with the latest technology. While the guns of 497 battery were towed, the SS could field a powerful force of self-propelled guns. These self-propelled guns brought greater mobility to the artillery formations of the Panzer divisions. The II SS Panzer Korps could boast two main types of self-propelled gun; the first of these was the Sd. Kfz. 124. In 1940, during the Battle of France, it was apparent that the Panzer II was unsuitable as a main battle tank. Though mechanically sound, it was both under-gunned and under-armoured. The chassis, however, proved serviceable for providing mobility to the 10.5 cm field howitzer. Existing chassis were converted to self-propelled artillery vehicles. Its full title was *Leichte Feldhaubitze 18/2 auf Fahrgestell Panzerkampfwagen II (Sf.)* ("Light field howitzer 18 on Panzer II chassis (self-propelled)"). It was better known as the *Wespe* (the German name for "wasp"). This was one of the most common German self-propelled artillery vehicles developed and used during the Second World War. It was based on a modified Panzer II chassis. The *Wespe* was very popular with their crews due to its reliability and high manoeuvrability. This made counter battery work difficult and dangerous for my father and his colleagues as the enemy could fire and move across country leaving the scene rapidly while the 25-pounders could only be moved by easily targeted roads making them vulnerable to counter-battery fire. The design for the *Wespe* was produced by Alkett, and was based on the proven Panzer II Ausf. F chassis. Amongst other modifications to the Panzer II, the engine was moved forward and the chassis was slightly lengthened to gain sufficient space for the rear-mounted 10.5 cm leFH 18 howitzer. The superstructure was lightly armoured, with 10 mm armour plate (enough to stop small arms fire) and was open at the top and to the rear. The vehicles were produced by FAMO's Ursus plant in Warsaw. The *Wespe* was in production from February 1943 until June 1944 when Soviet forces approached the frontier. By that time, 676 had been produced. An additional 159 were modified to serve as mobile artillery ammunition carriers. These guns had the advantage of being able to fire then move quickly to a new location across virtually any type of terrain and were more than a match for the towed adversaries which had to be hitched up and driven to a new location by road. The *Wespe* first saw combat in 1943 on the Eastern Front. It proved very successful, and Hitler ordered all production of Panzer II chassis to be utilized in the production of the *Wespe* alone, dropping other projects such as the Marder II self-propelled anti-tank gun.

The mobile artillery vehicles were allocated to the armoured artillery battalions (*Panzerartillerie Abteilungen*) of Panzer divisions and SS-Panzer divisions and along with the *Wespe* there was also the heavier *Hummel*, one of the best pieces of self-propelled artillery produced during the war. The *Hummel* (the German for "bumblebee") was equally popular with its crews and was even more deadly in a counter battery action. This heavier calibre gun was a highly effective piece of self-propelled artillery. It was based on the *Geschützwagen III/IV* chassis, armed with a 15 cm howitzer. It was used by the German *Wehrmacht* during the Second World War from early 1943 until the end of the war. The full designation was *Panzerfeldhaubitze 18M auf Geschützwagen III/IV (Sf) Hummel, Sd.Kfz. 165*. On February 27th, 1944, Hitler ordered the name *Hummel* to be dropped as being inappropriate for a fighting vehicle. The *Hummel* was designed in 1942 out of a need for mobile artillery support for the tank forces, the lack of which had first been felt during the invasion of the USSR. There were some self-propelled artillery vehicles already in service with the *Wehrmacht* at the time, but most were of limited value. The first option looked at was to mount a 10.5 cm leFH 18 howitzer on a Panzer III chassis, but this was rejected in favour of the same howitzer on a Panzer IV chassis. One prototype was built of this design. This design was again rejected, this time in favour of a more powerful solution: mounting the 15 cm sFH 18 L/30 howitzer on the specially designed *Geschützwagen III/IV*, which took elements of both the Panzer III (the driving and steering system) and Panzer IV chassis (the suspension and engine). The same chassis was also used for the Nashorn tank destroyer. The *Hummel* had an open-topped lightly armoured fighting compartment at the back of the vehicle which housed both the howitzer and the crew. The engine was moved to the centre of the vehicle to make room for this compartment. Late model *Hummels* had a slightly redesigned driver compartment and front superstructure, to offer more room to the radio operator and driver. Because the basic *Hummel* could only carry a limited amount of ammunition, the *Munitionsträger Hummel* ("ammunition carrier *Hummel*") was developed. This was basically a standard production *Hummel* without the howitzer (a 10 mm armour plate covering the gun mount) and with racks fitted to hold the ammunition. When necessary, these could still be fitted with the 15 cm howitzer of the normal *Hummel*; this could even be done as a field conversion. By the end of the war 714 *Hummels* had been built with another 150 ammunition carriers using the same design. The *Hummel* first participated in large scale combat at the Battle of Kursk, when some 100 *Hummels* were in service. They served in armoured artillery battalions (*Panzerartillerie Abteilungen*) of the Panzer divisions, forming separate heavy self-propelled artillery batteries, each with 6 *Hummels* and one ammunition carrier. These guns were also deployed by the II SS Panzer Korps in Normandy.

The SS self-propelled artillery was an obvious headache for the British, but the thing my father and so many other soldiers really hated was the infamous *Nebelwerfer*, a rocket firing weapon which fired six rockets in a close group. This was the 'Moaning Minnie' which spelt fear and destruction for anyone in the path of this vicious weapon. The *Nebelwerfer* ("Smoke Mortar") was another in the innovative series of weapons developed by the Germans which have become synonymous with the *Wehrmacht*. These weapons had been developed in the inter-war years and the name was used to fool observers from the League of Nations, who were observing any possible infraction of the Treaty of Versailles, from discovering that the weapon could be used for explosive and toxic chemical payloads as well as the smoke rounds that the name *Nebelwerfer* suggested.

The *Nebelwerfer* was initially developed by and assigned to the *Wehrmacht's* so-called "chemical troops" (*Nebeltruppen*). This weapon was given its name as a disinformation strategy designed to lead spies into thinking that it was merely a device for creating a smoke screen. Although they were primarily intended to deliver poison gas and smoke shells, a high-explosive rocket shell was also developed for the *Nebelwerfers*. By 1944 a variety of rocket launchers ranging in size from 15 to 32 centimetres were in action. The thin walls of the rockets had the great advantage of allowing much larger quantities of gases, fluids or high-explosives to be delivered than artillery or even mortar shells of the same weight. With the exception of the Balkan Campaign, *Nebelwerfers* were used in every campaign of the German Army during World War II. A version of the 21 cm calibre system was even adapted for air-to-air use against Allied bombers. The lower muzzle velocity of a mortar meant that its shell walls could be thinner than those of artillery shells and it could carry a larger payload than artillery shells of the same weight. This made it an attractive delivery system for poison gases.

Rocket development had begun during the 1920s and reached fruition in the late thirties. This offered the opportunity for the *Nebeltruppen* to deliver large quantities of poison gas or smoke simultaneously. The first weapon to be delivered to the troops was the 15 cm *Nebelwerfer 41* in 1940, after the Battle of France, a purpose-designed rocket with gas, smoke and high-explosive warheads. It, like virtually all German rocket designs, was spin-stabilized to increase accuracy. One very unusual feature was that the rocket motor was in the front, the exhaust venturi being about two-thirds down the body from the nose, with the intent to optimize the blast effect of the rocket as the warhead would still be above the ground when it detonated. This proved to greatly complicate manufacture for not much extra effect and it was not copied on later rocket designs. It was fired from a six-tube launcher mounted on a towed carriage adapted from that used by the 3.7 cm PaK 36 and had a range of 6,900 metres (7,500 yards). Almost five and a half million 15 cm rockets and 6,000 launchers were manufactured over the course of the war.

The 28/32 cm *Nebelwerfer 41* rockets were introduced in 1941, before Operation Barbarossa. They used the same motor, but carried different warheads. The 28 centimetres (11 in) rocket had a HE warhead, while the 32 centimetres (13 in) rockets were incendiary. The maximum range for either rocket was only 2,400 yards, a severe tactical drawback. Both could be fired from their wooden packing cases or a special wooden (*Schwere Wurfgerät 40* – heavy missile device) or tubular metal (*Schweres Wurfgerät 41* (sW.G. 41)) frame. Later, a towed launcher was developed that could take six rockets. Both rockets used the same launchers, but special liner rails had to be used for the 28 centimetres (11 in) rockets. A vehicular launch frame, the *Schwere Wurfrahmen 40* (sWu.R. 40), was also designed to improve the mobility of the heavy rockets. These were normally mounted on the sides of Sd.Kfz. 251 half-tracks, but they were also adapted for several different captured French tracked vehicles. The sWuR 40 was nicknamed the *Stuka-zu-Fuß* ("Foot Stuka"). Over six hundred thousand rockets and 700 launchers, excluding the sW.G. and sWu.R. firing frames, were made during the war. In total, 345 launchers were built from 1940.

The 21 cm *Nebelwerfer 42* rocket, which was introduced in 1942, had a longer range (7,850 metres (8,580 yds.)) and a simpler design than the smaller 15 cm rocket. It was only made with high-explosive warheads and was fired from a five-tube launcher that used the same carriage as the smaller weapon. Liner rails were used to allow it to fire the smaller 15 cm rocket.

Also introduced into service by 1944 was the 30 cm *Nebelwerfer* 42. This was intended to replace the 28 and 32 cm rockets, which had too short a range. Advances in propellant chemistry also reduced its smoke signature. It could be fired from all of the same platforms as the older rockets and many of the older launchers were converted to be used with the newer rocket by installing adapter rails, although it also had its own purpose-designed launcher, the *30 cm Raketenwerfer 56*. Some two hundred thousand rockets and 700 launchers were built during the war

To improve the mobility of the *Nebelwerfer* units, a ten-tube 15 centimetres (5.9 in) launcher was mounted on a lightly armored Sd.Kfz. 4 *"Maultier"* half-track chassis as the *15 cm Panzerwerfer 42 auf Selbstfahrlafette Sd.Kfz. 4/1* (based on the Opel *"Maultier"*, or "Mule", half-track). Three hundred of these were produced, split evenly between launchers and ammunition carriers. The Waffen-SS decided to copy the Soviet 82 millimetres (3.2 in) M-8 *Katyusha* rocket launcher as the 24-rail 8 cm *Raketen-Vielfachwerfer*. Its fin-stabilized rockets were cheaper and easier to manufacture than the German spin-stabilized designs and used cheaper launch rails. It was also capable of using the considerable stocks of captured Soviet rockets. Separate production lines were set up under party control as the army refused to convert any of its existing factories, but not many actually appear to have been made. Production quantities are unknown, but photographic evidence shows the launcher mounted on lightly armoured versions of the Sd.Kfz. 4 *"Maultier"* and captured French SOMUA MCG half-track.

These were the weapons which my father and his colleagues had such good reason to fear. Their missiles came howling down and exploded in a densely packed group which did tremendous damage and produced a shattering wave of concussion which could kill just from the force of the successive blast waves which sucked the oxygen from the lungs of its victim.

- CHAPTER IV -
THE ODON VALLEY BATTLES

*A*lthough the artillery of the *Wehrmacht* still packed a considerable punch, by the time the Normandy invasion had started the *Luftwaffe* had been virtually swept from the skies, and Germany itself was the subject of sustained bombing campaigns by the Allied air forces. This was damaging the German economy and overall caused significant harm to the morale of the German civilian population. In Normandy the Germans were subject to frequent and heavy artillery bombardments and they struggled to match this firepower. Despite having inferior rations, kit and equipment to the Allied forces, the *Wehrmacht* fought tenaciously, with great skill. Their courage in the face of far superior forces cannot be doubted.

The 53rd (Welsh) Division was placed under the command of Lieut.-General Sir Richard N. O'Connor of the VIII Corps, and were tasked with relieving the 15th Scottish Regiment and holding the ground they had gained. The VIII Corps were under serious pressure as the enemy counterattacked the Southern and Western flanks, through the 1st, 2nd, 9th and 10th Panzer Divisions. The 15th Division had suffered heavy casualties, but had virtually held all the ground that had been gained. In the action in the Southern portion of the salient, Lieut.-Colonel E. R. P. Ripley, Commanding Officer of the 1/5th Welch Battalion was to die in action.

The early days of July 1944 were to see the Division regroup, and by 8th July they moved into position between Gavrus and Baron, covering the Western face of the salient. Much fighting took place along this front, but nearly always confined to small raids and ambushes. The Division moved to XII Corps in time for the Second Battle of the Odon which was a series of operations fought by the British Army in mid-July 1944 against *Panzergruppe West* as part of the Battle of Normandy. Operations

Greenline and Pomegranate were intended to draw German attention away from the upcoming assault from the Orne bridgehead, codenamed Operation Goodwood. After four German infantry divisions arrived in Normandy, the objective was to prevent them from replacing German Panzer divisions deployed opposite the Second Army for operations against the U.S. First Army. No significant territorial gains were made but the attrition operations were strategically successful in keeping three German armoured divisions west of Caen, in the Odon river valley area, away from the Goodwood battlefield east of the Orne.

The three British armoured divisions and seven tank/armoured brigades, faced six Panzer divisions and three heavy tank battalions. The British units were at full strength but the German units had suffered considerable attrition and few losses had been replaced. The German defences had been prepared in depth, exploiting the terrain, minefields, a large number of long-range anti-tank guns and three *Nebelwerfer* brigades.

XII Corps and XXX Corps planned holding operations on the left flank in the Odon valley, from Tilly-sur-Seulles in the west to Caen in the east, to improve their positions and to deceive the German command, that the expected British offensive would be launched west of the Orne, while Operation Goodwood was being prepared east of the river. On 15th July, XII Corps was to attack from the Odon salient, to establish a secure jumping-off line, along the road running south-east from Bougy through Évrecy, for a later advance south-west towards Aunay or south-east to Thury-Harcourt. Next day, XXX Corps was to commence operations to take ground around Noyers, ready to reach the high ground to the north-east of Villers-Bocage.

XII Corps, comprising the 15th (Scottish) Infantry Division, reinforced by a brigade of 53rd (Welsh) Infantry Division and the 34th Tank Brigade, the 43rd (Wessex) Infantry Division and the other two brigades of the 53rd (Welsh) Infantry Division, was to attack in Operation Greenline at 9.30 P.M. on 15th July, using "Monty's Moonlight", searchlight beams reflected from clouds to illuminate the ground. The two 53rd Division brigades were to secure a start line for the 43rd Division to attack towards

Hill 112 and drive a corridor to the Orne River via Bougy, Évrecy and Maizet, ready to advance on Aunay-sur-Odon or Thury Harcourt should there be a German withdrawal. Further west, XXX Corps was to conduct Operation Pomegranate beginning on 16th July, in which the 49th (West Riding) Infantry Division on the right, was to capture Vendes and the surrounding area, in the centre the 59th (Staffordshire) Infantry Division was to capture the villages of Noyers-Bocage, Haut des Forges and Landelle and on the left the 53rd (Welsh) Division was to attack, ready for the corps to advance towards the high ground north-east of Villers Bocage.

On 29th June, during the British Epsom offensive, *Generalfeldmarschall* Gerd von Rundstedt the *Oberbefehlshaber West* ("Commander-in-Chief West") and *Generalfeldmarschall* Erwin Rommel the commander of Army Group B had met with Hitler at Berchtesgaden and been told to maintain the defence of Normandy and to organise a counter-offensive against the British salient. On their return from Germany, they received reports from *SS-Obergruppenführer* Paul Hausser, the commander of the 7th Army and the *Panzergruppe West* commander Leo Geyr von Schweppenburg urging a retirement from Caen to a new line beyond the range of Allied naval guns. The proposals were forwarded to Hitler and on 2nd July Rundstedt was sacked and replaced by *Generalfeldmarschall* Günther von Kluge. Geyr was dismissed and replaced by General Heinrich Eberbach two days later.

On 8th July Hitler issued a new directive requiring the front in Normandy to be maintained since the German forces lacked the tactical mobility for a battle of manoeuvre and an invasion in the Pas de Calais was believed imminent. Kluge made a tour of inspection and ordered that the existing positions be maintained, that they be increased in depth, by the use of every available man for labour and that a new counter-offensive by the seven Panzer divisions, be prepared against the Odon salient for 1st August, by which date the infantry divisions arriving in Normandy must have completed the relief of the Panzer divisions. The offensive was to be conducted on a 3 mile (4.8 km) front from Grainville-sur-Odon to Juvigny-sur-Seulles, to reach Luc-sur-Mer behind Caen. (Rommel thought the plan unrealistic and on 16th July wrote to Hitler predicting that the Normandy front would soon collapse. Next day he was strafed by Allied aircraft and wounded, which ended his service in Normandy).

Operation Greenline, 15th-17th July

On the left flank of the 15th Division, the crossroads at le Bon Repos and the higher ground overlooking Esquay-Notre-Dame were attacked by the 2nd Glasgow Highlanders of the 227th (Highland) Infantry Brigade ("227th Brigade"), supported by Churchill tanks of the 107th Regiment Royal Armoured Corps ("107th RAC") of the 34th Tank Brigade and the 141st Regiment RAC ("141st RAC") of the 79th Armoured Division, equipped with Churchill Armoured Vehicle Royal Engineers ("AVRE") and Churchill Crocodile flame thrower tanks. The Scottish advanced from the north-east, south-west over the northern slope of Hill 112, towards the defences of the III Battalion, 21st *SS-Panzergrenadier* Regiment. As the infantry emerged from dead ground they were met by massed mortar fire, which temporarily disorganised the battalion, as did a smoke screen placed on Hill 112, which had merged with fog and covered the area. The Scottish still managed to cross the start line on time at 9.30 P.M. and captured the SS survivors of a flame attack by the Crocodiles, on the road running from Croix des Filandriers to le Bon Repos. The advance continued downhill under Monty's Moonlight and covering fire from the 107th RAC Churchills, on higher ground just south of Baron. Esquay was captured by 11 P.M. but not held, as its position below a saucer of higher ground made it a shell-trap.

The two leading tank squadrons and two troops of Crocodiles from the 141st RAC were engaged while the third squadron waited in reserve behind the crest under frequent mortar fire during the evening and night. Four tanks were lost but many of the crews returned after dark. The troops dug in on the surrounding rises at positions determined earlier using reconnaissance photographs. The attack was interpreted by the Germans as a move on Hill 112 and Tiger tanks of 102nd *Schwere SS-Panzer Abteilung* were sent up the southern slope to repulse an attack that never came. Further west, the rest of the division had captured Point 113 but not Évrecy, which left the Glasgow Highlanders overlooked from both flanks, although German counter-attacks by infantry of the 21st *SS-Panzergrenadier* Regiment and tanks of the 10th SS-Panzer Regiment at first concentrated on Esquay, which had already been evacuated. The Germans counter-attack then fell on the positions around le Bon Repos, where two Panzer IVs were knocked out by 6-pounder anti-tank guns. The Scottish were pushed back several times, only for the medium artillery of XII Corps to bombard the Germans back out. On 18th July, 107th RAC had a skirmish with dug-in Tigers and two 88 mm self-propelled guns and lost four tanks on the ridge. The Highlanders maintained their positions for two days, before being relieved by a battalion of the 53rd (Welsh) Division.

The 44th (Lowland) Infantry Brigade ("44th Brigade") was to attack south-west from Tourmauville to take Point 113, Gavrus and Bougy in the Odon valley, while the 227th Brigade captured Esquay and then attacked Évrecy. The main 44th Brigade attack would then begin, with an attack by the 6th King's Own Scottish Borderers ("KOSB") on Point 113 and then attack by the 2nd Gordon Highlanders and the 10th Highland Light Infantry of the 227th Brigade on the left flank at 10.30 p.m., followed by an attack by the 8th Royal Scots with the 153rd Regiment Royal Armoured Corps ("153rd RAC") of the 34th Tank Brigade on the flank of the hill at 5.30 a.m. on 16th July, to take Gavrus and Bougy; Monty's Moonlight was to be deployed to assist the night advance. The 6th KOSB formed up on a start line behind the German outpost line and advanced directly into the German defences under the artificial moonlight. By morning the Scottish were dug in on the hill, one company finding itself 1,000 yards (910 m) forward of its objective, which disrupted German preparations for a counter-attack, before retiring to its objective.

At 5.30 a.m. on 16th July, the 8th Royal Scots ("8th RS") and the 153rd RAC advanced towards Gavrus, the tanks attacking to the side of the hill on the left flank, protected from the Germans in Évrecy by the ridge, to get behind the village and menace the German line of retreat, while the infantry overran the village. By 7.45 A.M. the 8th RS had taken the village and 70 prisoners. A similar attack was made on Bougy and another 100 prisoners were taken, after the garrison was routed. During the day several counter-attacks were made on the Scottish positions, which were repulsed by artillery barrages, with many German casualties. In the afternoon, the Germans counter-attacked twice with Tiger and Panther tanks accompanied by infantry. Mortar fire on forward positions was continuous throughout the afternoon and evening but no ground was lost and many casualties were inflicted on the Germans in a mutually costly defensive action. The tank crews fought or were at instant readiness for thirty hours without relief, from the zero hour until the German counter-attacks ended. The 6th Royal Scots Fusiliers ("RSF") were moved forward to Gavrus and the 8th RS formed up at Bougy. On the left flank, the situation deteriorated after the 227th Brigade attack on Évrecy failed; touch with the 6th KOSB became tenuous.

By dawn on 16th July the 15th (Scottish) Division had captured Bougy, Gavrus and dug in around Esquay and the western end of Point 113. On 17th July, the front line became quieter but the 44th Brigade was exposed by the success of the German defenders on the flanks and subjected to artillery bombardment. The 6th KOSB repulsed two attacks and the Germans defeated British attacks towards Évrecy. Two officers of the 8th RSF had led patrols towards Évrecy and found that German positions were still occupied. By the morning of 18th July the German positions were found to have been partly evacuated and the 6th KOSB pushed forward to the Bougy-Évrecy road. An attack by the 59th (Staffordshire) Division of XXX Corps, from the right (western) flank towards the positions of the 8th RS, made very slow progress. Four more German counter-attacks against the 44th Brigade were defeated. During the night the brigade was relieved by the 71st Brigade, 53rd Division and returned to Le Haut du Bosq, suffering several casualties on the way. The 9th SS-Panzer Division was brought up from reserve and by the end of the day had restored the front line, except at Hill 113.

The 158th Brigade from the 53rd (Welsh) Division, under command of the 15th Division and the 147th RAC were due to attack early on 16th July. The attack was postponed, because minefields around Baron had not been cleared; several flail tanks and two Churchill tanks had been disabled by mine explosions. On the next night the attack was cancelled due to fog and the operation began late on 17th July. To attack Évrecy required a long advance down a forward slope to the village. The attack was poorly prepared and the infantry battalion had already been depleted by casualties, a composite company being formed from one officer and fifty men and a second company consisting of only a composite platoon. The infantry were too tired to keep up with the tanks, which had to move quickly when brought under 88 mm fire from the village. About 150 prisoners were taken but mortar fire forced the infantry back to their start line. The 53rd (Welsh) Division captured Cahier and defeated several big counter-attacks. More attacks by XII Corps gained no ground and during the evening of 17th July the British force on Point 113 withdrew, ending operation Greenline.

By 21st July the 1/5th Welch found themselves holding high ground at Baron to the East of Garus. The two forward Companies were on high ground towards Le Bon Repos (Hill 112). During the afternoon and evening the enemy launched three Infantry attacks supported by Tiger tanks. The first two were beaten off, but the third, supported by six Tigers, overran one company and part of the other. The men who had not been overrun were mostly casualties, and the enemy established themselves at the cross roads at Bon Repos where they dug in. In this action, 3 officers and 115 other ranks of the 1/5th Welch were reported missing in action. Two days later, the 4th Welch carried out a reprisal raid, consisting of two Companies supported by Crocodiles (flame throwing tanks), artillery, mortars and small arms fire. This was highly successful and they progressed as far as Esquay. The enemy suffered heavy casualties and some prisoners were captured. In all the fight for Hill 112 took over two weeks to complete.

The baptism of fire had been intense and the awful reality of war hit home at the outset of the campaign as I discovered from my father's own words:

"Within a few nights of landing we had our first casualty. One of our Troop Commanders was in a semi derelict tower as an observation post. A German gun scored a direct hit, and he was killed. We were undergoing shell and mortar fire on odd occasions, but nothing too severe. After one fairly hairy night, I had orders to take all my men, in small groups as they could be spared, to a certain position on our left. Not having the vaguest idea why this order had been given, I took the first group myself. The site before us was certainly an upsetting one. In a very small, shallow slit-trench a figure was crouched, bending forward. The back of his neck had been sliced open and a large lump gouged out. To say that it was not a pretty sight is a complete understatement. It was the simplest and most salutary lesson I was ever to receive. I know that that poor fellow's death, in those circumstances, was to save many.

For weeks we moved around, forward, sideways, whatever the orders were. We knew that our foothold on the continent was continually being improved, strengthened and enlarged, but the infantry had to fight hard for whatever ground they gained. One of our moves was to a spot overlooking Caen. The Canadians had been attacking it for quite a while, but the stubborn resistance still held them out. With the additional firepower from a number of our units, they eventually triumphed. The following day we drove through Caen to our new position. I have never seen a more desolate scene. The town had been subjected to the fire of numerous artillery units for days on end, as well as a number of bomber attacks. There were still some civilians living there and the entire place, buildings and humans, seemed to have a thick coating of dirty grey dust. It was really a heart-breaking sight.

The whole of July went by. We, as gunners, really had it easy compared to how the infantry were faring. We moved from A to B and then to C, but they were just open areas, with one spot being like any other. But we knew from the amount of firing we did to support the infantry that they were having a very busy and dangerous time. A little news kept filtering down about how they were faring, and about the losses. Sometimes light, sometimes heavy, but seldom none. But *virtually every incident in which they took part resulted in victory, some taking longer than others. Eventually the effect really began to tell on the enemy."*

- CHAPTER V -
THE FALAISE POCKET

$\mathcal{B}$y 3rd August, it was clear that the enemy had started the withdrawal from the River Orne. The Allied advance began with the 53rd Division on the left and the 59th on its right. By the 6th the 53rd had secured a position by the river between Amaye and Feuguerolles and the 59th a bridgehead at Grimbosq. Although Von Rundstedt was advocating a speedy withdrawal, Hitler issued orders to begin a counter attack which commenced at Mortain, on the Western edge of the corridor on 7th August. Five Panzer Divisions were deployed in the counter attack and General Montgomery, seeing this as an opportunity to destroy a great deal of the enemy forces, closed the Eastern front of the corridor, directing part of the American 3rd Army on Argentan and Falaise. His ploy proved a massive success with the bulk of the German forces being destroyed in the "Falaise" pocket, leaving the Allies to cross the Seine almost unopposed.

On 12th August the 53rd Division crossed the River Orne at Grimbosq, with the 1st East Lancashire capturing Bois Halbout and the 1/5th Welch Fresney Le Vieux after intense battles. Some 250 enemy prisoners were captured. At the same time, Allied forces were pushing forward towards Falaise, leaving the 53rd Division to cut the roads leading out of the town.

16th August 1944 is a day which will endure in the memories of the 53rd for ever. During intense action at Balfour, Captain Tasker Watkins was to earn the first Welsh Victoria Cross of World War II. Leading an assault on a machine gun post, after all the other officers were killed in the approach, Watkins continued to lead the group and won his VC for leading a bayonet charge against 50 armed enemy infantry and then single-handedly took out a machine-gun post to ensure the safety of his unit. The official citation reads as follows:

"While commanding a company of the Welch Regiment in North-West Europe on August 16th, the battalion was ordered to attack objectives near the railway at Balfour.

Major Watkins' company had to cross open cornfields in which booby traps had been set. It was not dusk and the company came under fire. The only officer left, he placed himself at the head of his men and, under short range fire, charged two posts in succession, personally killing or wounding the occupants with his Sten gun.

On reaching his objective he found an anti-tank gun manned by a German soldier. His Sten gun jammed, so he threw it in the German's face and shot him with his pistol before he had time to recover.

The company had only some thirty men left, and was counter-attacked by fifty enemy infantry. Major Watkins directed the fire of his men and led a bayonet charge, which resulted in the almost complete destruction of the enemy.

At dusk, orders were given for the battalion to withdraw. The orders were not received by Major Watkins' company, who found themselves alone and surrounded, in depleted numbers and in failing light.

Major Watkins decided to rejoin his battalion by passing around the flank of the enemy position through which he had advanced, but, while passing through the cornfields once more, he was challenged by an enemy post at close range.

He ordered his men to scatter and himself charged the post with a Bren gun and silenced it. He then led the remnants of his company back to battalion headquarters.

His superb gallantry and total disregard for his own safety during an extremely difficult period were responsible for saving the lives of his men and had decisive influence on the course of the battle."

Still expecting von Kluge to withdraw his forces from the tightening Allied noose, Montgomery had for some time been planning a "long envelopment", by which the British and Canadians would pivot left from Falaise toward the River Seine while the U.S. Third Army blocked the escape route between the Seine and Loire rivers, trapping all surviving German forces in western France. In a telephone conversation on 8th August, the Supreme Allied Commander General Dwight D. Eisenhower recommended an American proposal for a shorter envelopment at Argentan. Montgomery and Patton had misgivings; if the Allies did not take Argentan, Alençon and Falaise quickly, many Germans might escape. Believing he could always fall back on the original plan if necessary, Montgomery accepted the wishes of Bradley, as the man on the spot and the proposal was adopted.

The Third Army advance from the south made good progress on 12th August; Alençon was captured and von Kluge was forced to commit troops he had been gathering for a counter-attack. Next day, the 5th U.S. Armoured Division of XV U.S. Corps, advanced 35 miles (56 km) and reached positions overlooking Argentan. On 13th August, Bradley over-ruled orders by Patton, for a further push northwards towards Falaise, by the 5th U.S. Armoured Division. Bradley ordered the XV U.S. Corps to "concentrate for operations in another direction". The U.S. troops near Argentan were ordered to withdraw, which ended the pincer movement by XV U.S. Corps. Patton objected but complied, which left an exit for the German forces in the Falaise Pocket.

With the Americans on the southern flank halted and then engaged with Panzer Group Eberbach and with the British pressing in from the north-west, the First Canadian Army, which included the Polish 1st Armoured Division, was ordered to close the trap. After a limited attack by the 2nd Canadian Infantry Division down the Laize valley on 12th/13th August, most of the time since Totalize had been spent preparing for Operation Tractable a set-piece attack on Falaise. The operation commenced on 14th August at 11.42, covered by an artillery smokescreen that mimicked the night attack of Operation Totalize. The 4th Canadian Armoured Division and the 1st Polish Armoured Division crossed the Laison but delays at the Dives River gave time for the Tiger tanks of the *Schwere SS-Panzer Abteilung 102* to counter-attack.

Navigating through the smoke slowed progress and the mistaken use by the First Canadian Army of yellow smoke to identify their positions, when the strategic bombers used yellow to mark targets, led to some bombing of the Canadians and slower progress than planned. On 15th August, the 2nd Canadian Infantry Division, 3rd Canadian Infantry Division and the 2nd Canadian (Armoured) Brigade continued the offensive but progress remained slow. The 4th Armoured Division captured Soulangy against determined German resistance and several German counter-attacks, which prevented a breakthrough to Trun. Next day, the 2nd Canadian Infantry Division entered Falaise, against minor opposition from Waffen-SS units and scattered pockets of German infantry and by 17th August, had secured the town.

At midday on the 16th August, von Kluge had refused an order from Hitler for another counter-attack and in the afternoon Hitler agreed to a withdrawal but became suspicious that von Kluge intended to surrender to the Allies. Late on 17th August, Hitler sacked von Kluge and recalled him to Germany; von Kluge then either committed suicide or was killed by Jürgen Stroop an SS-officer, for his involvement in the bomb plot of 20th July. Von Kluge was succeeded by *Feldmarschall* Walter Model, whose first act was to order the immediate retreat of the 7th Army and Fifth Panzer Army, while the II SS Panzer Corps with the remnants of four Panzer divisions, held the north face of the escape route against the British and Canadians and the XLVII Panzer Corps with what was left of two Panzer divisions, held the southern face against the Third U.S. Army.

By 17th August the encirclement was incomplete. The 1st Polish Armoured Division, part of the First Canadian Army, was divided into three battle groups and ordered to make a wide sweep to the south-east, to meet American troops at Chambois. Trun fell to the 4th Canadian Armoured Division on 18th August. Having captured Champeaux on 19th August, the Polish battle groups converged on Chambois and with reinforcements from the 4th Canadian Armoured Division, the Poles secured the town and linked up with the U.S. 90th and French 2nd Armoured divisions by evening. The Allies were not yet astride the 7th Army escape route in any great strength and their positions were attacked by German troops inside the pocket. An armoured column of the 2nd Panzer Division broke through the Canadians in St. Lambert, took half the village and kept a road open for six hours until nightfall.

Many Germans escaped and small parties made their way through to the Dives during the night.

Having taken Chambois, two of the Polish battle groups drove northeast and established themselves on part of Hill 262 (Mont Ormel ridge), spending the night of 19th August digging in. The following morning, Model ordered elements of the 2nd SS-Panzer Division and 9th SS-Panzer Division to attack from outside the pocket towards the Polish positions. Around midday, several units of the 10th SS-Panzer Division, 12th SS-Panzer Division and 116th Panzer Division managed to break through the Polish lines and open a corridor, while the 9th SS-Panzer Division, prevented the Canadians from intervening. By mid-afternoon, about 10,000 German troops had passed out of the pocket.

The Poles held on to Hill 262 (The Mace) and were able from their vantage point, to direct artillery fire on to the retreating Germans. Hausser, the 7th Army Commander, ordered that the Polish positions be "eliminated". The remnants of the 352nd Infantry Division and several battle groups from the 2nd SS-Panzer Division, inflicted many casualties on the 8th and 9th battalions of the Polish Division but the assault was eventually repulsed at the cost of nearly all of their ammunition and the Poles watched as the remnants of the XLVII Panzer Corps escaped. During the night there was sporadic fighting and the Poles called for frequent artillery bombardments, to disrupt the German retreat from the sector.

German attacks resumed the next morning but the Poles retained their foothold on the ridge. At about 11.00, a final attempt on the positions of the 9th Battalion was launched by nearby SS troops, which was defeated at close quarters. Soon after midday, the Canadian Grenadier Guards reached Mont Ormel and by late afternoon, the remainder of the 2nd and 9th SS-Panzer Divisions had begun their retreat to the Seine. The Polish casualties at Mont Ormel were 351 killed and wounded, with eleven tanks lost. For the Falaise pocket operation, the 1st Polish Armoured Division listed 1,441 casualties including 466 killed. German losses in their assaults on the ridge were c. 500 dead and 1,000 men taken prisoner, most from the 12th SS-Panzer Division. Scores of

Tiger, Panther and Panzer IV tanks were destroyed, along with many artillery pieces.

By the evening of 21ˢᵗ August, tanks of the 4ᵗʰ Canadian Armoured Division had linked with Polish forces at Coudehard and the 3ʳᵈ and 4ᵗʰ Canadian Infantry divisions had secured St. Lambert and the northern passage to Chambois; the Falaise pocket had been sealed. From 20-50,000 German troops minus heavy equipment, escaped through the gap and were reorganized and rearmed, in time to slow the Allied advance into the Netherlands and Germany.

The Battle of the Falaise Pocket ended the Battle of Normandy with a decisive German defeat. Hitler's involvement had been damaging from the first, with his insistence on hopelessly unrealistic counter-offensives, micro-management of generals, and refusal to countenance withdrawal, when his armies were threatened with annihilation. More than forty German divisions were destroyed during the Battle of Normandy. No exact figures are available but historians estimate that the battle cost the German forces c. 450,000 men, of whom 240,000 were killed or wounded. The Allies had achieved victory at a cost of 209,672 casualties among the ground forces, including 36,976 killed and 19,221 missing. The Allied air forces lost 16,714 airmen killed or missing in connection with Operation Overlord. The final battle of Operation Overlord, the Liberation of Paris, followed on 25ᵗʰ August and Overlord ended by 30ᵗʰ August, with the retreat of the last German unit across the Seine.

The area in which the pocket had formed was full of the remains of battle. Villages had been destroyed and derelict equipment made some roads impassable. Corpses of soldiers and civilians littered the area along with thousands of dead cattle and horses. In the hot August weather, maggots crawled over the bodies and hordes of flies descended on the area. Pilots reported being able to smell the stench of the battlefield hundreds of feet above it. General Eisenhower recorded that:

> 'The battlefield at Falaise was unquestionably one of the greatest "killing fields" of any of the war areas. Forty-eight hours after the

closing of the gap I was conducted through it on foot, to encounter scenes that could be described only by Dante. It was literally possible to walk for hundreds of yards at a time, stepping on nothing but dead and decaying flesh. Fear of infection from the rancid conditions led the Allies to declare the area an "unhealthy zone". Clearing the area was a low priority though and went on until well into November. Many swollen bodies had to be shot to expunge gasses within them before they could be burnt and bulldozers were used to clear the area of dead animals.

The international army boundary arbitrarily divided the British and American battlefields just beyond Argentan, on the Falaise side of it. Patton's troops, who thought they had the mission of closing the gap, took Argentan in their stride and crossed the international boundary without stopping. Montgomery, who was still nominally in charge of all ground forces, now chose to exercise his authority and ordered Patton back to his side of the international boundary line. For ten days, however, the beaten but still coherently organized German Army retreated through the Falaise gap.'

By 22nd August, all German forces west of the Allied lines were dead or in captivity. Historians differ in their estimates of German losses in the pocket. The majority state that from 80,000-100,000 troops were caught in the encirclement of which 10,000-15,000 were killed, 40,000-50,000 were taken prisoner, and 20,000-50,000 escaped. In the northern sector, German losses included 344 tanks, self-propelled guns and other light armoured vehicles, as well as 2,447 soft-skinned vehicles and 252 guns abandoned or destroyed. In the fighting around Hill 262, German losses totalled 2,000 men killed, 5,000 taken prisoner and 55 tanks, 44 guns and 152 other armoured vehicles destroyed. The 12th SS-Panzer Division had lost 94% of its armour, nearly all of its artillery and 70% of its vehicles. With close to 20,000 men and 150 tanks before the Normandy campaign, after Falaise it was reduced to 300 men and 10 tanks. Although elements of several German formations had managed to escape to the east, even these had left behind most of their equipment.

After the battle, Allied investigators estimated that the Germans lost around 500 tanks and assault guns in the pocket and that little of the extricated equipment survived the retreat across the Seine.

By the 18th August the 53rd (Welsh) Division had closed in to the West and South of Falaise and captured a great number of enemy prisoners. The following day the gap was finally sealed when the Polish Armoured Division joined up at Chambois, South-east of Falaise, with the American troops coming up from the South.

The scene around Falaise was one of utter carnage. The German Armies of the West had perished, or were captured, and suffered a blow from which they never fully recovered. The 53rd spent the next few days in a mopping up operation, before moving to an area near Evreux, in preparation for the long hard trek across France to the Low Countries.

In the aftermath of Falaise, as the enemy forces retreated, weather conditions improved allowing the Allied Air Forces to inflict heavy casualties on their vehicles. On August 20th alone, the 2nd Tactical Air Force destroyed 471 wheeled vehicles and 33 tanks and damaged a further 865 vehicles and 57 tanks. This was a fairly typical haul for them at this time.

As the 53rd advanced across France and Belgium they were supported by the 4th Armoured Brigade. Opposition was met regularly, and though sometimes stubborn, was rarely prolonged. Most opposition was met at bridges, cross roads and villages. The Brigades of the Division leap frogged each other as they advanced.

At this point it is pertinent to record the casualties suffered by the 53rd from the day of landing to the end of August 1944, a total period of less than one hundred days:

	Officers	Other Ranks
Killed	52	533
Wounded	145	2711
Missing in Action	18	360

A total of nearly 4,000 casualties. Amazingly the Division had taken a total of 3,823 enemy troops prisoner, a figure that just about matched their own casualties.

My father's diaries recount a couple of tales from this period:

"Two incidents from this period stick in my mind, one fairly humorous, the other obviously not. To the rear of one of my gun positions near Falaise, quite some distance away, was a fairly dark looking object. I decided to investigate – carefully. To my surprise it was the front portion of an RAF bomber. There were three crew members still inside, in a mummified state. I chose not to move them, but notify the War Graves Commission of their exact location so that they could be properly cared for.

The other occasion concerned my Troop Sergeant Major. We were doing one of our night drives. We were all absolutely shattered, we'd had very little sleep. We were halted, just waiting events when T. S. M. Dilley (who was a real old soldier of many years' service) came out of his jeep and begged me to take over the driving of his vehicle so that he might have a short nap in the back of my truck. He was sure that he'd fall asleep otherwise. I acquiesced, and changed vehicles. Another lad came and joined me as my passenger. After quite a while the signal to proceed was given. As soon as the jeep moved I knew I'd been stung. There was a puncture in one of the back wheels. In a jeep the tools are kept in small boxes on top of the back wheels. The back of the jeep was absolutely crammed with stuff which we had to move before we could reach the tool boxes. After that we had to change the wheel, and all the while the regiment was getting further away, and we had no idea where we were heading. These night drives were simply follow my leader and keep hoping. Of course old Dilley swore that he was perfectly innocent. "The puncture must have happened after I stopped," he said. He certainly never had the same chance to catch me again. We sped on until late in August we crossed the Seine near Rouen. Then early in September we crossed the Somme at Picquigny, a few miles from Amiens, then on to Saint Fol and Bethune. It was here that another incident occurred.

I was a member of a small 'recce' (Reconnaissance) party. I was dropped off by myself to go into an adjacent field and make preparations for the arrival of the guns which would follow on in a few hours. I did not have long for it to get a little lighter so that I could start my preparations. Away to my right I could see the faint outlines of a few houses, I then noticed a slight stationary figure watching me. He began approaching slowly and I could see that he was wearing light mauve breeches, resembling a farmer. He was very hesitant until it became a little lighter and he could see me more clearly. Then he ran towards me quite excitedly. He asked if I was 'Anglais' and when I replied yes he embraced me and sobbed. I was able to assure him that the Germans had retreated from the whole area and were miles away. He then left me and ran towards the little hamlet and shouted madly until everyone was awake and had heard the good news. People began rushing towards me, dressing as they came. It was then for the first time that it really sank in as to how these people had suffered through years of occupation. I was being smothered by them all and to cap it all, my guns began to arrive. I had to beg them to stand clear while the guns were put into their positions.

All that day I was being grabbed by people who simply had to shake my hand or kiss me. They spent the whole day talking to the lads and looking at the guns. It was fortuitous that we had no firing instructions otherwise I don't know what would have happened. Late in the afternoon a shy young girl, hanging onto her parents hands, shyly handed me a 'photo' of herself, on the back of which she had written, in French, 'Souvenir of the day of my Liberation, Bethune, 5th Sept. 1944. Emilienne Cousin.' Due to the good auspices of a newspaper editor in LIEGE, in Sept 1994 I again met Emilienne with her husband and little grand-daughter. They were accompanied by the daughter of the first man to see me that day, as well as her husband. Unfortunately the man himself was dead."

The photograph my father was given that day in 1944 is featured in the photographic section of this book.

- CHAPTER VI -

THE ADVANCE TO HOLLAND

*W*ith the comprehensive defeat suffered by the German Army at Falaise, resistance against the early Allied advance was ineffective and the Seine was crossed swiftly, with the Allied troops making good progress through Belgium and into Holland before they met any serious defence. However, although the German defence might have been short in number, they fought tenaciously and with great courage. Their defence was stronger in the North of Europe, with some of the American advance further South meeting little resistance. The Allied forces had support from the French resistance, who despite their undoubted harassment of the retreating enemy forces, were not always as accurate as they could have been with the provision of information.

On the 21st August, the 53rd Reconnaissance Regiment with the 4th Armoured Brigade fought in support of the 2nd Canadian Corps and found stubborn resistance from the enemy, who employed a number of Tiger tanks. Despite this, around 1,800 prisoners were taken that day.

By the 24th, the 53rd were still being held up near Mounai and Broglie, just west of the Seine. "Wasps", carriers equipped with flame throwers were brought into action, and this was as a result of the first successful deployment of these weapons by the 4th battalion of the Royal Welsh Fusiliers in their raid on "The Triangle" on 2nd August. On the 25th the Division continued their advance towards Acquigny-Ecardinville-Evreux-Dacquepus. The advance was difficult due to the terrain, the debris of the fierce fighting and did not arrive until the 26th. The 53rd crossed the Seine on the 30th, at Muids, some 20 miles South of Rouen. Progress was good, and by 1st September they were overrunning Flying

Bomb emplacements at Pontremy and Berguenfuse. The next day they crossed the Somme at Picquigny with little resistance. The only thing that hampered their advance was the speed that their vehicles could carry them.

On September 7th, the Division crossed the border into Belgium at Armentieres and by midday they were into Coutrai. The liberated townsfolk flocked around their liberators with small boys pleading for "cigarettes for papa". The next day they advanced to Antwerp which had already been liberated by the 11th Armoured Division a few days earlier. To their surprise the German forces, having suffered serious defeats as the advance progressed, had left the Belgian city virtually undefended. As they guarded the city, German counter attacks were intermittent and ineffectual. For the first time since they landed in France some the Allied forces were actually able to relax. On the 13th September the liberating troops were visited by the recently promoted Field Marshal Sir Bernard Montgomery.

In my father's words:

"Anyway, back to the main story. We carried on through Armentieres and as far as Antwerp in Belgium. The armoured Div. had driven in and the 53rd Div. were the first foot-soldiers to enter. The area of Antwerp, South of the Albert canal was free of Germans, but they were settled on the North bank and on the Walcheren Islands in the estuary. We were given our gun positions, but things were pretty quiet. We now saw our first real signs of civilisation since landing in France. There were shops open, actually selling things!!

I was dumbfounded to see rich-looking cream cakes on sale. There was a beautiful public bathing pool with one large retractable wall that opened up to flood the pool with sunshine. It was a wonderful break to walk around the streets with so little damage which we had been forced to endure in. For example, in some we had been subjected to an objectionable amount of enemy shell-fire or rocket-fire. The horrible experiences were, at night, being subjected to action from the 'Moaning Minnies' which is what we called their multiple rocket-

launchers. As the rockets flew towards you, they set up a hideous very loud screaming sound!! Not very pleasant! Fortunately, they didn't happen too often. After the 'breakout' we were at least able to see signs of humanity and even the odd civilian evident. But soon the Germans began the odd spot of shelling onto the town itself. We had arrived in Antwerp on the 8th Sept. and were to move out around the 15th Sept. starting the operation to drive a narrow corridor up through Holland to the Nijmegen area."

By this time, General Eisenhower had taken direct command of the forces and Field Marshal Montgomery had only the 21st Army Group under his control. Montgomery believed that the Germans were shattered by their defeat in France and that a swift attack on a narrow front would take the Allied troops across the Rhine and into Germany, bringing the war to an end in 1944. The attack would take place in the North, with other operations being temporarily suspended. Eisenhower had other thoughts though. He wanted to attack on a much broader front and destroy the German Troops West of the Rhine. As Supreme Commander, Eisenhower's plans prevailed.

In preparation for this next assault, the ground troops were to push forward towards the River Waal around Nijmegen. Montgomery estimated he could commence his offensive by September 17th and it was arranged for three Airborne Divisions to be dropped on a line linking Eindhoven to Arnhem. Following this line of attack were the troops of XXX Corps, while VIII Corps were to guard the Eastern flank on the right, and XII Corps were to guard the Western flank on the left, broadening the base of the salient.

Upon arriving in the Arnhem area, the division began the task of refitting. The majority of the remaining armoured vehicles were loaded onto trains in preparation for transport to repair depots in Germany. On Sunday, 17th September 1944, the Allies launched Operation Market-Garden, and the division would become heavily involved in the subsequent Battle of Arnhem. The British 1st Airborne Division was dropped in Oosterbeek, to the west of Arnhem. Realizing the threat, Bittrich (now commander of the II SS Panzer Corps) ordered *Hohenstaufen* and *Frundsberg* to ready themselves for combat. The division's armour was unloaded from the trains and workshop units worked frantically to replace the tanks' tracks, which had been removed for transportation. Of the division's armoured units, only the division's reconnaissance battalion, equipped mostly with wheeled and half tracked vehicles, was ready for immediate action.

Bittrich ordered *Hohenstaufen* to occupy Arnhem and secure the vital bridge. Harzer sent the division to the city, encountering stiff resistance from the *Roten Teufel* (Red Devils), as the Germans came to call the British paratoopers. The Reconnaissance Battalion, a 40-vehicle unit commanded by *Hauptsturmführer* Viktor Eberhard Gräbner, was sent south over the bridge to scout the area around Nijmegen. Gräbner had that day received the Knight's Cross for his actions in Normandy.

While the Reconnaissance Battalion was scouting to the south of Arnhem, Colonel John Frost's 2nd Battalion of the British 1st Airborne Division had advanced into Arnhem and prepared defensive positions at the northern end of the bridge. Gräbner returned from his scouting mission to the south on the morning of 18th September, and ordered about half of his reconnaissance unit, numbering about 22 armoured cars, half-tracks, and a few trucks, to attack north across the bridge. Gräbner's exact intentions remain a mystery, but he apparently either hoped to recapture the bridge or to race through the British positions to assist the rest of the division in its defence of Arnhem. Either way, the attack was a complete disaster. The Paras were ready, and after allowing the first four vehicles to pass, they opened up with PIAT anti-tank weapons, flamethrowers and small arms fire. In two hours of fighting, the Reconnaissance Battalion was virtually annihilated, losing 12 vehicles out of 22 in the assault and around 70 men killed, including Gräbner. This action is depicted in the film A Bridge Too Far.

Throughout the eight-day battle, the division operated mostly in and to the west of Arnhem, fighting with Frost's battalion and reducing the pocket containing the remainder of the 1st Airborne, which had become encircled near Oosterbeek. The battle of Arnhem was a victory for *Hohenstaufen*. With the assistance of other German formations, the division had destroyed an elite British airborne outfit, which was badly outnumbered and only lightly armed. Despite the intensity of the fighting, the soldiers of *Hohenstaufen* and *Frundsberg* treated the captured paratroopers courteously, although there are reports of cold-blooded executions by some SS members, and Bittrich remarked that the tenacity and fighting prowess of the Red Devils was not to be matched, even by the Soviets.

The 53rd Welsh Division were to attack on the right flank, tasked with forcing a crossing of the Junction Canal North of Lommel, 36 miles East of Antwerp. By September 15th the 7th Armoured Division took over responsibility for the security of Antwerp and the 53rd Welsh began moving on.

As elements of the 53rd Reconnaissance Regiment moved up towards the canal, with the 158th Brigade, who were to make the assault crossing, completed their reconnaissance. The crossing was to be carried out on a two battalion front, either side of a demolished bridge, just North of Lommel. The 7th Royal Welch Fusiliers on the right and the 1st East Lancashire Regiment on the left. The Divisional Engineers were then to construct a new bridge alongside the broken one.

Supporting fire began late on the morning of the 16th. Seven Field Regiments were deployed alongside two Medium regiments, with 4.2 Mortars and Machine guns on the flanks. The first boats were launched at 11.30 P.M.

Despite losing a few boats, the initial crossing was successful. However the darkness of the night, coupled with the wooded nature of the country and heavy rain made it difficult for Companies to find their objectives. Heavy opposition was encountered on the right, but by late afternoon on the 17th, the bridgehead had been established. Mopping up the few remaining enemy troops took some time. Most of these troops were German Paratroops who fought tenaciously and very few of the prisoners taken were unwounded.

The 1/5th Welch crossed the canal that evening, but the Battalion's Commanding Officer, Lieut.-Colonel H. T. Gibson was wounded and ultimately died as a result of these wounds. Having previously fought with great distinction in Crete and North Africa, this was a big loss to the Division.

At the same time the troops of the 15th Scottish Division were making their crossing some way to the West. Heavy resistance was encountered on all fronts.

On the 18th, the 160th Brigade, with the 6th Royal Welch Fusiliers in the lead, crossed the Junction Canal and passed through the bridgehead, followed by the 71st Brigade on the 19th. The next two and a half weeks saw the whole Division push North in a series of hard fought battles.

The 21st saw the 4th Royal Welch Fusiliers attack, and ultimately capture the village of Wintelre, killing some 60 Germans and taking a further 144 prisoners. Unfortunately Brigadier Blomfield was seriously wounded and was replaced by Brigadier M Elrington a few days later.

The 160th Brigade passed through the bridgehead on September 18th moving on to Wilreit-Luykgeste, the 4th Welch made a successful attack to clear a wood losing several officers and men. By the 23rd Postel was captured and on the 24th, moving North, they reached the outskirts of Reusel. The Germans offered stiff resistance and an advance by one Company of the 6th Royal Welch Fusiliers only managed to occupy the Southern fringe of the village. A further assault on the 25th was unsuccessful and it was not until the 6th October that the village was ultimately captured. Orders were frequently given in Welsh to keep the Germans from understanding them. Having captured Reusel, the Brigade moved North East to a defensive position at Elst, between Nijmegen and Arnhem.

While all this action was taking place, the XXX Corps had been driving forward to secure a bridgehead over the Rhine further west. The Airborne Corps had secured most of their objectives, but the ground troops had struggled to make their progress towards the Rhine. The remnants of the 1st British Airborne Division and the Polish Para Brigade, who had landed in the Arnhem area, had to be withdrawn south of the Rhine. While the attempt to secure a bridgehead over the Waal at Nijmegen had succeeded that over the Rhine had failed.

The next task for the 53rd Welsh was to protect the corridor which had been established through Eindhoven and Grave with its apex at Nijmegen, by this time winter conditions were beginning.

This time was classed as the Division's stay on the "Island" as the Nijmegen bridgehead was called. It was a period when they came under heavy and continuous bombardment form the enemy's artillery and mortar fire. They were relieved on the 17th October by the 50th Division, in readiness for their assault on the town of 's-Hertogenbosch.

My father's memories of this period are brief, but include a reunion with an old school friend. It is amazing to think that this could take place at such a time:

"We had now gone through two spheres of war. In Normandy we had experienced a very enclosed type of feeling, which had been completely changed after the 'breakout'. As people who manned the guns, we were never able to see our targets or even know what our targets actually were. When things had quietened down the T.C. would be able to put us in the picture to some extent. We were usually told how the battle had progressed. Normally we would only be aware that we were in some field and that the enemy would be somewhere in front of us. Our memories of the various, numerous gun positions which we had occupied were therefore very vague and were defined only by the conditions

Field Marshal Montgomery planned that his troops, the 21st Army Group would force a narrow corridor, the length of Holland and would arrive at Nijmegen on the river Waal. This operation started about the 17th Sept. As the world knows, the operation was not completely successful. We took Nijmegen and our Battery was on the 'Island' between Nijmegen and Arnhem for quite some time. I must mention here that whilst waiting to cross the bridge to the 'Island', I dismounted from my vehicle to stretch my legs, and who happened to be on the pavement, but Eric Melton, an old school chum who was now a member of the R.A.M.C in the Polar Bear division. A quick chat and we were on our respective ways. Such was life!"

- CHAPTER VII -
THE BATTLE FOR 'S-HERTOGENBOSCH

*T*he next period in the war was to see the 53rd Welsh take part in the attempt to liberate the German stronghold which had been established at the Dutch city of 's-Hertogenbosch. Before I go into the detail of what was to be one of the hardest fought battles of their war, it is pertinent to consider the words of Major Riehl, the German Garrison Commander, following the capture of the city. He stated, "I was ordered to hold the town at all costs. The speed of the 53rd Division's advance came as a complete surprise and I was impressed by the resolute manner of the way the infantry crossed the River Dommel and the prompt manner in which the Sappers bridged the river for the passage of the anti-tank guns."

The assault on 's-Hertogenbosch represented the first time since landing in Normandy some four months earlier that the Division would go into a battle as a whole. Up until this point, their fighting had seen them operate as diverse and sometimes isolated units. This was to change with their attempt to capture the capital of the Noord Brabant when they entered the fray as a complete Division.

Following the failure of the Allied troops to secure a crossing over the Lower Rhine at Arnhem, Montgomery's immediate task was to open the port of Antwerp to Allied shipping. This task was given to the 21st Army Group. Up until this time most of the supplies were still being brought by road from the French ports, some 200 miles behind the front. The transport resources were stretched to breaking point and the situation could not be allowed to continue. Two operations were considered necessary:

1. The Scheldt had to be cleared through the occupation of the

Dutch mainland coast south of the estuary and occupying the Dutch islands of Walcheren and South Beveland.

2. Protecting the Northern Flank of the corridor leading to the Nijmegen Bridgehead by closing up the Lower Maas from the West of Grove to its mouth.

XII Corps was given the second of these tasks. The Corps plan was for the 53rd Welsh and the 7th Armoured Division, followed up by the 51st (Highland) Division if required to advance against 's-Hertogenbosch from the North East clearing the town and surrounding countryside. Attacking from the South East, the 15th (Scottish) Division was to capture Tilburg. The enemy forces consisted of three Divisions, reinforced by a fourth on the day before the operation commenced, all in fairly good shape by the standards of that time.

's-Hertogenbosch was heavily defended. The Germans regarded its retention as vital, providing as it did, protection for the withdrawal and supply route of the enemy forces still defending the Scheldt against the Allies. Four battalions of the 712th German Division held the area, with about nine companies holding the town and the remainder guarding the likely approaches.

Commanding officer Major-General Ross had the following plan:

The attack would be made from East to West, from the direction of Oss.

160th Infantry Brigade, supported by the 5th Dragoon Guards with "crocodiles" (flame throwing tanks) and "flails" (tanks equipped for detonating mines) north of the railway – Oss-'s-Hertogenbosch.

71st Infantry Brigade to advance south of the railway astride the road from Heersch to 's-Hertogenbosch.

158th Infantry Brigade held in reserve, ready to pass through with the 53rd Reconnaissance Regiment and one Squadron of the 5th Dragoon Guards to seize the canal bridges in the town if possible.

At 6.30 A.M. on the 22nd October the advance commenced. The 160th Brigade made good progress quickly clearing the village of Nuland with the first troops reaching Kruisstratt by 1.30 P.M. The 71st Brigade, on the left, were unsupported by armour and progress was slow. In the afternoon, the Divisional Commander reinforced the success of the 160th Brigade by pushing through the 53rd Reconnaissance Regiment and the 1st Battalion The East Lancashire Regiment. Having passed through, they were hampered when they encountered a minefield and the 2nd Monmouths continued the advance.

The 23rd October saw the advance continue when the 2nd Monmouths of the 160th Brigade passed through the East Lancashires and pushed on to Rosmalen. By the afternoon the Division was in a position to attack 's-Hertogenbosch and that evening General Ross issued orders for the next day. The 1/5th Welch and the 1st East Lancashires were to advance along the railway during the night and get into the North Eastern outskirts of the town by first light. Simultaneously, the 7th Royal Welch Fusiliers were to push down towards Hintham with a view to capture the bridge. To help them in this task, the 6th Royal Welch Fusiliers were to advance on Hintham from the North. To support them a massive Artillery programme was arranged comprising over 200 guns of which 75% were 25 pounders and the remainder medium and heavy.

By 10 P.M., A Company of the 6th Royal Welch Fusiliers had outflanked the village and entered from the West. They held out against continuous attacks through the night.

In the early hours of the 24th the Welch and East Lancashires began their march through difficult terrain. Making good progress the Lancashires reached a position just to the North East of the town and soon after the 1/5th Welch passed through to take the canal bridge. This platoon then came under heavy fire from a German self-propelled gun, which they put out of action by an anti-tank gun borrowed from the East Lancashires. Straight after this however, two more self-propelled guns were brought forward and pinned them down. The Germans blew the bridge behind them and casualties were heavy with the survivors being taken prisoner later that day.

Meanwhile the East Lancashires were having more success inflicting heavy casualties on the German troops as they retreated down the road from Hintham to 's-Hertogenbosch, oblivious of the fact that two Battalions of British troops had already arrived in the town. By 11.30

that morning, the East Lancashires had been joined by a squadron of tanks of the 5th Dragoon Guards which had moved in along the railway line. Their job was to secure the two bridges over the canal, but they only managed to secure one intact, the Germans having blown up the other. The Battalion then took up a defensive position between the bridges.

The 7th Royal Welch Fusiliers together with two squadrons of the 5th Dragoon Guards advanced along the Hintham road. Making rapid progress they passed through Hintham by 11 A.M. to relieve A Company of the 6th Royal Welch Fusiliers. Small pockets of resistance were overcome on the way through, with many German prisoners being taken captive. They also captured three 75 mm guns. By early afternoon they have secured the factory area to the East of the town. All bridges over the Zuid Willems canal had now been destroyed but the lock was still intact. Supported by tanks and crocodiles, A Company of the 7th Royal Welch Fusiliers moved across the lock and overcame an enemy post in a nearby house. B Company followed on and a strong bridgehead over the Canal was secured. Through the night the 555th Field Company constructed a Class 40 Bridge over the Canal.

By the 25th with the battle going well, the British forces suffered a setback. The 6th Battalion Royal Welch Fusiliers were unsuccessful in their attempt to cross the Canal as a result of the Germans bringing up reinforcements during the night. To counter this resistance, the 1st Battalion East Lancashires were brought up around the Southern flank and captured the bridge. As this was unfolding, the 1/5th Welch crossed the Class 40 Bridge and cleared the area to the North. Following heavy fighting, The East Lancashires finally made it to the River Dommel by around 8 P.M. to find both bridges had been blown. By nightfall two Platoons of the 1/5th Welch reached the bridge to the West of the Canal to find it only partially destroyed.

The plan for the 26th was for the 158th Brigade to cross the River Dommel and complete the clearance of the town. The 1/5th Welch were to rush the partially demolished bridge and the East Lancashires were to move on another bridge which it now transpired was only partially destroyed. The 7th Royal Welch Fusiliers were held in abeyance ready to move on either of these fronts.

Around 11 A.M. the 1/5th Welch with covering smoke and mortar but no artillery rushed the bridge. The assault caught the enemy napping and 25 prisoners and two Spandau machine guns were captured. A bridgehead was formed but came under violent counter attack and heavy fire through the day. It was only with the greatest difficulty that the bridge could be crossed and repairs started.

As a result of this fierce resistance, the 7th Royal Welch Fusiliers were deployed past the bridge held by the East Lancashires, who began the move Northwards to link up with the 1/5th Welch, which they had managed by 10 P.M. The 7th then moved slowly North East towards the Railway Station which was burning furiously. They continued to mop up various buildings helped by the light from this fire.

The German garrison had resisted fiercely, but every street and house had to be cleared. The defences were well planned and demolitions were carried out with the usual German efficiency. As the battle wore on however, German resistance began to wane with morale suffering and physical exhaustion setting in. Many prisoners had been taken, and casualties were high. By the end of the day, the capture of 's-Hertogenbosch was nearing completion.

On the 27th the 7th Royal Welch Fusiliers commenced a mopping up operation on the Western fringe of the town. Resistance was light and many prisoners were taken including the German Commander.

Elsewhere, resistance was stronger with three German tanks, five S.P. guns and a Company of Infantry to the fore, advancing on the railway station from the West. B Company engaged them with small arms and mortar fire causing the Infantry to seek shelter in houses. All available weapons and a smoke screen were then deployed against the armoured vehicles and of the eight tanks and S.P guns two were knocked out by anti-tank fire, one was abandoned and the rest withdrew. Four of the S.P. guns were later captured by the 1/5th Welch, three of them intact. By the evening of the 27th all resistance had ceased and the battle was over. The 160th Brigade relieved the 158th apart from the 7th Royal Welch

Fusiliers, with the 158th withdrawing to the East of the town. For his role in the battle, Major Dick Hughes was awarded the Military Cross, his citation reads:

> *"Major Hughes is Battery Commander of 497 Field Battery which is affiliated to 2nd Battalion Monmouthshire Regiment.*
>
> *During the operations of 22nd/25th October 1944, culminating in the capture of 's-Hertogenbosch, 2nd battalion Monmouthshire Regiment advanced on a narrow front along the only road available on the exposed right flank. Throughout the four days Major Hughes was continually up and down this axis reconnoitring Observation Posts and organising fire support to enable the advance to continue, showing complete disregard for his own safety and a determination to provide the maximum artillery support at all costs. By his energy and vigilance he managed, when communications were bad, to get fire orders back to the guns not only of his own battery but to those of other Observation Posts supporting the forward battalions, thereby largely contributing to the success of the artillery support as a whole.*
>
> *But for his outstanding courage and devotion to duty during these critical days, the advance on the right flank would not only have cost many more casualties to our own tanks and infantry but might also have been considerably delayed."*

Colonel Brooke and Brigadier Coleman were both awarded the DSO for their roles in the same battle. The History of the 2nd Battalion The Monmouthshire Regiment recorded the action thus:

> *"The spirited action by the 2nd Monmouths contributed in no small degree to the capture on the following day of 's-Hertogenbosch by the 158 Brigade and was recognised by the award of the D.S.O. to Lt. Col. Brooke, who was also personally congratulated on the Battalion's achievements by both the Army and the Corps Commanders when he met them in the town while the fighting on the 24th was still going on. In its advance of nearly 7,000 yards in two days, the 2nd*

Monmouths had destroyed two German Battalions, a result largely ascribable to the unfailing support of tanks and "Crocodiles," and the extremely quick and accurate shooting of 133rd Field Regiment, R.A. (Panteg), and in particular of 497 Battery, whose shells were often in the air within one minute of a call for fire. It was in fact a triumph of teamwork, with every man engaged doing his full share with skill, courage and endurance!"

A year after the liberation of Den Bosch, Major General Ross, along with some of the troops of the 53rd Welsh returned to the town and presented the Burgomaster with a shield engraved with the crests of all the units which took part in the liberation of the town. In return he was awarded the Freedom of the town. The shield is proudly on display in the town hall, along with a book of memorial listing the details of all the 147 soldiers who lost their lives in the struggle to free the people of Den Bosch. The windows of the room where the shield is displayed have also been engraved with the names of the fallen soldiers in a fitting epitaph to the memory of the bravery with which they fought.

My father's record of this battle is brief but poignant.

"On the 17th Oct. we withdrew from the 'Island' and went S.W. of Grave whilst liberation of 's-Hertogenbosch was planned. This city was the capital of the large area of North Brabant which now had to be taken to protect the narrow corridor which had been created. It was known that the city was extremely well defended because it protected vital German supply routes.

At 6.30 A.M. on the 22nd Oct. this memorable battle started. Five tremendous days of battle followed and eventually on the evening of the 27th, all resistance was virtually defunct. Hard-fought battles took place at dozens of vital points and each individual battle was costly. During October the division lost: 145 men killed, 705 men wounded and 83 men missing. These were principally suffered at Den Bosch. On the 24th Oct a platoon of the 1/5th Welch fought their way over a Canal Bridge. They were initially menaced by a S.P. gun, (self-

propelled). Soon two more S.P.s supported the first. In the meantime the bridge behind them had been destroyed. Many were killed and by evening the survivors were taken prisoner.

The gallant gentleman in charge of this platoon was Capt. (later Major) David Ronald Morgan. This whole operation had been accompanied by the fiercest artillery fire of the war. In one day of 24 hours, each of my four guns had fired the unbelievable sum of one thousand rounds. This works out at approximately one shell per gun every one and half minutes. Since the arrival in Normandy in June, it has been estimated that the infantry have been out of contact with the enemy for only four days. The Press, back home, recorded this victory as a tremendous success for the Division! Ever since, the people of Den Bosch and those of the 53rd. have built up and maintained the greatest rapport. They have a 53rd. War Memorial there, and there is a simple 53rd Div. Cross in the Cathedral of St. Jan."

It is interesting to read the account of the battle for 's-Hertogenbosch from the German viewpoint. The following passage is a translation of the report by General-Lieutenant Neumann, Commander of the German 712th Infantry Division. It clearly demonstrates the importance of the allied artillery in overcoming the resistance of the German defenders of the town. I have quoted this account at length as General-Lieutenant Neumann expands upon the effect of the incoming artillery fire. It is quite sobering for me to reflect upon the fact that the man who wrote this account was on the receiving end of the relentless curtain of shells fired by my father's guns. I was also struck by the brief description of the battle for the bridge. The machines my father described as S.P. Guns were actually the famous *Sturmgeschütze* which were a form of infantry support tank. These vehicles played a major role in the set-back which the men of the 53rd suffered in the fighting for the bridge.

"In the period from 17.10.44 the higher command had formed the impression that prior to 712. Inf. Division's establishing its perimeter east of 's-Hertogenbosch the enemy presumably had shifted its forces.

There were two possible scenarios: either the British 7th Armoured Division, which was positioned opposite our Division during late September, was pulled back and swapped for a different British Inf. Div. added to the British XII Corps, or the XII Corps had changed position in the area opposite our Division. Together with the British 7th Armoured Division and a further added Div. an attack further West might therefore take 's-Hertogenbosch and threaten the German 15th Army's flank if not cutting it off from its supply lines.

It was therefore necessary for the area to be cleared from the enemy by force.

The assumption that the British 7th Armoured Division had not completely moved from the frontline was confirmed by the 712. Inf. Div. This was confirmed along the frontlines by the movement of numerous tanks and reconnaissance vehicles. It was even assumed, after multiple shock troop infiltrations during night operations that the opposite side had strengthened their Division's right flank regiment. The enemy was alert and it was very difficult to bring in prisoners. Finally we received confirmation about the enemy's situation during the night of 19th October from two prisoners captured along the road, 's-Hertogenbosch-Hees. A Lieutenant (severely wounded and later deceased) and a Sergeant of the British 7th Armoured Division were brought in as prisoners. In the afternoon of 21st October, as we later discovered our own highly visible traffic was attacked by our own artillery in area Kaathoven.

The enemy's artillery activity proved to be minor until 19th October when four enemy batteries began shelling the area north of the river Waal during the night of 19th October from the area north of Oss were shelled with the help of the Divisional artillery engaging in heavy bombardments. Thus it could be concluded that there was no weakening of the enemy's artillery strength, but rather that they were regrouping their artillery for a major effort.

Our reconnaissance troops had already encountered strong dug in enemy tank positions, these continued to deployed in the night of 21st October. As a result they were unable to fulfil their objective, bringing in prisoners. When in the end the situation regarding the enemy's position reached the Division at 03.15 hrs on 22nd October a powerful and thunderous British artillery barrage was opened on the area south of the Zuid-Willemsvaart.

The intensity of this artillery barrage clearly showed it was meant to clear the way for an imminent and major enemy assault.

At the commencement of the battle the 712th Division could deploy the following forces:

a) the regular Infantry of the Division plus the Feldersatz-Btl. (Field replacement Battalion) of the Division. It was for the most part deployed at the front line along the Maas river, although also this battalion entirely consisted of Luftwaffe recruits with only three to four weeks of army training.

b) Artillery: The Division had at their disposal: 61st battery with 17 guns and 1-s. Battery with 2 guns calculated according to the number of guns only 65% had one ammunition supply available!

c) Anti-tank: The Division possessed 3 x 8.8 cm Pak (Panzerabwehrkanone) Anti-tank guns and also 3 x 7.5 cm Pak 40 and 5 medium anti-tank guns.

Furthermore each of the battalions was issued with 12 Panzerschreck (anti-tank rocket launchers) and around 100 Panzerfausts. Which were single use pre-loaded anti-tank weapons

d) Engineers: As Engineers the Div. only had a weak company Pionieer Engineers of the 59 I.D. available of which about 35 Uffz. (officers) and soldiers of the old Pi.Btl.712 Nachkommandos (rearguard of the Wehrmacht) from the coastal defence were added to fill in the ranks so the 1./Pi.Kp.159 (Kp, Corps) comprising a combined force of more than 100 men, though lacking in almost every type engineering equipment.

e) Communication troops were sufficient in relation to this type of battle, and because 150 km of 185 km Division network was in use (by ground cable) only 35 of the 70 available lengths of cable were still to be installed. During this it became more and more evident that the Division lacked mobility as it was equipped as a 'Bodenständige'

Division (troops lacking sufficient transportation to move around on the battlefield). This was not sufficient for easy movement in the coming engagement.

Once the battle had started it soon became evident that the communication network was not up to the job.

f) Supply troops and transport troops had been badly depleted and could hardly fulfil their duties. The problem was the lack of sufficient large transport for heavy loads that was only partly solved by collecting most of the troop transports from the rear area.

The Division was deployed over an area some 27 km wide of which half was very difficult for tank movement. The positions however had been further strengthened and fortified during the previous three weeks. In addition belts of 400 T- and 1000 S-mines and several barriers fashioned from cut down trees had been constructed; but no other form of defence had been built.

The fear for the enemy armour was not a factor for Fusilier-Btl.712 and II./G.R.745 (Grenadier Regiment) which were battle hardened formations adept in anti-tank actions, while at I./G.R.732 and Felders.Btl.347 could be described as partially battle-hardened and reasonably well versed in anti-tank actions, while the other poorly organized Battalions could be best described as not being hardened towards enemy armour.

It must be mentioned that the Division has lost twenty Infantry-Regiment and Battalion Commanders since May '44, with the result that Commanders on the 22nd October were, for the most part, inexperienced and not really up to the job during their period of command.

22nd October

During the Early morning heavy enemy fire was only experienced in the sector south of G.R.732 (Grenadier Regiment), this heavy fire increased shortly after 06.00 hrs and extended as afar as the Div. Command post. The sector of G.R.745 however received no incoming *artillery fire which led the Division to conclude that it could expect a large offensive on both sides of the Zuid-Willemsvaart shortly.*

At 06.00 hrs after a heavy artillery bombardment the enemy advanced along both sides of the road Veghel-Berlicum with 2 Companies of infantry and 12-15 tanks to support attack. The attack was halted as a result of combined artillery fire from the main line of resistance positioned near the advanced secure boundaries in which also the left side of 59.I.D. Artillery section took part in. The tanks were deployed shortly after.

At 07.10 hrs After a half hour artillery bombardment the enemy advanced over a wider front and attacked the sector of Fusilier-Btl.712 between the road, 's-Hertogenbosch-Hees and the railway line, 's-Hertogenbosch-Nijmegen, with about 50 armoured vehicles, amongst them were numerous flame throwing tanks. As a result of the poor visibility it was difficult to execute a joint artillery attack especially after the effects of the tremendous opening bombardment that damaged the communication equipment – the phone line network in the area was also almost entirely destroyed.

It was no surprise therefore that the 50 armoured vehicles were able to infiltrate the front, but the Main Line of Resistance held out. It was only after some hours that the enemy was able, by systematically smoking out dug in anti-tank measures, to force a gap in the lines at Nuland. The enemy however lost at least 6 tanks in this sector because of the fearlessness of numerous Grenadiers equipped with the Panzerfaust and medium anti-tank guns. Because the battle area was very favourable for deployment of the Panzerfausts it can be concluded that the losses were probably a lot higher, though the division has no proof for this logical assumption, other than the fact that these soldiers bravely did their duty and posts and defended themselves – most of these men however should be considered as having been killed in action.

The Division decided to keep strengthening of the main resistance line by the deployment of III/G.R.732 (G.R. Grenadier Regiment) with the addition of hundreds of volunteers. It was resolved not to reduce the number of troops in this sector nor to consider a fall back position, even though the forward position covered a 7 km wide front with just 250 men, of which 40% were raw recruits.

For this Luftwaffe-Btl. Ewald (without the recruit company), which had been positioned at 's-Hertogenbosch in case of an airborne assault and for the security of the Battle Commander, was alerted and also summoned up was the Gren. Rgt.745 (Regiment) which was ordered to leave behind just one battle ready reserve company, Btl. Wittstock, that occupied a line of resistance at the hamlet Bruggen, occupy the so-called 2nd line of resistance south-west of Nuland.

At 09.30 hrs the enemy again commenced an attack on the south wing with support of several tanks and simultaneously attacked I./ G.R.732 at Nieuwekampen. During this attack our own artillery fire was destroyed. I./G.R.732 reported that the tanks at Nieuwekampen were allegedly advancing behind German prisoners of war that were used as shields. As a result of this act, both here deployed medium Pak could not attack the enemy and were put out of action.

At Fusilier-Btl.712 the enemy used the same trick but here the evidently "German prisoners" opened fire just in front of the MLR so it became clear that it was considering a shameful deception of British soldiers in German uniforms.

Around 11.00 hrs the enemy was ready to break out from the gap at Nuland that was temporarily closed again by a counterattack at about 12.00 hrs by the battalions; Btl. Stabes, Fus.Btl.712 and I./ Fus.Btl.712. But the enemy broke through after a pre-bombardment lasting about half an hour and attacked with at least 2 Btl. of Infantry and about 40 tanks on both sides along the railway line. The enemy was engaged in bitter fighting at the local defensive positions but it could not be prevented – the artillery was not able anymore to give support by using the desirable loads of ammunition – that the enemy advanced to the defensive position north of the railway and even crossing it. In heroic close combat against enemy armour the Regiment command post G.R.745 held on until the last men.

There were further enemy attacks between 11.00-16.00 hrs at

multiple places varying from 2 Companies up to Battalion size, regularly supported by 5-8 tanks. On one occasion 3 tanks had broken through at the street from Veghel to Berlicum with the infantry split in two and heavy casualties inflicted amongst the infantry along the MLR by own defensive fire. At Doornhoek and south of the woods at Hooge Heide a bigger breakthrough had taken place.

There the deployed 8.8 cm Pak were simultaneously attacked and destroyed by 5 tanks. This part of the MLR is, except from a few still fighting soldiers, apparently totally destroyed. At Nieuwe Kampen the enemy also succeeded with 5-6 tanks to push through until south of the command post of I./G.R.732 so the connection in the middle of the woods positioned 1./G.R.732, was cut off.

Further north the MRL stayed intact until the edge of the woods 800m south-west of Nuland where the line bent several hundred meters further to the north. Here the brave Fusilier-Btl. lead by Hptm. Siebecker (Hauptmann, Captain) held the line from 23.10 hrs to 04.00 hrs until the withdrawal order was given to the defensive position (new MLR).

It was completely preventing the Div. to counterattack and mobile anti-tank weapons to close the gap in the MLR so the Div. was forced to conclude that the defensive position should be considered now as the MLR. The Engineers were already deployed during the morning to create roadblocks through fallen trees and booby-traps and other obstacles with the little reserve of mines that were left.

Because of counterattacks of Btl. Ewald along the defensive position in the woods to the north and near the Division's army school barracks from the West the enemy that had penetrated the defensive position into the west, was forced to turn around. Btl. Wittstock has vacated the defensive position north from Kruisstraat after enemy pressure; no forces are at hand to close this gap.

At the railroad crossing 1 km south of Kruisstraat infantry supported by 6 tanks was spotted east-west of the defensive position adjacent to the woods. One shock troop attack during the night supported by artillery failed with heavy losses to own troops.

Though the Division in the evening was able to fight back this first day of heavy enemy attacks on the defensive position against a strong British Armored Division with a full Infantry Division counting about 25-30 Batteries and divisional and army artillery from every caliber, it was doubted that these more or less unorganized troops were able to hold the new Main Line of Resistance during another day of heavy battle. Sadly it was noted that the Division was out of Pak. The North flank of the defensive line north of Kruisstraat was opened wide. The artillery ammunition is becoming scarce. The Division is expecting a concentrated attack on the area Berlicum and Rosmalen concentrated on both sides of the rail line.

It has become clear that our troops inflicted heavy bloody losses to the enemy after their first attacks and also on this day 15 enemy tanks and an armoured reconnaissance vehicle have been destroyed. Also our own losses were considerable. The overall mass of the Division Battalions kept occupying their positions, they fulfilled their assignments to defend these to the last men.

23rd October

In the night strong harassing fire that at times increased to artillery barrage fire.

Reinforcements that were added were:

1./Pz.Jg.Abt.256 (Anti-Tank Division 256) with 5 x 7.5 cm Pak 40 (mot.Z.)

1./G.R.481 (arrival last parts finally at 07.00 hrs)

4./A.R.185 (Artillery Regiment 185) (fire ready around 09.30 hrs)

Stab I./A.R.159 with 1. and 9./A.R.159 (Stab = HQ or staff) (fire ready round 10.00 hrs).

During the night our own artillery gave harassing fire on suspected enemy assembly area's and locations.

07.00 hrs – The enemy attack began as expected on the rail crossing south of Kruisstraat. After artillery and fog bombardments 3 tanks broke through the defensive position south of the railway.

Further tanks broke through the line 500 m north of the main road, 's-Hertogenbosch-Hees. As a result of the foggy morning and because of enemy artillery support by own troops proved difficult. Also here again it was noticeable that the lack of communication equipment was to our disadvantage.

At the position of I./G.R.481 at Bruggen, for the retaking of section Kruisstraat-Hoefgraaf canal, a battalion moving in a rather narrow area under the protection of the fog suffered a strong enemy tank attack with multiple flame throwing tanks. Several tanks advanced to Rosmalen but were forced to turn around because of combined fire. Btl. Wittstock together with I./G.R.481 pressed through from Rosmalen again until Bruggen and, without informing the Division, pressed on until Het Gewande. The result hoped for, closing the gap at the north wing, failed. On the contrary, a breakthrough of numerous tanks took place again in the area of G.R.732. Nevertheless, the area around Rosmalen remained the most threatened area. At 12.45 hrs 2 (Sturmgeschütz)/Pz.Jg.Abt.256 (Panzer. Jager. Abteilung. 256) without 1st platoon was, according to the request of 11.00 hrs made by n.Kdo.LXXXVIII.A.K. (General Command 88 Army Corp), deployed at both sides of Kruisstraat for retaking the Main Line of Resistance.

The Division had, from its own resources, provided this Sturmgeschütz company with fuel so it could be expected that they would soon be ready to march. The accompanying infantry was provided with 2 VB's, (Vorgeschobener Artillerie-Beobachter, Forward Artillery Observers) from both the artillery-battalions and the plan of attack was discussed with the involved Commanders so a presumption for success was given. These Commanders were specially ordered to close all gaps. To the south adjacent troops kept to their orders and accompanied the attack. Because of incomprehensible causes – apparently difficulties during refuelling – the Sturmgeschützen finally arrived around 16.00 hrs at the Division's defensive position at Hintham, at the time when the Batteries of A.R.1712 (Artillery Regiment 1712) were already at Rosmalen partly involved in close combat with enemy tanks and infantry. On this dim day there was the danger that the attack, at the beginning of darkness, would not fully develop. During the hours of preparation the frontline at G.R.732 was broken through by enemy tanks and infantry troops at multiple places. The opponent was increasing his artillery activity since noon. It was not a rarity that the enemy artillery dropped 800-1000 shells on single districts or expected defensive positions.

When our multiple Sturmgeschütze, accompanied by infantry seated on top of the Sturmgeschütze, approached Rosmalen at 16.30 hrs from the south for the attack, they came under attack from our own artillery with over a 1000 shells and suffered considerable losses. 2 Sturmgeschützen were put out of action by direct artillery hits. Heavy tank battles developed around Rosmalen. While half the Sturmgeschützen accompanied by infantry bypassed Rosmalen to the east-west and progressed forward onto Bruggen, the other half was engaged in a heavy battle with tanks that wanted to destroy our counterattacking west flank. This Sturmgeschütz group came in oppression and called back the infantry accompanied Sturmgeschützen in the dawning dusk. As a result the infantry could not continue their attack and also because they suffered significantly under enemy artillery. At Rosmalen a super heavy tank (dreadnought), 1 Sherman tank and 1 armoured reconnaissance vehicle were destroyed. The Sturmgeschützen were pulled back to serve as corps reserve as ordered by the Gen.Kdos. (General Command) after a further Sturmgeschütz was put out of action by multiple direct anti-tank hits in the northwest part of 's-Hertogenbosch.

While the focus of the division with all the heavy weapons was focused to support the attack on Rosmalen, Bruggen, Kruisstraat around 17.30 hrs, British infantry penetrated at Hintham coming from the southeast numbering about 50, occupied the houses and could not be driven out again because of lack of power as parts of the Div. Stabes (Divisions HQ) the communications battalion 712 and the Stabsbatt.Art.Rgt.1712 (HQ of Artillery Regiment 1712) were deployed elsewhere as an alarm unit. In this critical stage the newly added Battalion – Balzereit arrived around 18.30 hrs and was assigned to push north along Hintham to take over the protection of the artillery positions in the area around Rosmalen and to resume the communication with parts of Gr.Rgt.732. Btl. Balzereit did not fulfil this order, partly because it was annihilated by artillery fire during darkness. It lacked the Division being in communication with the troops deployed at the front. The special reconnaissance patrols couldn't penetrate, either because they couldn't get through because of the enemy or they just couldn't find the troops any more. Communication equipment was partly shot to pieces and telephone lines were destroyed.

At 20.00 hrs the enemy artillery barrage started on the location of the Division's Command post in the west part of Hintham without pausing until 04.40 hrs. There was no doubt this was espionage because the largest number of shells fell precisely on the Command Communication – Ic and IIa Bunker. According to stopwatch counts that were hastily repeated by an artillery-battalion Commander during the artillery attack, in the night of the 23rd and 24th of October , with a number of Batteries, the enemy had fired about 50,000 shells up to the calibre of 17 cm on the Division's Command Post. The military damage inflicted is certainly in no relationship to the expenses incurred!

Though it was apparent that the artillery partly fought a lost battle during close combat with tanks and infantry and the infantry also was defeated, the Division Commander decided to defend his command post and to fulfil his assignment until the end. Only after orders by the General Commander, the command of the HQ, the remainder of the communications division and the staff of Art.Reg.1712 left the burning remains of Hintham by foot and parallel the attacking British forced around 06.15 hrs on the 24th to organise a new defence in 's-Hertogenbosch.

Arriving within 's-Hertogenbosch the Division obtained knowledge that a strong British force had attacked and taken the large road bridge along the main north-south road passage. The battle commander

Captain G. H. Davies.

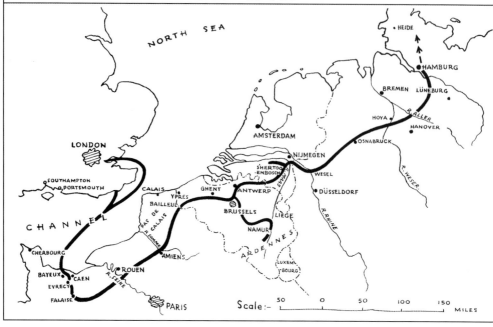

THE PATH OF THE 53(WELSH) DIVISION
- JUNE 1944 to MAY 1945.   Folding Map

Officers of the 133rd Field Regiment, Royal Artillery, 1944. My father (circled) can be seen standing second from the left on the back row.

Mondrainville, July 1944.

Evercy from Mondrianville, July 1944.

Major Dick Hughes with OP Carrier.

Bombardier Loach moving through Evreux. Sergeant Simpson is pictured in the background on a bicycle.

Bombardier Loach at Evreux.

A knocked out German gun.

Hill 112, 29ᵗʰ July 1944.

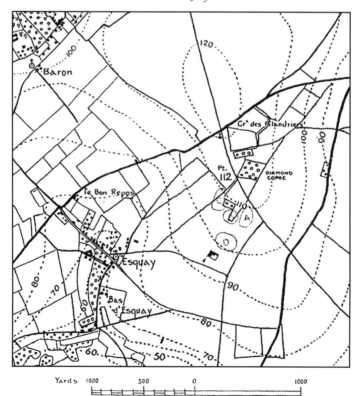

A photograph of Emilienne Cousin on the day of the liberation of Bethune, 5ᵗʰ September 1944. On the right, the inscription on the reverse of the photograph.

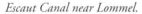

Escaut Canal near Lommel.

A Churchill flail tank used for exploding mines.

A Churchill 'Crocodile' flame-throwing tank in action.

The famous 25-pdrs. of 497 Battery in action.

My father, the island at Nijmegen, October 1944.

Major Hughes in Reichswald.

Colonel Brooke (left) pictured at Den Bosch.

Battery Commander's half-track.

Photographs from the camera of a deceased SS Officer my father came across in March 1945.

Captains Bishop and Martin with Major Hughes at Hiltrop.

Captains Thomson, Holmes, Davies and Bishop undertaking pistol practice.

Captain Joss Martin.

Colonel Brooke at Verdun.

Bocholt after the battle.

Officers of 497 Battery and American nurses at Harburg, 1945.

Rees and Griffin (my father's batman).

Officers of 497 Battery, Harburg 1945.

My father sitting on cases full of liquor taken from the Kriegsmarine barracks, Harburg.

Lieutenant Huw Drummond at Harburg.   *Captain Dennis Bishop at Harburg.*

My father alongside Captain Dennis Bishop photographed firstly on the left at the lake at Harburg and latterly on the right on VE Day 1945.

German surrender cable.

<u>Message Form</u>

Date – time of origin

071115B May 45

From   53 Welsh Div Arty

To   81 83 133 Fd Regts   71 A tk Regt   25 Lua Regt
        344 SL (ML) Bty

- -

RAO 30 (.) CONFIDENTIAL (.) a rep of the GERMAN HIGH COMD signed the unconditional
surrender of all the GERMAN land sea and air forces in EUROPE to the ALLIED
EXPEDITION ARY FORCE and simultaneously to the SOVIET HIGH COMD at 0141 hrs central
European time 7 May under which all forces will cease active ops at 0001B 9 May (.)
effective immediately all offensive ops by Allied Expeditionary Force are to cease
and tps are to remain in present posns (.) moves involved in occupational duties
will continue (.) due to difficulties of comn there may be some delay in similar
orders reaching enemy tps so units will continue to take full def precautions (.)
NO repeat NO release will be made to the press pending an announcement by the heads
of the three governments (.) all infm

- -

IN CIPHER   PRIORITY

F. Steedman   IMMEDIATE

had already initiated the first steps for the retaking. The General Commander had therefore ordered the remaining Sturmgeschützen of the 2nd (Sturmgeschütz) Pz.Jg.Abt.256 to support. During their push the British were driven back and many enemy soldiers were brought in as prisoners after the battle.

It was now important to build a new MLR along the Zuid-Willemsvaart. The forces to our disposal were: Company Zetzman (A scratch Company built out of scattered-troops), the Recruit Company of Battalion-Ewald and further local Companies of the 59th Infantry Division. In addition there were remnants of Field Battalion 347 around 10.00 hrs who, without being attacked, occupied the defensive position between the canals south-west of Berlicum from 22.10 hrs in the evening. Battle ready sections of 712 Infantry Division were not available during this period. Several little groups were able to retreat whilst fighting. Also three artillery pieces and 60-70% of the Artillery Division personnel could partly retreat whilst fighting in close combat. Orders by the Commanding General of 88 Army Corp to the address of the Battle Commanders explained thereit was also envisaged that there would have to be an expansion to form a second defensive line at the north-south canal that in a later stage could be expanded into a main line of resistance. Also the west bank of the 's-Hertogenbosch-Maas canal (north-west of the city) should be occupied and developed into a mainline of resistance.

The Division established a collecting point for stragglers. Battalion Wittstock was shifted from Het Gewande passing Empel to the south behind Hedel in the defensive canal position north-west of 's-Hertogenbosch. They were again and again provided with all the small detached Divisions Infantry groups that fought their way back to the lines. There was the following section structure:

a) Section Battle Commander 's-Hertogenbosch.

b) Section Battalion Wittstock from the north-west exit of the city until the canal fork centre north of Engelen.

c) Section Battlegroup Fuchs with Bridgehead Hedel and Maas Section.

There were successful shock troop attacks deployed in the part of the city east of the Zuid-Willemsvaart. During this day altogether 2 senior lieutenants and 44 men were brought in as prisoners.

The enemy constantly gave harassing artillery fire and small artillery attacks in the city parts west of the Zuid-Willemsvaart. Moreover he closed in with strong forces of infantry and armour.

During the day the following artillery was brought back into position: The remainder of I./A.R.159 and I./A.R.1712 that had shifted north went into position north of the Maas while the compiled battery of II./A.R.1712 went to the sector Vlijmen. During the evening the following Artillery reinforcement was ordered: 4./A.R.185, that already had taken position in the section Hedel, was again ordered to section Vlijmen by means of Hedel and also 5./A.R.185 was newly positioned here, so that in the sector Vlijmen an Artillery Group was created existing out of 4./, 5./A.R.-185 and 6./A.R.1712, while north of the Maas I./A.R.159 with 1./A.R.159 and 1./A.R.1712 and the newly introduced Artillery Section Ubel, (I./A.R.347) with 2 s.F.H. (Heavy Field Howitzer) and one 1st F.H.Battery were placed in position. Still to be expected was IV./A.R.256 with 2 Batteries each with 6 s.F.H.18. Field Howitzers.

The difficulty was the command of this Artillery and because the Artillery was positioned north of the Maas the Division decided against the command by the Art.Reg.Stab (Staff of the Artillery Regiment) in Hedel as is normally the practice, but give direct orders to Artillery group Kratzer itself because technical communication problems were to be expected. However, that the Command of the Artillery in its whole failed almost completely in adequate communications was not foreseeable. Though troops were deployed to construct a phone line connection between Division-Art. Rgt. it lasted 25 hours before one was created in the afternoon of 25.10. but was destroyed again 3 hours later because of permanent Artillery fire and a connection could only be constructed again after 39 hours by completely redirecting the lines route and changing the command posts location! Thus the division had to rely on encrypted radio traffic with the artillery V.B. accounts (*Vorgeschobene artillerie Beobachter*), (forward artillery observers) could not be sent to the threatened sectors because also they were without communication equipment. Also the Communication Division could not help out because they possessed no more cable. The few remaining artillery radios – as already was known for weeks – mostly did not function at the decisive moments. Thus the Division could only give the Infantry's battle artillery support by giving prearranged artillery fire though the tense ammunition situation of 24. and 25.10. was still complicated though decreased after some time. It became evident that for the battle not only the number of Batteries and Gun tube amounts is decisive but that an artillery division fully equipped with observing and communication equipment and abundant ammunition supplies can support the troops far much better than 4 sections that can only give prearranged artillery support after radio requests by the Division.

These problems have collaborated decisively in the Battle for 's-Hertogenbosch.

At 16.30 hrs the Battle Commander of 's-Hertogenbosch reported that the enemy had crossed the Zuid-Willemsvaart at the south-east exit of the city with a shock troop of about 40-50 men and approached the 59 Infantry Divisions position. The immediate ordered counter attack suffered from the enemy's tactic at the east bank by a positioned row of firing tanks that prevented our shock troops to come closer.

After orders from the Battle Command, that could only depend on sending runners to the front, the break through point was closed and a crossing of further enemy forces in the vicinity of the destroyed lock bridge was neutralised. The Division in retrospect believed that the enemy had still reinforced itself overnight. However, from 22.00 hrs the Battle Commander also called aside its reserves, for under the command of the 59.Inf.Div. Btl. Gramse, coming from St.Michielsgestel in a westerly direction, that couldn't gain a connection with the 59.Inf.Div. and therefore asked for the temporary reestablishment of the blown bridge at the south edge of the city, to make it possible for Btl.Gramse to cross over. For this a bridge head had to be created. In doing so it was achieved that the whole of Battalion Gramse could cross over including one light battery and one 8.8 cm Flak gun. Following this the bridge was destroyed again.

The preparations made by the Division for a counter attack to take place in the early hours of the morning against the enemy bridgehead in the south-east were ready. The enemy's breakthrough had to be cleared along the south bypass road with support of the Division mandated s.Pz.Jg.Abt. 559. The Battle Commander reported to the Division at 07.05 hrs 25.10.44 that looking back at the personal Corp order that he received, explaining that the north-south canal was now the MLR and that along the Zuid-Willemsvaart only combat outposts could be deployed, he did not execute a counter attack because their commanding Sturmgeschütz Commander reported on grounds of reconnaissance reports coming from the area that they were attacked by enemy tanks that were awaiting far away across the other side in covered positions without really being able to help out. The Battle Commander reported that he furthermore could dominate the crossings points flank and that the point where the enemy had broken through was now firmly closed. This later proved to be not adequate enough as the enemy drove us out by smoking out our corner bases south of the Zuid-Willemsvaart by frontal attack with flame throwing tanks and anti-tank guns and able to cross further troops under the protection of heavy artillery fire. At 10.35 hrs the Battle Commander reported that enemy armoured vehicles were reported within the bridgehead.

When the enemy shortly after attacked our defensive position with heavy artillery support the Battle Commander decided to create and move in a new defensive position that ran straight through the city. The Division was only notified of these facts after they already had been executed. After the enemy moved in with tanks in its extended bridgehead and used them in his attack, the Battle Commander ordered to retreat from the entire Zuid-Willemsvaart canal defence line that by now was systematically smoked out and cut to the rear by an enemy attack in north-west direction to move in and occupy a new defensive line that ran from about the St. Michielsgestel bridge, across the Markt, straight into a north-west direction. Around 15.30 hrs the enemy attacked the combat outpost's right flank coming over the road from St.Michielsgestel with tanks and infantry and pushed them back under heavy fire. Following this he built a crossing again at the destroyed bridge by using a bridge laying tank, and now rolled in to the city from the south with tanks and vehicles and pushed on determinedly in the direction of the north-south canal bridges for an attack. The Battle Commander called back the outposts in the MLR on his own initiative at 16.00 hrs and ordered the bridges to be blown. This order was not adequate for 3 of the 4 bridges. At the southernmost wide bridge however an artillery barrage from 11.00 hrs had damaged the detonator charge and explosives. Every measure taken by the General Command and the Division to re-attach new explosives (bombs) was ineffective. Therefore a concentrated anti-tank point was deployed here; because the danger existed that enemy tanks would try to cross the poorly blown bridge.

Sadly the Staff Battle Commander of 's-Hertogenbosch was relieved for another assignment in the evening of 25.10. It later became eminent that by then Oberst Dewald, had been assigned to replace Major Riedel, an old reserve officer of the Luftwaffe, he was in no way adequate for this task. The Division on the other hand was not in the position to assign a better energetic leader that could fill in the place of Battle Commander. This person as the new Battle Commander is, as afterthought surveys showed, the main reason for the collapsing of the 's-Hertogenbosch front, as this person gave withdrawal orders in contrary to multiple orders and orders in writing, witnessed phone conversations and personal obligations by the Division Commander. After the post office building and with it the amplifier was blown a further commanding problem arose. Since 25.10 in the afternoon the Division, that was without communication radios, could only depend on a, at the phone line end point at Grootdeuteren dugout, and exposed heavy field cable that because of the constant ongoing artillery fire could be used only a few minutes a day. Because of this the Division had to rely on frequently sent out communication officers. These though often brought important messages much too late. Only after an initiative taken by the General Command during the night of 25/26.10 a troublesomely formed communications group could be deployed in support of the Battle Commander.

The enemy brought heavy artillery attacks down on the west part of the city during the night of 25th October. This was considered in preparation for the expected attack to break through to the west.

In the afternoon of 24th October men of A Comp. 7th Bat. Royal Welch Fusiliers stormed the lock crossing at the Zuid-Willemsvaart in the city and formed a bridgehead on the other side of the lock. Later that night a Class 40 bridge was constructed so tanks and armoured vehicles could cross into the city.

The German Luftwaffe reserve officer Major Riedel was a prisoner of war. This Officer was 's-Hertogenbosch's last Battle Commander after he replaced Oberst Dewald who on 25th October took over the command of the frontlines at Zaltbommel. According to these documents Major Riedel was mainly responsible for the fall of the 's-Hertogenbosch front.

26th October

In the morning the artillery fire declined. Deployed in the Main Line of Resistance were: in sector 's-Hertogenbosch (Commander Major Riedel) right subsector: F.E.B 347 (Felders Ersatz Battalion) added with 4./F.E.B.1712. left subsector: Btl. Ewald added with Sammel-Company (a company put together of soldiers from different units) a fighting force counting about 450 men. The equipment with M.G. (Machine Guns) was remarkably low, some of the company's even counted one M.G.! 4./F.E.B. 1712 counted a fighting force of 100 men 2 M.G.!

In contrast to the view of the Chief of the General staff of the General Command, who meant to believe that in 's-Hertogenbosch liberation parties took place, the enemy continuously strengthened *itself with infantry and armour at the east bank of the north-south canal.*

At 11.30 hrs strong artillery fire with fog grenades on the Main Line of Resistance, the positions at the destroyed bridges were simultaneously controlled by enemy tanks deployed on the east bank. Under cover of this fire the enemy succeeded in crossing the canal at two points with infantry shock troops counting 30-40 men and to infiltrate the Main Line of Resistance.

Because of counterattacks which were immediately executed one enemy shock troop was destroyed/driven back over the 80 to 100 cm deep canal and the other for the greatest part was also wiped out. While these counter measures were initiated and shock reserve troops were moved from less threatened areas, the enemy crossed at other positions over the poorly blown south bridge at the canal and advanced in the direction of the west bank and infiltrated the main Main Line of Resistance. The enemy was able to create a crossing at the south bridge by means of a bridge laying tank under the protection of artillery fire and fog grenades. Two tanks could cross over this bridge around 14.00 hrs and advanced as far as the railroad embankment and from there covered their advance route to the west and north with fire. The Adjutant of Felders Battalion 347 attempted to contact its right neighbour (Battalion Gramse) to discuss a joint counter attack. He was able to advance until past Vught, without being able to find any members of Battalion Gramse at the Dommelcanal, the main road, the railroad and along the Afwateringscanal. At concentration camp Vught he observed a tank maintenance and repair platoon with 10 enemy tanks!

The enemy closed in with its lead troops from the south under heavy artillery support and with the use of phosphor and fog grenades. Individual strongpoints in houses were held, while a strengthened trench line supported with Sturmgeschützen was built by the Battle Commander in the area south of the train station. Because of the lack of artillery ammunition for the Group Vlijmen our own defence gradually weakened. Early in the morning the Division initiated drops of ammunition stocks from Artillery Group Hedel to Artillery Group Vlijmen but this had not been completed. s.Pz.Jg.Abt.559 already had suffered sensitive losses. The strengthened trench line at the train station could be held for the most part. The enemy suffered heavy losses by the counterattack. 5 enemy tanks were probably destroyed.

On 26th October British tanks attacked the German positions at the Wilhelmina square and Willems Bridge in 's-Hertogenbosch in support of the 1st East Lancs.

27th October

During the night the south-west part of 's-Hertogenbosch was subjected to our own harassing artillery fire, but this couldn't prevent the opponent from reinforcing his forces with tanks and infantry during the course of the night. Parts of Artillery Group Kiewitt went into position in the sector south of Heusden during the night. The commander of A.R.191 and the commander of s.Pz.Jg.Abt.559 and 59.Inf.Div had discussed the support for our own counterattack starting from the train station area to the south to regain the main line of resistance. The 59.Inf.Div refused to give support from the south in the form of infantry support and based on the communication attempt made by the executive officer of F.E.B.347 the left flank of the 59.Inf. Div would by then already have shifted more to the west anyway.

The start of the attack was ordered for 08.10 hrs after the south-west part of the city was subjected to destructive artillery fire from 08.00 hrs until 09.10 hrs by A.R.1712 (artillery group north of the Maas, Art Group Vlijmen) and from 4 Batteries of the 59.Inf.Div and III./A.R.139. This order could only be conveyed to Art.Rgt.1712 (Art.Group north of the Maas) by radio.

The enemy realized we were preparing an attack and had the area from where we would deploy devastated by a heavy concentrated artillery attack. Our own Infantry suffered heavy bloody losses during this attack. Nevertheless, supported by 3 Sturmgeschützen and 2 Jagdpanthers the Infantry attacked through two streets into a southerly direction to regain the main line of resistance at any price. The attack however was hampered by strong defensive fire whereby in particular the numerous enemy Pak (anti-tank guns) laying in ambush stopped our push. One Jagdpanther and two Sturmgeschütze were put out of action.

To cover the failure of the Battle Commander the Division ordered the north-west adjacent Battle Group Schulze to immediately put a company with a battle strength of at least 50 men under the command of the Battle Commander. The Artillery kept the order to give harassing fire on to the south-west part of 's-Hertogenbosch. After rumours, it became apparent on 28th October that the Battle Commander, against all orders, had already given orders for a withdrawal in the morning but according to his own statement at 14.30 after battle for the last row of houses at the canal he had attached himself to the rest of Battle Group Schulze that consisted of two officers and about 30 men who were still able to fight.

He immediately received an order from the Division Commander to fight his way back into the city with the company from Battle Group Schulze (battle strength 68 men) or otherwise he should report himself for Court Martial at the Division. It was promised that he would be provided with a further company of stragglers that in the meantime were collected by the Divisional Staff and were geared up by the Nat.Soz.Fuhr.Offz. (Nationalsozialistische Führungsoffiziere: Political Officers promoting propaganda for the National Socialist Party) and were provided with weapons and ammunition by Section. Ib. At this stage there still had to be parts of F.E.B.347 Battalion Ewald and remnants of other groups in 's-Hertogenbosch. Finally at 18.00 hrs the enemy broke through with Infantry all the way up to the army barracks west of the town and not suitable for tanks was the railway underpass at the south-west exit of the city and all the way up to the sports arena at the train station. Because of combined artillery fire the enemy was held up and could not get any further and retreated.

The Division ordered Battle Group Schultze to order the company *of stragglers, which was accompanied by a strong force of shock troops and were marching on to Engelen, to be commanded by an energetic commander and to report to the Battle Commander. In the evening it appeared that, as ordered by the Battle Commander, the Commander of FEB 347 had pulled out around 16.30 hrs. An order messaged by radio directed to the Commander of FEB 347 that told him to hold out at any cost was only partly received. Some brave groups though continued to stay in the city. It became apparent after 28th October that the shock troops deployed at the north-west exit of the city encountered heavy resistance in the factory area. Numerous soldiers returned back to Battle Group Schultze but were separated during the night because of enemy artillery attacks. There was no news concerning the fate of Battle Commander Riedel. There are reports that he was wounded in action. The Division assessed that because of its poor position and the available battle weary troops the retaking of 's-Hertogenbosch was impossible. It was important to prevent the enemy breakthrough to the west. Therefore the Division deployed the former troops of bridgehead Hedel, 2 Companies of Lw.Bodenpersonal (Lw, Luftwaffe, Air Force – Bodenpersonal, ground personnel) to the area of Bokhoven to occupy a defensive position at the road fork (1 km east of Vlijmen) along the causeway leading north-east to Engelen, while 1 Company of FEB 1712 remained at the east boundary of Vlijmen taking frontal positions along both sides of the main road which they had occupied since the 25th.*

The bridge 1.5 km to the east of Vlijmen was prepared for demolition and was to be blown if enemy amour should approach regardless of our troops at Groot-Deuteren.

The build-up of the defensive position was accomplished without enemy action. It was apparent that the enemy pulled back some of its forces as no tanks were sighted anymore since the evening of 27.10. The MLR's right flank was located at the south-west corner of the harbour, at the north-west exit of the city. Here the deployed companies were constantly under the attack of machine gun, mortar and artillery fire and suffered ongoing losses.

The Division held the defensive position at the flooding areas at the causeway Vlijmen-Engelen and the ditches in front of the right flank and the enemy's almost coverless areas for approach were favourable for defence. The enemy finally tried to cautiously advance with 2 armoured reconnaissance vehicles along the road, 's-Hertogenbosch-Vlijmen around 17.00 hrs but after the bridge was blown the vehicles pulled back. A shock troop, that was advancing from the MLR's right flank at the north-west edge of the city with the intent to connect with the forward deployed troops at Groot Deuteren, was able to destroy 2 military utility vehicles at Groot Deuteren and capture and bring back important enemy maps.

The division pull back of own units out of the defensive position west of 's-Hertogenbosch followed in the night of 28-29.10. What's left of the Division after this is:

Division Staff (losses more than 25%)

Signal Battalion 712 (losses more than 30%)

1 strong mixed Infantry Battalion from G.R.732, 745 and Fus. BTL.712

Staff of A.R.1712 with 1 mixed Staff detachment with, 1 Battr.F.K.39 with 3 Guns

1 Battr.1.F.H.18/40 with 3 Guns and 2 Personnel battr.

20 men from the command road positioned Pz.Jg.Kp.712

Felders.Btl.1712 with Staff and 3 Companies (the 4th Company is lacerated in the battle in 's-Hertogenbosch)

Medical troops (2/3 of Medical Company 712 taken prisoner by the British on 24.10. in 's-Hertogenbosch)

During the Battle from 22-27.10.44 the 712th and troops assigned to the 712th at least destroyed;

29 tanks (of which 14 by Panzerfaust), 1 tank shot immobilized and 2 armoured reconnaissance vehicles destroyed.

The division summarizes the following result after the big battle.

The Infantry of our own Division was already defeated during the first days of the big battle by two complete and well equipped British Divisions (of which one Armoured Div.). While carrying out the orders the Division adequately defended itself. The not organically organized air force-battalions could not consolidate during the battle and because of this fell apart.

The Division was not adequately equipped with communication equipment to act as a static division, especially the Command of the Artillery suffered because of this. It already became clear in October, during several shock troop deployments that the communication radios for the Artillery usually failed. Furthermore, the greatest part of the communication radios of the VB (forward deployed artillery observers) failed.

Furthermore it became apparent that after three big battles the men had become careless.

The scattered troops did not deploy fully battle hardened men and the worst soldiers are for the greatest part scattered. The Division prevented the enemy push through over 's-Hertogenbosch to the west because of their sacrificing battle.

Our own artillery was much too weak at the beginning of the big battle and the ammunition stock not sufficient. Later on the Staff of the Artillery Regiment was not in the position to command and lead their Artillery Battalions by use of radio equipment.

The Panzerfaust 44 proved sufficient though it doesn't replace the heavy anti-armour shells. Also the Infantry Division needs a Sturmgeschütze as a mobile weapon in the point of the attack.

The new British flame-throwing tank greatly contributed to the success of the enemy because the infantry soldier at only some instances could defend himself against this weapon with a Panzerfaust.

There was a shortage in M.G. equipment. During the beginning of the battle the Divisions Companies only had the use of 5-6 M.G. and were for the greatest part already destroyed during the artillery's pre-bombardments.

A further cause for the great losses for the Division is to be found in the command. Since May until 21.10.44 and also during the big battle the Div. 22 Commanders and Battalion Officers of the Artillery were either lost in battle or transferred. During the course *of the big battle, 1 Regiment Commander, 1 Regiment Officer and 2 Battalion Officers of the divisions own troops were missing. More unfavourable was the situation for the Companies and Platoons. Therefore it's necessary for the Division to relieve them and form new ones. Therefore a sufficient build up period is favourable to let the replacements and officers get used to one another and to let them get used to the new structure and new weapons. A refresh in deploying forces with only march battalions will at this moment, for the state the Division is in, not be a foundation for a full worthy Battle Division. After redeployment of these forces the Division will be in the position again to fulfil its obligations and to achieve proud successes again.*

Distributor: 15 Army, cc. General Command of 88 Army Corp, General Command of 84 Army Corp, Ia/War diary."

- CHAPTER VIII -
THE ONSET OF WINTER

After the successful liberation of Den Bosch, the 53rd were to move on to take part in the operations on the river Maas. The Assault on the Dutch Islands of South Beveland and Walcheren had already begun, with Canadian troops, the 52nd (Lowland) Division and Commando formations and this was to be the last point in opening up the Scheldt estuary, securing the supply route through the port of Antwerp. The Germans had now regrouped after their earlier defeats in France and were putting up stubborn resistance. The countryside was interspersed with streams and canals making life very difficult for the tanks, and the Germans had also flooded large tracts of land. The onset of winter brought heavy rain making life even more difficult.

The Allies found themselves facing two Panzer Divisions and a Parachute Division on the Eastern Flank of the salient at Nijmegen in what Montgomery described as a spoiling tactic.

The assault had begun on the 27th October, while the 53rd were still in 's-Hertogenbosch, and was carried out by the U.S. 7th Armoured Division. This Division held a front with its left on the Helmond-Venlo railway, thence South along the Deurne Canal to its junction with the Noorer Canal, then South-West along that Canal to Nederweert and from there South-East along the Wessem Canal to the Maas at Wessem – a very twisty line extending for nearly 30 miles. Clearly an Armoured Division on a front of this length could not offer effective resistance. Nevertheless, considering the difficulties of the country, the Germans made rapid progress. The town of Meijel was captured and by the 28th an ugly situation had developed. The formation most readily available to counter this thrust was the 15th (Scottish) Division which was moved through Eindhoven to plug the hole around Meijel. They began moving on the 28th. The next formation to hand was the 53rd (Welsh) Division, which had completed the capture of 's-Hertogenbosch on the 27th October.

By the 30th October the situation on VIII Corps front had been stabilized, but on the following day the 53rd Division began moving to the right flank of the Corps sector which was still only lightly held. By the 31st the Division had occupied a position along the Wessem Canal as follows:

On the Northern flank of the Division was the 7th U.S. Armoured Division and on the Southern the 113th Cavalry Group of the 29th U.S. Armoured Division.

The enemy was holding the line of the Wessem Canal, but had patrols forward, and in the area of the town of Wessem he had established posts west of the Canal. Major-General Ross immediately gave orders for his men to seek out and destroy any enemy West of the Canal and to prevent any Germans crossing it. Patrols were to be sent to the East side.

The enemy in this area consisted of two Battalions of former members of the German Air Force and proved to be very tough and enterprising customers, especially on the front of the 71st Brigade where they had a footing West of the Canal. On the night of the 1st/2nd November the East Lancashire Regiment had a sharp fight with a strong raiding party and on the afternoon of the 3rd the Oxford and Bucks beat off a raid by some 40 Germans.

On the 3rd November two most welcome communications were received by Divisional Headquarters. The first stated that Major T. Watkins, 1/5th Battalion, the Welch Regiment had been awarded the Victoria Cross, and the second was a message to Major-General Ross from the Commander, 2nd Army, General Sir Miles Dempsey, which ran as follows:

"Will you please give your splendid Division my very sincere congratulations on the way they carried out the operations which led up to your capture of 's-Hertogenbosch. I was delighted that the part played by the 53rd (Welsh) Division could be made public in connection with the battle. You truly go from strength to strength."

About this time units of the Division received substantial officer and other rank reinforcements.

The Divisional plan was divided into four phases:

Phase I – The crossing of the Wessem Canal about Grathem by the 160th Brigade and the formation of a bridgehead to the East.

Phase II – The capture of Baexem by the 158th Brigade.

Phase III – The seizure by the 71st Brigade of the area around Horn.

Phase IV – The mopping up of the whole area. The plan included the construction of four bridges over the Wessem Canal.

The operation began at 4 P.M. on the 14th November with an assault crossing on the left by the 51st (Highland) Division. It met with little opposition apart from mines. Once again the role of the artillery in this action should not be overlooked. Around 400 guns were involved, supported by tanks and Crocodiles. Their initial job was for the guns to soften up the opposition, before the tanks and Crocodiles advanced. The guns opened fire at 19.00 and bombarded the enemy for an hour before ceasing fire. At 20.00 dozens of searchlights illuminated the enemy positions, and the Crocodiles added to this as their fearsome fire was projected across the river, adding to the glare.

After a brief, but intense, bombardment Brigadier Coleman's 160th Brigade assaulted at 10 P.M. On the left the 4th Welch met little resistance, and on the right the left Company of the 2nd Monmouthshires got across fairly easily. Their right Company was, however, held up; but a third Company was quickly put through on the left and this, by moving South, opened up the other crossing. Mines – particularly *"Schu"* Mines (small anti-personnel mines which, being made of wood, did not react to mine detectors, the victim usually lost a leg or a foot, and some cases proved fatal) – gave a lot of trouble. The number of casualties as result of these mines was mercifully small, but over 2,000 Schu mines were subsequently lifted from the area.

By midnight a shallow bridgehead had been established and the 2nd Monmouthshires had cleared a start line for the 6th Royal Welch Fusiliers to advance further, so as to enlarge the bridgehead sufficiently for the Sappers to begin bridge building.

The 6th R.W.F. were to have a difficult passage. It was a very dark night and they had great difficulty in finding their boats, due to the Monmouthshires having changed the crossing place owing to heavy opposition at the original one. Eventually they got across, but were held up by a stream which had become swollen, and only just fordable, owing to the exceptionally wet weather. Yet by midnight they had two Companies on the start line. After a short bombardment they advanced against shelling, mines, and slight small arms fire, and reached their objective. The two rear Companies then passed through and the further objective was secured.

In the early hours of the 15th the ferrying of anti-tank guns, jeeps and other vehicles by "Buffalo" began; but it was a difficult business owing to the steep banks and to mines. Several "Buffaloes" were put out of action, but the anti-tank guns were in position by first light. At 1 P.M. the 7th R.W.F., from the 158th Brigade, passed through the bridgehead and were soon in position covering the old road bridge on the Weert-Roermond road, and in touch with troops of the 51st Division. By 6.15 P.M. a Company of the 6th R.W.F. had occupied Grathem.

Meanwhile to the South the 7th Armoured Division had captured Panheel Lock, in a small, but very important, operation designed to make sure that the level of the water in the canals would remain constant throughout and therefore not interfere with the crossing by assault boats and "Buffaloes". On the evening of the 15th November the 6th R.W.F. moved South without opposition and joined up with troops of the 7th Armoured Division.

After dark on the 15th the second phase of the operation began, when the 158th Brigade passed over the bridges, which had by then been erected, and occupied Baexem against negligible opposition.

Civilians reported that the Germans had evacuated the place a few days before owing to its waterlogged condition.

Phase III began at 7 A.M. on the 16th November and soon after the 1st Highland Light Infantry (71st Brigade) entered Horn. The only enemy occupants were two snipers, who were quickly disposed of. Civilians reported that the Germans, with a number of guns, had withdrawn from the area on the previous night. The same afternoon (the 16th) the 1/5th Welch (158th Brigade) moved on to Nunhem and Buggenuni to the North East of Horn.

About the same time the 160th Brigade further South occupied Heel (4th Welch) and Beegden (2nd Monmouthshires), where they liberated several Royal Air Force prisoners of war who had been in hiding there.

Thus by nightfall the 53rd Division had cleared the area up to the line of the Maas between the Canal and River junction at Wessem and Buggenum – a distance of 6 miles in a straight line, but many more as the river flows – except for a small area around the Western defences of Roermond.

The next few days were spent in patrolling, adjusting defensive positions and in making preparations for eliminating the enemy covering Roermond.

It was at this time that the 53rd Reconnaissance Regiment, now at Weert, was placed at 6 hours' notice for operations in Belgium in aid of the Civil Power. This was in connection with the disarming of certain personnel of the Belgian Resistance and Partisan movements who had been ordered to hand in their arms by the 25th October. Many had not done so and there was considerable anxiety about the attitude and behaviour of some of the less responsible elements. In the event the Belgian authorities themselves dealt with the situation and the 53rd Reconnaissance Regiment was not called upon.

It is of general interest to record that on the 18th November the town of Geilenkirchen, some 16 miles to the South, was attacked by troops of the 43rd (Wessex) Division in the XXX Corps – the first British troops to carry the war on to German soil.

On the 21st November Brigadier Elrington's 71st Brigade carried out operations to clear the enemy from his small bridgehead west of the Maas covering Roermond. One Squadron of the East Riding Yeomanry, one "AVRE" Squadron and a Troop of "Flail" tanks were allotted to the Brigade. The task was a formidable one involving the crossing of open, and partially waterlogged, ground intersected by a deep stream and an anti-tank ditch. When these obstacles had been surmounted the enemy had to be assaulted and destroyed – the whole operation to be completed in one night if possible.

The attack, which began at 7.30 p.m., was directed against the small village of Weert and some brickworks held by Germans covering the Roermond Bridge. The 4th R.W.F. captured Weert and after an intricate bridging operation the 1st Oxford and Bucks passed through to the brickworks which were taken with great expedition and with a bag of 100 prisoners.

By the 23rd flooding had become progressively worse. Many posts were almost completely isolated and movement in the forward areas often involved wading waist deep in water. As a result many adjustments had to be made in the defensive lay-out and in some places posts had to be withdrawn from the immediate vicinity of the river. On this day the 160th Brigade was relieved by the 7th Armoured Division in the Heel-Beegden area and moved north to Kessel where it extended the left of the 53rd Division by taking over the front held by the 153rd Brigade of the 51st (Highland) Division.

On the 27th the left was still further extended to Baarlo when the 160th Brigade took over the front of the 154th (Highland) Brigade.

The Divisional front now extended from the Roermond bridge on the right to Baarlo on the left, a distance of about 12 miles, with the 71st Brigade right, 158th Brigade centre and 160th Brigade left.

On the 26th and 27th November the Division was sharply attacked by German aircraft and suffered some casualties.

On the 30th November the 71st Brigade, (with the 53rd Reconnaissance Regiment attached) extended their position south to include the large town of Maeseyk. The Division was now on a very extended front of over 20 miles, but the flooded condition of the country made any major enterprises by the enemy out of the question.

The 30th November was also notable for a visit from the Supreme Commander, General Eisenhower, who talked informally with many officers and men of the Division and looked at equipment.

Another series of reliefs took place on the 7th December when the 227th Brigade of the 15th Scottish) Division took over the Northern

Sector from the 160th Brigade, which in turn relieved the 71st Brigade in the South. The 71st then went into Divisional reserve at Bree.

The Welsh Division was to remain on the Maas until a week before Christmas. It was a quiet period, but not an uneventful one for the forward troops. On the 6th December the 4th R.W.F. (71st Brigade) had attacked a lock in the loop of the Maas South of Roermond. Seventeen prisoners were taken; but the enemy counter-attacked during the night and fighting continued until dawn on the 7th.

The 1/5th Welch (158th Brigade), in particular, engaged the enemy in a number of patrol clashes around Buggenum, and the following incidents are of interest. One day during the second week in December the Welch observed a party of Germans dressed in white smocks, marked with a Red Cross, embark in a boat with an outboard engine and cross the river, where they recovered some wounded men. No action was taken against them. Similarly a few days later, after a standing patrol of the 1/5th Welch had suffered casualties from mines, the enemy permitted the Battalion pioneers to sweep a path through the minefield for the Medical Officer and a party of Stretcher Bearers. It was pleasing to think that after five years of total war at least some front line soldiers were capable of acts of humanity of this kind.

On the 15th December preparations began for the departure of the Division from the Maas, where it had spent a very trying period, although not one of very heavy fighting. Casualties had been comparatively light since leaving the 's-Hertogenbosch area at the end of October. Now the Division was to move to an area East of Antwerp in order, as it was said, to rest, refit and carry out special training for future operations.

On the 17th December the 158th Brigade was relieved by a Brigade of the 15th (Scottish) Division and the 160th Brigade and 53rd Reconnaissance Regiment by part of the 11th Armoured Division.

By this time a very smooth running amenity and entertainment organization existed in the Division. It was unfortunate that an Officers Club, and a Cafe for other ranks, was just about to be opened in Weert when the Division received orders to leave the area.

By the 18th December, however, events were shaping elsewhere which were to upset all plans for rest and training. Within four days the 53rd (Welsh) Division was to be on the move again, in an unexpected direction. The German offensive in The Ardennes, Hitler's last bid for victory in the West, had begun.

In my father's words:

"Most of November and the first half of December was spent in the area of Roermond and Venlo on the river Maas. It was possibly classed as a fairly quiet period, but there were numerous skirmishes both sides of the river.

We were now to be withdrawn in order to rest, refit and carry out special training for future operations. We scarcely had time to draw breath at Bree, when an 'O' group was called (to issue urgent orders). On the 16th Dec, the Germans had put in an attack in the Ardennes and thus initiated the 'Battle of the Bulge'. The next day we had a pitiful premature Christmas dinner. The ration of turkey was said to be TWO OUNCES per man! Whether this was live or dead weight, I don't know, it's the only figure I heard quoted. The ration was so painful; the officers said they would forego this wonderful share-out. I mention later, the fact that I witnessed an American Christmas dinner. So, we set out for the Ardennes to help our wonderful American Allies. The weather had turned really cold and when we got there our gun position was completely snow-covered. The only extra equipment which we'd received to help us fight the wintry conditions was a petty little one-person sleeping tent issued to each of us. The temperature was basically below freezing and the wind was biting. Due to the atrocious conditions, there were many road accidents, so the Americans had introduced 'Wrecker Gangs', which patrolled the area in their lorries and dealt with all damaged and abandoned vehicles.

One day the Major from a sister Battery called in to telephone his unit. On the road in front of my troop, just around a corner his Jeep had a puncture and had no spare wheel available. So he had contacted his unit to send a vehicle with men and a spare wheel to see to his Jeep. It seemed absolute ages before the relief vehicle arrived and reported that they could not find the Jeep. I won't say what the Major called the 'idiots', who had passed his vehicle and were too blind to see it. All they ever found was a body of a Jeep. In about twenty minutes the 'Wreckers' had taken everything. The wheels, seats, engine and every working part had disappeared!

It was actually then that we had to take over an American gun position. I went along first to gather all the technical information and my guns would follow later. Their 'cookhouse' was fifty yards or so behind the actual guns. I was talking to their Captain when one of his sergeants approached, carrying the large tray on which was his Christmas dinner. The Captain looked at it and said 'hardly worth walking back for'. As well as a mountain of goodies, that tray held a complete leg and several slices of turkey breast. That one G.I. had been given more turkey than my entire troop had received. I did wonder if we were fighting the same war.

My guns arrived and the Yanks were departing. I pointed out to the Captain that they had not yet picked up a mound of 60 to 80 pairs of brand new boots and a pile of almost 100 'Compo' packs. 'If they aren't in your way, we'll leave them.' How I managed to hide my enthusiasm, I just don't know. A 'compo' pack was a good-sized cardboard box which contained rations for seven men for three days. And what rations! Tins of bacon, corned beef hash, rich Christmas-style fruit puddings, the like of which we hadn't seen for years. Everything was fairly split between the four gun crews and the Command Post personnel. We all managed to find a pair of boots to fit, and were able to have a second breakfast for ages. The extra food certainly helped us to cope with the shocking conditions. Snow, cold, wet and we were living in the open air. No accommodation of any kind. One evening David Thomson, my troop Commander came down from his O.P. (Observation Post). He was absolutely over the moon. He had just received a telegram to let him know that his wife had given birth to a daughter – their first child, and both were well.

Whilst in Antwerp I had managed to purchase a few miniatures of Benedictine. On exceptionally cold nights, when firing was necessary, I had shared the odd tot with my Command Post Crew, just a little sip each to keep the cold at bay. That night we used them all to ensure that Mother and child were properly 'toasted'. Diana's birthday was the 28th Dec.

Very early one morning I saw something which I shall never forget. In each of our vehicles, on the passenger side there is a circular hole in the roof (a Bren gun ring) so the passenger can stand up and observe. We were travelling North with a very deep river valley on our left and beyond that a mountain which was a little higher than the one on which we were travelling. Dawn was not very far away. Although we remained in darkness, a beam of light shone across the valley and illuminated a scene of the Crucifixion on the opposite side. The three figures on the crosses were beautifully colourful and the whole scene sparkled and glittered. I wondered how many coincidences had to coincide for us to be exactly there at that exact moment. The whole world was in darkness except for that scene. It was worth going to the Ardennes if only to see that."

- CHAPTER IX -
THE ARDENNES -
THE BATTLE OF THE BULGE

*B*y mid-December the Germans had succeeded, thanks to the heavy autumn rains and severe winter weather, in slowing the Allied advance, in forming a solid front and in limiting the invasion of the Fatherland to minor areas. We had seen how the enemy was capable of conducting a local offensive on a considerable scale, and the stubborn manner in which he fought in defence. Now he was about to assume the offensive with the object, albeit a vain hope, of gaining a major victory in the West.

The German high command had succeeded in refitting about eight Panzer Divisions in the West, to a scale of approximately 100 tanks each, of the latest "Panther" and "Tiger" types. The enemy had also managed to increase his total Field Force in the West from the equivalent of some 23 Divisions in August, to about 70 Divisions in December.

Hitler planned to risk the reserves thus built up in an all-out offensive which, by means of a surprise thrust, was to drive across the River Meuse towards Antwerp and deprive the Allies of their main bases at Liege, Brussels and Antwerp. If fully successful there were rich prizes to be won; but even if only partially successful much might be gained, or so it was argued. It was just conceivable that it would induce the Americans and the British to grant a separate peace: it would provide a breathing space for the development of the series of new weapons, of which the V1s and V2s were the forerunners, and it would give time for some of the new dispersed, and underground, factories to come into production.

After the battle of Arnhem, *Hohenstaufen* moved to Paderborn for a much-needed rest and refit. On 12th December 1944, the division moved south to the Munstereifel. It was to act as a reserve for Sepp Dietrich's 6th SS Panzer Army, a part of the Ardennes offensive (*Unternehmen: Wacht am Rhein*). The 6th Panzer Army was tasked with attacking in the north, along the line St. Vith-Vielsalm. Initially, only the divisional reconnaissance and artillery units were involved in the fighting, but on the 21st December the entire division was committed.

When the attack in the north stalled, the division was sent south to assist in the attacks on Bastogne. *Hohenstaufen* was involved in the fighting around Bastogne, taking heavy casualties from the American defenders, and losing much equipment to the incessant attacks of Allied ground attack aircraft. On 7th January 1945, Hitler called off the operation and ordered all forces to concentrate around Longchamps; the division was involved in holding this area, as well as keeping lines of communication open with the 5th Panzer Army to the south.

In the event none of these hopes was fulfilled. The offensive met with considerable initial success and it postponed the Allied offensive in the Rhineland by some weeks. But eventually the German troops were heavily defeated and their refurbished Panzer Divisions almost completely destroyed. The Germans had used their last reserve and when, three months later, the Allies crossed the Rhine there were no effective forces to oppose them.

The spearhead of this offensive was the Fifth Panzer Army and the Sixth SS Panzer Army, each of four Panzer and some Infantry Divisions, which were to attack in the centre. The two Panzer Armies were to be flanked on the North by the Fifteenth Army and on the South by the Seventh Army, both consisting of Infantry Divisions.

These four Armies comprised Army Group B under the command of *Feldmarschall* Model, with ultimate responsibility resting on *Feldmarschall* von Rundstedt, the Commander-in-Chief in the West.

The attack, which was prepared with the greatest secrecy, was to be delivered between Malmedy in the North and the River Moselle just West of Trier in the South. This front, of approximately sixty miles, was held by the United States VIII Corps, consisting of no more than four Infantry and one Armoured Divisions.

The blow fell on the 16th December and, in its initial stages, made rapid progress against the thinly held front. Although the situation which developed was regarded as serious, there were no signs of panic and General Eisenhower and his Army Group Commanders handled it in a spirit of confidence. It was decided to place the two American Armies (1st and 9th), which were North of the "bulge", under Field Marshal Montgomery, leaving General Omar Bradley's 12th Army Group with only its Third Army.

General Eisenhower's plan to deal with the situation was to halt the enemy advance before it crossed the Meuse and to counterattack the salient with the First United States Army from the North and the Third United States Army from the South.

In this plan the XXX British Corps (43rd Wessex, 51st Highland and 53rd Welsh Divisions – plus three Armoured Brigades and other Corps Troops), under Lieut.-General Sir Brian Horrocks, was given the immediate task of securing the Meuse crossings between Namur and Liege.

This was the general picture and we can now turn to the role of the 53rd (Welsh) Division.

We left the 53rd Division in the area West of Antwerp where it hoped to remain for a short time resting and refitting after the strenuous fighting on the Maas. Soon after arrival in this area reconnaissance began for a move to the neighbourhood of Eindhoven, but this was cancelled, and the reconnaissance parties recalled, when the German offensive began.

During the night of the 18th/19th December the Divisional Area was disturbed by reports, which proved groundless, of landings by enemy parachutists. On the following night orders were received for one Brigade to proceed at once to the River Dyle South of Louvain and for the remainder of the Division to be prepared to move at mid-day on the 20th.

In accordance with these orders the 160th Brigade, with the 53rd Reconnaissance Regiment (Lieut.-Colonel L. Williams) attached, moved from its billets in the Herenthals area at 8 A.M. on the 20th December. Its destination was the area South of Louvain, where the East

Riding Yeomanry, of the 33rd Armoured Brigade, came under Brigadier Coleman's command. On arrival a Squadron of the Reconnaissance Regiment was pushed forward to Namur where it found everything normal. Posts guarding the City's four river bridges were established.

On the afternoon of the 20th Major-General Ross held a conference at which he disclosed that the rest of the Division was to follow the 160th Brigade that night, with the task of holding a position on the River Dyle in order to form a firm base for operations to be conducted by the rest of the XXX Corps.

The right flank between Genappes and the River Dyle was held by the 53rd Reconnaissance Regiment.

Main Divisional Headquarters was at Tervueren, Rear Headquarters at Steerebeck and the Divisional Administrative Area North-East of Brussels.

During the afternoon the 29th Armoured Brigade, which had hurried over from West Belgium, came under Major-General Ross's command, and was given the task of relieving detachments of the Tank Replacement Centre and other hastily collected units which, on Field Marshal Montgomery's orders, had been sent to hold the line of the Meuse between Namur and Givet.

Up to this time information about the progress of the enemy offensive was very sketchy: the Division had to be ready for almost any eventuality and prepared to carry out any role. However, by midday on the 22nd the situation was much clearer. The enemy advance had been slowed and the shoulders of the "bulge" were holding. Earlier plans for a possible withdrawal of the Division towards Brussels were put out of mind and the 29th Armoured Brigade was ordered to hold the Meuse crossings without consideration of withdrawal. About the same time the Division received a substantial reinforcement of one Field Regiment, two Anti-Tank Regiments and one Light Anti-Aircraft Regiment. In addition the 5th Army Group Royal Artillery, consisting of two Medium, one Heavy and one Heavy Anti-Aircraft Regiments, was placed in support.

By the 24th December the German offensive had been halted and General George Patton's Third U.S. Army was preparing for its attack from the South. It had seemed that the 53rd Welsh would have a quiet Christmas, but this was not to be. On Christmas Eve instructions were received from XXX Corps, which resulted in the following force being dispatched in the early hours of Christmas Day to hold the line of the Meuse between exclusive Namur and Givet, and take the offensive against any enemy seen on the East bank.

On arrival the Divisional Commander was to take under his command the 29th Armoured Brigade and a considerable force of Artillery, which included an A.G.R.A. and an Anti-Tank Regiment.

This measure had been made necessary by delay in the arrival of the 6th Airborne Division who had been earmarked for this task. In the meantime the rest of the 53rd Division was to remain on the Dyle under the Command of Brigadier G. B. Sugden (158th Brigade) and was to be known as "SUGFORCE".

The force was established on the Meuse by about 4 P.M. on Christmas Day with the 1st Highland Light Infantry about Dinant, the 4th Royal Welch Fusiliers at Givet and the 1st Oxford and Bucks in reserve at Rosee (10 miles West of Dinant). The 53rd Reconnaissance Regiment patrolled the river to the North between Dinant and Namur. Brigade Headquarters was at Serville (6 miles West of Dinant) and Divisional Headquarters at Mettet (15 miles South-West of Namur).

East of the river Detachments of the 29th Armoured Brigade, which had come under command of the Division at 10.30 A.M., on the 25th, reported that they had destroyed a German "Panther" tank, and three other vehicles, and taken 93 prisoners. These must have been among the most Westerly German troops, or possibly a detachment which had lost its way in the confused fighting at the apex of the "bulge."

No sooner had the 71st Brigade Group arrived in the new area, and before it had completed its deployment, than news came in that advanced elements of the 6th Airborne Division were arriving, and that the Brigade would be relieved and probably return to the Dyle on Boxing Day.

Moves and counter-moves, and a variety of roles, were to be the order for the next few days. The relief of the 71st Brigade by the 6th Airlanding

Brigade was completed by 10 A.M. on the 26th. The Brigade then concentrated in the area Florennes-Philippeville (some 15 miles West of Dinant), the 1st Oxford and Bucks remaining at Rosee. Divisional Headquarters remained, for the time being, responsible for this Sector with the 6th Airlanding Brigade and the 53rd Reconnaissance Regiment on the river and the 71st Brigade in reserve with counter attack roles against Namur, Dinant and Givet.

About mid-day on the 27th the 6th Airborne Division took over the sector, and Headquarters 53rd (Welsh) Division returned to Tervueren.

On the 28th the 71st Brigade moved again, this time to positions around Namur. This was a particularly unpleasant move, in thick fog and over icy roads, and the tail of the column did not reach its destination until 6 P.M. Almost immediately a warning order for another move arrived, to Ciney (8 miles east of the Meuse at Dinant) where it was expected that the whole 53rd Division would go into action. The chances of the Highland Light Infantry celebrating Hogmanay in traditional fashion seemed remote.

Finally on the 31st the Brigade received orders to relieve the 84th United States Division in the Marche area (12 miles South East of Ciney) and reconnaissance parties set off that afternoon.

Meanwhile "Sugforce", the temporary name given to the rest of the Division, had spent a quiet and pleasant Christmas on the Dyle, in cold but clear weather. With the return of Major-General Ross and his Headquarters on the 27th the 158th Brigade received warning to relieve part of the 2nd United States Armoured Division on the River Lesse about Houyet and Ciergnon (about 10 miles East of Givet on the Meuse). This move began on the 28th and was completed on the following day. The rest of the Division, less the 71st Brigade and the 53rd Reconnaissance Regiment, which it will be remembered were still on the Meuse, followed on the 30th and the 53rd then took over the whole front of the 2nd United States Armoured Division, from Houyet to Aye, a distance of about 13 miles.

Mention should be made of the very severe, and difficult, weather conditions during all these moves. There was snow on the ground and the roads were in an icy condition by day and by night. Track vehicles, in particular, experienced great difficulty and in the move of the Division South of the Meuse many had to spend the night on the road.

Owing to differences in American and British organization, and some differences in tactical conception, a clear-cut take over in the new area was not possible and some adjustments had to be made, including the construction of new defences.

As previously explained the 71st Brigade had already been ordered to the area and was expected to come into reserve on arrival, although this arrangement was soon upset by further alterations in XXX Corps plans involving different disposition for the 53rd Division.

During this period the Allied Air Forces were taking a heavy toll of the enemy in the "bulge", and in an effort to neutralize this, the German Air Force was also very active. The 53rd Division was not, however, subjected to any serious air attacks.

When it became apparent that the German offensive had shot its bolt the main task of the XXX British Corps was to relieve American troops on the Meuse, and at the apex of the bulge, and thus release them for offensive operations against the flanks of the enemy salient. This had involved many moves and almost daily changes in dispositions; but on the 1st January Corps Headquarters issued orders for the last stage in the reorganization of the front. Already the Corps had relieved two Divisions of the American VII Corps and they were now to relieve a third.

The Corps front ran approximately from Wellin on the right, through Marche to Hotton on the left. This was to be held by the 6th Airborne Division on the right and the 53rd (Welsh) Division on the left sector from Aye to Hotton.

The necessary chain of reliefs was completed by 10 A.M. on the 2nd January 1945. Movement of vehicles continued to be hampered by the snow and ice, many of the tanks abandoning the slippery roads and preferring to move across country. The moves were further complicated by the congestion caused by outgoing American units, and by the switching of supply channels involved in side-stepping Eastwards.

It is interesting to record that during the whole period in the Ardennes leave to the United Kingdom, and local leave to Brussels, continued without interruption. Approximately 6 officers and 109 other ranks went on home leave.

The United States VII Corps began their attack on the left of the Division on the 3rd January, and a warning order was received that the Welsh Division would attack on the 4th in order to keep abreast of the American advance. The American plan was for their VII Corps to break through on the axis Barvaux-Grandmenil-Houffalise and join up with the 3rd American Army moving north from Bastogne. The XXX British Corps was to conform with the American advance by clearing the triangle Marche-Laroche-Hotton. On the right the 6th Airborne Division was also to advance.

British Intelligence reports gave an accurate picture of the enemy. On the East of the 53rd Division's area of attack was the 116th Panzer Division and to the West the 9th Panzer Division, with the boundary between them just East of Marche. The main opponent – the 116th Panzer Division – had suffered heavily in the offensive and was thought to be able to raise no more than six Infantry Battalions, or troops available as Infantry, each about 300 strong.

The 2nd Monmouthshires were under command of the 158th Brigade. The 53rd Reconnaissance Regiment, still under the 6th Airborne Division, was linked up with the 71st Brigade. Its Headquarters was in the King of the Belgians' Chateau at Ciergnon. Additional Artillery, in the form of two A.G.R.A.s, (with a total of six Medium and one Heavy Regiment), the 127th Field Regiment and two Batteries of the 73rd Anti-Tank Regiment, were placed in support of the Division.

The advance of the 158th Brigade began at 8 A.M. on the 4th January in a heavy snow-storm which was to last most of the day. The 1/5th Welch attacked in the left centre and the East Lancashires on their right. By 10.15 A.M. the Welch had secured the woods between Menil and Waharday; but, such was the snow and mud, that the only supporting weapons which could be got forward were the Mortars, and the machine-guns of the Manchesters, and these only by manhandling. The

Commanding Officer, Lieut.-Colonel Nelson Smith, and his Intelligence Officer, Captain W. T. Owen, were both wounded by mines. The East Lancashires on the right were similarly handicapped by the shocking state of the ground, but reached their objective by mid-day. One of their Platoons disposed of four German posts, and another detachment stalked, and knocked out, an enemy S.P. gun with a Personal Infantry anti-tank gun.

The 2nd Monmouthshires, under Lieut.-Colonel F. H. Brooke, advanced at 10.30 A.M. to clear the thickly wooded country to the West of the River Ourthe. Little opposition was encountered at first until the defile at Rendieux-le-Bas was reached. Here they came under heavy fire covering a road block. The supporting artillery was unable to fire effectively owing to difficulties over crest clearance, and the attack was held up.

On the fronts of the 1/5th Welch and East Lancashires the opposition from enemy Infantry and Tanks was only moderate; but shell fire was heavy, and mines and booby traps plentiful.

By 1 P.M. the 160th Brigade had concentrated in and around Hotton for their part in the attack in the wake of the 2nd Monmouthshires.

At the same time the 71st Brigade attacked in its sector, with the 1st Oxford and Bucks (Lieut.-Colonel F. H. Howard) on the right and the 1st Highland Light Infantry (Lieut.-Colonel T. McLeod) on the left. The 4th R.W.Fs. task was to patrol vigorously towards Hargimont and to watch the right flank of the Division.

By 5.30 P.M. both attacking Battalions were firmly established on their objectives, but not without stubborn fighting and in face of difficult conditions. The Oxford and Bucks captured some 20 prisoners, but at about 3.30 P.M. were sharply counter-attacked by a party of Germans. The attack was beaten off; but Major F. C. Vickers, Commanding D Company, was killed. The H.L.I. were heavily shelled during the advance and also much troubled by mines.

At 5.30 P.M. the 2nd Monmouths reverted to the Command of their own Brigade – the 160th. The Battalion was still held up some 200 yards from the defile at Rendieux-le-Bas. The approach along the road was suicidal without effective fire support and there was no room to deploy off it. A number of attempts were made by another route, but the terrain was too difficult and they were not successful. The capture of Rendieux-le-Bas was regarded as important for supply purposes during the next phase of operations, and the Divisional Commander ordered that further attempts to capture the place be made during the night.

Meanwhile the 7th R.W.F. (Lieut.-Colonel G. F. T. B. Dickson) passed through the 1st East Lancashires, and the 1/5th Welch pressed on towards Waharday. Both Battalions were slowed up by mines and the shocking state of the ground, and neither had succeeded in capturing their objectives by nightfall. There had been no opportunity for reconnaissance of these objectives or to prepare a night attack. The Battalions, therefore, dug in for the night in the snowy woods, with the temperature at many degrees below freezing.

About this time an appeal was made for "Weasels" to ease the supply problem. These were tracked vehicles of American manufacture, about the size of a Bren Carrier, and specially designed for operating in conditions of snow or mud. They had an additional advantage in that they did not detonate many types of German mines. Twenty of these vehicles were promised by Headquarters XXX Corps and arrangements made to collect them during the night. Others were promised later. Major-General Ross also succeeded in obtaining the release from the 6th Airborne Division of the 53rd Reconnaissance Regiment and the unit moved to Marche during the night of the 4/5th January.

The situation at nightfall on the 4th was that the Americans on the left, having reached Beffe at noon, were pressing South against Infantry and Tank opposition. On the right the 6th Airborne Division was meeting resistance South of Rochefort.

At about 7 P.M. a tragic accident occurred. Brigadier G. B. Sugden, the Commander of the 158th Brigade, was killed when travelling in a scout car with his G.S.O.3, Captain R. C. H. Smith. The car skidded on the ice and overturned. Lieut.-Colonel R. E. H. Hudson (83rd Field Regiment) assumed temporary Command of the Brigade, pending the arrival of Lieut.-Colonel K. G. Exham, from the 6th Royal Welch Fusiliers.

The day's fighting had given the Division an idea of what offensive operations during winter in the Ardennes entailed. The troops had no special clothing, boots or snow camouflage suits, and no special transport immediately available. In the woods, and most of the country was wooded, it was often difficult to negotiate the snow-ladened and wet undergrowth if one left the track. Map-reading was largely a matter of guess-work. Many of the troops had been in the open for three or four days before the advance began and this fact added to the magnitude of their achievements.

The weather on the 5th had not greatly improved although it became clearer and suitable for flying.

The pre-dawn attack by the 2nd Monmouthshires made some progress, but the defile defied capture, although repeated efforts were made against it throughout the day, including one made with aircraft (Typhoon) support.

On the front of the 158th Brigade slow, but steady, progress was made. The East Lancashires reached their objective without opposition, but the 7th R.W.F. had trouble with some enemy S.P. guns.

During that afternoon (the 5th) plans were made for resuming the offensive on the following day. However, at 5.30 p.m. the enemy made a heavy counter-attack, with about 400 Infantry supported by tanks, against the left forward Company of the 7th R.W.F. The Company was completely overrun and there were only 18 survivors. The centre Company was also heavily involved and forced to withdraw after running out of ammunition. The withdrawal was carried out in good order and the right Company was then ordered to conform. These forward Companies went back to an area in rear of the reserve Company and the Battalion then regrouped. The enemy did not follow up.

It was at this time that Major Hughes developed a new fireplan, codenamed "April". It called for a massive assault utilizing all available guns, delivering 5,820 shells in just twenty minutes. An initial assault using this fireplan took place at 01.00, with a second assault timed at 05.30, prior to the launch of the of the infantry assault. Due to a drop in temperature between the two fireplans, some of the shells fell short of the ridge, causing casualties among the troops of B Company.

It was now clear that the 7th R.W.F., who had suffered heavy casualties, were in no condition to take part in the next day's offensive in which they were to play a leading part. The Divisional Commander therefore postponed the operation and, as a precautionary measure, ordered the 4th Welch (160th Brigade), with one Squadron of the East Riding Yeomanry, to move to the area of the 158th Brigade and come under its command. During the same night (5/6th January) the 53rd Reconnaissance Regiment moved to Bourdon in Divisional reserve, and the 6th R.W.F. to Marche. At midnight the first batch of "Weasels" arrived in the Divisional area.

The 6th January was a very cold day. Some adjustments in dispositions were made, the main ones being the relief of the 4th R.W.F. by the 6th Airborne Division to the West of Marche, and the relief of the 2nd Monmouthshires in front of the Rendieux-le-Bas defile by the 53rd Reconnaissance Regiment.

A new plan was then made for the 7th January. The 4th Welch (still with the 158th Brigade) were to attack on to the high ground South-West of Waharday, followed on the right by an attack by the East Lancashires on Grimbiemont. The 71st Brigade were to attack on the right of the East Lancashires. On the evening of the 6th the Division was informed that after the next day's battle the 51st (Highland) Division would move into the lead. About the same time Brigadier J. O. Wilsey arrived to take command of the 158th Brigade. It was arranged that Lieut.-Colonel Exham would remain at Brigade Headquarters on the following day in an advisory capacity.

At 9 A.M. on the 7th January the 4th Welch (Lieut.-Colonel R. G. F. Frisby), supported by the 144th R.A.C., began their attack. The attack met with considerable opposition; but was nevertheless a complete success and by 11.30 A.M. the objective had been captured.

The attack of the East Lancashires began at 12 noon after an unfortunate setback on the Start Line, when a shell landed on the Command Group of Battalion Headquarters, killing the Adjutant and Intelligence

Sergeant and wounding some members of the Intelligence Section. Moreover, not a single tank of the supporting Squadron succeeded in reaching the Start Line, owing to the condition of the ground. Nevertheless, as is their custom, the Infantry moved forward on time. The advance was uphill and in the open. By 2.20 p.m. Grimbiemont had been captured; but the two leading Companies (A and D) had suffered heavily and were reduced to about 25 men each. After the capture of the village a troop of tanks managed to get forward and assisted in its defence. In this engagement the East Lancashires' losses were 18 killed and 71 wounded. During the period 1st to 7th January they amounted to 11 officers and 232 other ranks.

The attack of Brigadier Elrington's 71st Brigade had also started at 12 noon. The objective was the line of the Hedree stream to the West of Grimbiemont. The advance was made in a South Easterly direction, with the 1st H.L.I. on the left and the 1st Oxford and Bucks on the right. By 2.20 p.m. the Brigade had captured 95 prisoners. Their own casualties were comparatively light in spite of fairly heavy shelling and some sharp fighting. As had been the case on previous occasions the Artillery were hampered by the difficulties of crest clearance and the Battalions relied very largely on mortar fire for close support. The 3 inch Mortars of the Oxford and Bucks fired 1,000 rounds in 30 minutes.

On this day the 53rd Division captured a total of 155 prisoners, and enemy killed were estimated at about 70.

During the afternoon the 160th Brigade relieved the 1/5th Welch with the 2nd Monmouthshires and took over the left sector – with the E. Lancashires under command and the 6th R.W.F. reverting to command.

That evening the Divisional Commander sent messages of congratulation to the 7th Bn The Royal Welch Fusiliers, 1st Bn. The East Lancashire Regiment, 1st Bn The Oxfordshire and Buckinghamshire Light Infantry and 1st Bn The Highland Light Infantry on their fine achievements.

Night patrolling was carried out in several inches of snow, and in bitterly cold weather. There were indications that the enemy was pulling out and these were confirmed when on the following day the 2nd

Monmouths occupied Waharday unopposed, and the Reconnaissance Regiment found the much disputed road block covering Rendieux-le-Bas clear of the enemy and entered the town against only slight opposition.

At 12 noon on the 8th January command of the Divisional Sector passed to the 51st (Highland) Division. The 71st Brigade, 53rd Reconnaissance Regiment, 1st Manchesters, 33rd Armoured Brigade and part of the Divisional Artillery and Engineers remained with the 51st Division for the time being. To minimize movement on the still icy roads all support weapons and ammunition in the forward areas were handed over on the ground to relieving units.

The rest of the Division moved north to the area South of Liege. Headquarters 53rd Division opened at Tilff and the 158th Brigade was at Nettine in Corps reserve.

On the 9th January the other formations and units began to move north and by the 10th the whole Division was concentrated in the area to the South of Liege. Although the weather remained cold the troops spent a very pleasant time in the friendly Belgian villages. On the 14th the Division took over the role of counterattack Division on the First American Army front. Plans for counter-attack in various areas were drawn up, but in the event they were not required.

By the 16th January 1945, exactly one month after the German offensive began, the American 1st Army in the North and their 3rd Army in the South were pushing forward in a counter-offensive against the flanks of the "bulge". Hitler's two Panzer Armies had not only been halted, they were about to be destroyed. By mid-January the enemy had lost 120,000 men and 600 tanks, and by the end of the Allied counter-offensive 220,000 German soldiers had been put out of action, including 110,000 as prisoners of war. This defeat destroyed the German Army's last strategic reserve. Although the offensive delayed the Allied advance to the Rhine by some six weeks it seems probable that in the long run it shortened the war. It certainly fitted in well with General Eisenhower's theory that the German Armies should be destroyed west of the Rhine.

Nevertheless, the Germans fought with their customary skill and valour. It was a measure of their military prowess that after five and a half years of war – and following their terrible defeats and losses in West and East – they should have been able to organize, and assemble, a force of this size and carry out such a vigorous offensive.

On the 17th January 1945 orders were received for the 53rd (Welsh) Division to move on the 19th to Eindhoven. The next task was to prepare for the Battle for the Rhineland.

It is interesting to note that my father had to stay on for a couple of days prior to moving out. I have no more details but his diary records the following:

> "The great worry of the Ardennes was now over, so we were all travelling back to the small village of Embourg which was very near Liege. However, David and I had to stay behind in Namur to give evidence in a Court-Martial. We had to report to the American Town-Major to be allocated accommodation. We were taken to the Chateau of a Titled Belgian Diplomat. He was stuck in occupied France, his wife and children were in Namur. The butler came to our room to tell us that the Countess was inviting us to join her for dinner. We knew that food was in very short supply, so we gave him two tins of corned beef from our rations. The chef concocted a lovely meal from the bully beef and the countess asked the butler what on earth the main course was. When he explained, the poor lady burst into tears, they hadn't seen meat for ages."

- CHAPTER X -
THE REICHSWALD FOREST - OPERATION VERITABLE

By mid-January it was clear that the German offensive in the Ardennes had been checked and was likely to involve the enemy in very heavy losses in men and equipment. Nevertheless, the Allied high commanders were impatient to resume the offensive and carry the war into Germany. The first step to be taken was the clearance of the Rhineland – the country between the rivers Maas and Rhine – as a preliminary to an assault crossing of the Rhine. This was the operation which the XXX Corps was about to undertake when the German attack in the Ardennes began, and which had to be postponed when the Corps was sent West to guard the crossings over the Meuse. Now that the threat in the Ardennes was over the XXX Corps, under Command of the First Canadian Army, was to re-assume its Rhineland role. For this operation the assault Divisions were to be the 51st (Highland), 53rd (Welsh), 15th (Scottish), 2nd Canadian and 3rd Canadian. The 43rd (Wessex) and Guards Armoured Divisions were to be in reserve. The importance of the Nijmegen bridgehead – the Island – was now apparent as it afforded a starting point East of the Maas for a drive South between the Maas and the Rhine.

On the 19th January 1945 the 53rd Division (less the 71st Brigade Group and the 53rd Reconnaissance Regiment) left the neighbourhood of Liege for an area just east of Eindhoven in the area of the First Canadian Army. The remainder of the Division followed the next day. The move was carried out in extreme cold and in face of a biting wind.

During the Ardennes operations the First Canadian Army had been planning and making preparations for the Rhineland offensive. A colossal tonnage of stores had been collected and much work done to improve communications. A comprehensive camouflage scheme was developed, as well as a "cover" plan to give the impression that an offensive in a Northerly direction, towards Utrecht, was contemplated.

The Nijmegen bridgehead, from which the offensive was to start, had two serious drawbacks. It was liable to heavy flooding and the approaches by road were confined to the two bottlenecks over the Maas at Grave and Mook. The weather and the question of the flooding of the rivers Maas, Niers and Rhine were constant sources of anxiety at this time.

The German defences were well developed and consisted of three main lines. Most Westerly was a zone of defences from the junctions of the Rhine and Waal and thence running south to the west of the Reichswald Forest. This consisted of a belt some 2,000 yards deep, covered by an anti-tank ditch and including many fortified villages. This line continued South along the East bank of the Maas as an almost continuous system of earthworks with strongly fortified areas at Venlo and Roermond.

Further East was the Siegfried Line. From the Nijmegen-Cleve road it ran South through the Reichswald Forest; then South-East to cover the towns of Goch and Geldern – both well-fortified – and then due South to the Roer. The defences had been recently greatly strengthened in the Reichswald Forest, although when our troops entered the zone they did not find them as formidable as had been expected.

The third line ran from the Rhine opposite Rees to the fortified town of Geldern and thence south. This was called the "Hochwald Layback" and joined the main line on the North bank of the Roer, a few miles from Linnich.

The German front between Duren and Nijmegen was known to be held by nine Divisions, and it was believed that three Panzer and two Para Divisions were available in reserve in the Northern sector.

"Operation Veritable", as it was called, was planned in three phases:

Phase I – A breakthrough by XXX Corps. This was to be an attack on a five-division front, with the right approximately at Mook, in the order from right to left – 51st (Highland), 53rd (Welsh), 15th (Scottish),

2nd (Canadian) and 3rd (Canadian). All Divisions were to attack simultaneously except the 3rd (Canadian) which was to follow some hours later.

Phase II – The capture of Goch by the 43rd (Wessex) Division and exploitation by the Guard Armoured Division. The opening of the road Goch-Gennep-Mook by the 51st (Highland) Division.

Phase III – The capture of Geldern and a general swing Eastwards by the XXX Corps to the Rhine. If possible the bridge at Wesel was to be captured intact by a mobile column.

During the first days of February arrangements were made for the forward move, and by the 7th the Division had crossed the Maas and was around Nijmegen – mainly in billets.

Orders for the operation had been issued on the 4th February and all Officers of the Division were briefed by Major-General Ross. Early on the 7th the details of the battle were explained to the men and the rest of the day spent in final preparations and in completing the reconnaissance of Assembly Areas in the woods North and West of the Dutch frontier town of Grosbeek which lay in pitiful ruins. The weather had not been kind: the long period of hard frost had broken and the going was indescribably bad. Unfortunately all the main roads through the Forest ran parallel to the front of advance, and communications forward would be mostly along tracks – not a very pleasant prospect. "Weasels", which had proved so valuable in the Ardennes, had been issued on a scale of 25 per Infantry Brigade to assist in maintenance in the forward areas.

In describing the operations which follow it has been impossible to give details of the very intricate and flexible Artillery programmes which formed part of every phase of the battle. The opening bombardment was very heavy, lasted for four and a half hours and was accompanied by what was known as a "Pepperpot". The object of the latter was to saturate the enemy defences on the front and flanks with heavy and prolonged fire from all types of flat trajectory weapons. This form of support, which was used on several occasions, was under the command of Lieut.-Colonel H. B. D. Crozier, 1st Manchesters, the troops taking part being the 1st Manchesters, C. Squadron Notts Yeomanry, 196

Battery of the 73rd Anti-Tank Regiment and three troops of the 25th Light Anti-aircraft Regiment.

The attack, along the Northern part of the Reichswald Forest, was to be made due East, the opening phase being on a one-Brigade front.

The 71st Brigade was to seize the Brandon Berg feature and the high ground to the South-East.

160th Brigade (with 1st East Lancashire Regiment from the 158st Brigade attached) was then to pass through the 71st, break into the Siegfried Line and then, leaving the East Lancashires astride it, push on and seize the Stoppel Berg feature.

The 158st Brigade would then pass through the 71st and, taking back the East Lancashires under command, occupy and mop up the area of the Siegfried Line between the 71st and 160th Brigades.

It was a very important feature of the Corps plan that troops of the Division should be astride the road leading south from Frasselt through the Forest by 4 P.M. on the 8th February, and that the Stoppel Berg feature should be occupied by 8 A.M. on the 9th.

At 5 A.M. on the 8th February 1945 more than one thousand guns opened up along the XXX Corps front.

At 9.30 A.M. the 71st Brigade, led by the 4th R.W.F. and preceded by a barrage, began the advance. The first objectives were captured with comparative ease as the Artillery and the "Pepperpot" had done their job well. The "Flails" which preceded the attack became bogged at an early stage, but the supporting tanks of the 147th R.A.C. managed to keep up. By 12 noon the 4th R.W.F. were some 1000 yards from the edge of the Forest and the 1st Oxford and Bucks and the 1st H.L.I. passed through. Good progress followed and by 1 P.M. the anti-tank ditch had been bridged at two places. At about 2 P.M. the leading troops reached the Forest and, although the going then became more difficult, they soon reached their objectives. The Oxford and Bucks captured the main Brandenberg feature and the H.L.I. took the feature to the South. By 3.30 P.M. the Brigade had achieved its main task. The H.L.I. were then ordered to push on to the spurs running East towards the Kranenburg-Hekkens road. Casualties in the Brigade had been very light. Some 30 enemy had been killed and about 200 prisoners taken, mostly from the 84th Infantry Division, but a few from the 180th. When later Tactical Headquarters, 71st Brigade moved up to the edge of the Forest they were shelled and the Brigade Major, the G.S.O.3, and two other ranks were wounded.

And so the 53rd (Welsh) Division carried the war on to German soil.

On the left the 15th (Scottish) Division had made good progress but on the right, where the enemy had been recently reinforced, the 51st (Highland) Division encountered stiff opposition.

At 4.30 P.M. the 180th Brigade was ordered to advance from its Assembly Area in the Grosbeek woods. Their task was to be a more difficult one than the 71st's. From the outset they were hampered by the shocking state of the roads, and the tanks, which had to move off the road, were constantly getting bogged. On entering the Forest the tracks were so bad that it was not until nearly midnight that the two leading Battalions, the 6th R.W.F. (left) and the attached 1st East Lancashires (right), were ready to attack. The 6th R.W.F. had to advance along a track under shell and mortar fire and when the Commanding Officer, Lieut.-Colonel K. G. Exham, arrived at the forming up place he found that his rear-link wireless set had been knocked out. Unable to communicate with Brigade Headquarters, and having no news of the deployment of the East Lancashires, he decided not to give the enemy a breathing space, but to attack at once with his Battalion and its attached Squadron of the 9th Royal Tanks.

On the right the East Lancashires were also meeting difficulties. On arrival at the edge of the Forest at dusk the Commanding Officer, Lieut.-Colonel G. W. P. N. Burden, found the road blocked with vehicles. He succeeded in getting two "Weasels" and another vehicle through and the Squadron of the 9th Royal Tanks were able to get round by means of a slight detour. The tanks, however, became bogged inside the forest and the Battalion deployed and went forward alone. The attack was through very difficult forest country with thick undergrowth, in which the leading Companies kept direction by means of compass bearings, which had been carefully worked out previously. The operation was also greatly assisted by "Movement Light" (an innovation brought into use towards the end of the war. A cloudy sky, preferably low cloud, was necessary, the clouds being used as "reflectors" for searchlights playing on them at suitable angles. By this means conditions of twilight could be artificially produced over a considerable area, which was employed extensively on the whole Corps front. Opposition was negligible. The 6th R.W.F. were through the Siegfried Line by midnight and by 1 A.M. on the 9th they had reached their first objective.

To the South the East Lancashires met with some opposition, but successfully reached their objective. The Kranenburg-Hekkens road had been secured unopposed and was held by two Companies. After capturing a tractor taking ammunition to a Russian-type gun, which was also captured, the Battalion went through two lines of trenches which lay some 150 yards beyond the road. Later the Battalion was counter attacked, but held its ground. Casualties were very light.

Meanwhile the rain had increased and this, with the additional traffic, reduced the forest tracks to an indescribable condition. The troops were carrying out a major offensive under the worst possible circumstances. By the end of the first day the 53rd Division had captured 272 prisoners out of a Corps total of about 1,100.

The next phase was the advance, through the 6th R.W.F., of the 4th Welch followed by the 2nd Monmouthshires. This movement was made with the left on the Northern edge of the Forest, with the object of capturing the hills leading to the Stoppel Berg. The advance, which was much delayed by the bad going, continued steadily in the rain throughout the latter part of the night. An attempt by the Monmouths to move outside the Forest near Schottheide was frustrated by German S.P. guns – which were later dealt with by the 15th (Scottish) Division. The 4th Welch assaulted their objective and had captured it, against only slight opposition, by 9 A.M. The Monmouths passed through and, somewhat to their surprise, captured the Stoppel Berg feature unopposed. A few tanks had succeeded in accompanying the Infantry and these seem to have completely demoralized the enemy. Some 70 prisoners were taken without a fight.

The 6th R.W.F. advanced from the Siegfried Line at 11 A.M. and forming up in the area of the 4th Welch assaulted the feature east of the Stoppel Berg, near the North-Eastern edge of the Reichswald. Overcoming minor opposition they occupied their objective and captured 50 prisoners. Exploiting rapidly to the edge of the Forest the leading troops were able to observe enemy tanks and a number of vehicles moving North-East along the road to Materborn and Cleve. These were engaged by our own tanks and the Divisional Artillery.

This completed the task of the 160th Brigade for the time being.

It will be remembered that the 1st East Lancashires, of the 158th Brigade, had already gone forward with the 160th Brigade and were now positioned in the Siegfried Line just east of the road leading south from Frasselt. At 2 A.M. on the 9th the rest of the 158th Brigade began to move forward. The 1/5th Welch (Lieut.-Colonel J. S. Morrison-Jones) were in the lead. By 7 A.M. the Battalion was being seriously delayed by congestion of traffic on the tracks just inside the Forest, and had passed many vehicles bogged down in the mud. Leaving his Carriers and supporting Armour behind the Commanding Officer decided to push on to the objective – the high ground West and North of the Gelden Berg feature. It would seem that by this time the enemy had partly recovered from the first shock and, owing to the advance of our own troops, was not being subjected to the same weight of Artillery fire as earlier in the battle. The Infantry met with considerable opposition from Spandau and Mortar fire. Later when the Armour (147th R.A.C.) arrived a plan was quickly made and the objective captured.

Meanwhile the 7th R.W.F. had relieved the 6th R.W.F. (160th Brigade) on the North edge of the Forest and, as related, the latter began advancing at 11 A.M. to their objective on the East edge of the Reichswald.

By 4 P.M. on the 9th the Division had captured all its objectives, although mopping up continued. Prisoners were still being taken in the area some days later.

It had been an operation against the weather rather than the German enemy: an operation in which timings, and other details of the plan, were frequently upset by the shocking conditions. Several bold decisions were made by Infantry Commanders to advance without tank or artillery support. The success of the operation was very largely due to the flexibility of the Division which, as on other occasions, always seemed able to produce a good improvised solution when the original plan went wrong.

With the completion of the tactical side of the first stage of the operation the question of supply became one of paramount importance. After the 158th Brigade had entered the Forest, on the morning of the 9th, it was decided to close the main Divisional axis to traffic for a time, in an attempt to clear the congestion and improve its condition. Men of the 71st Brigade toiled all day assisting the 244th Field Company to improve communications. In the evening the conclusion was reached that the only way of keeping the route open was to provide very large maintenance parties. These were found by, among others, the Mortar Company of the 1st Manchester and from personnel of Anti-Tank and Light Anti-Aircraft Batteries. Early on the 10th February the 71st Brigade provided an organization for the control of traffic – which excluded from the route all vehicles except those with the highest priority. Traffic to the forward areas had to go via Frasselt – to the North of the Forest and in the 15th (Scottish) Division's area.

For the troops the Reichswald was an extremely uncomfortable battle. Casualties were fairly heavy in a few units, but were on the whole light.

On the flanks the two Scottish Divisions, with whom the 53rd had been so intimately associated on other occasions, were battling forward. To the North the 15th (Scottish) Division had broken through the Nutterden defences of the Siegfried Line and by the evening of the 9th the leading troops were on the Materborn feature. A plan made earlier for the 160th Brigade to help in the capture of this feature was, therefore, cancelled. The 43rd (Wessex) Division, following up, reached Nutterden by midnight 9/10th February.

On the right flank the 51st (Highland) Division were meeting stiffer resistance and were also held up by the bad going. After capturing the Freudelberg, and mopping up South of Riethurst (at the Western corner of the Reichswald) they advanced to the Nijmegen-Goch road.

The 10th February was a very wet day and the Division spent it in patrolling and regrouping, with two objects in view, namely to establish a "front" along the Cleve-Hekkens road, and to position the Division in a favourable manner to continue the advance in a South-Easterly direction and clear the rest of the Forest.

The most notable engagement of this day was when a platoon of the 6th R.W.F. on patrol – and supported by another platoon of the same Regiment – fought a short action with a party of enemy Parachutists on the Northern edge of the Forest, West of Materborn, and inflicted heavy casualties on them. This was the first time Parachutists had been encountered in the Reichswald.

Severe fighting continued on the flanks. To the immediate North the 43rd (Wessex) Division, who were trying to turn the North-East corner of the Reichswald, were meeting stubborn resistance from Parachute troops. The Division was also handicapped by the floods on their axis of supply – the Nijmegen-Cleve road – which was under water to a depth of two feet in many places. Further North the Canadians, operating in amphibious vehicles, were mopping up the "Island" villages and had reached the Rhine in several places.

To the South the 51st (Highland) Division were still meeting fierce resistance on the Nijmegen-Gennep road.

The next task of the 53rd (Welsh) Division was to clear the rest of the Reichswald Forest while the 43rd Division fought its way down the East side, and the 51st pushed on through Hekkens to Kessel, and also captured Gennep.

Having recovered from the first shock – and surprise that an offensive should be conducted in such unfavourable weather – the Germans were now trying to establish a front across the Forest, from South of Materborn along the road running South-west to Hekkens and thence to Gennep. This front was being held by the 16th Para Regiment (6th Para Division) on the North; the 20th Para Regiment (7th Para Division) centre and the 2nd Para Regiment (2nd Para Division) to the South. These arrangements were not made in time, however, to prevent his right being turned.

The Divisional plan, in what may be termed the second stage in the capture of the Reichswald Forest, was to establish the 160th Brigade (left) and the 158th Brigade (centre and right) across the Forest and East of the Cleve-Hekkens road. Subsequently the 71st Brigade was to relieve the 158th, and the 158th and 160th would then push on and occupy up to the Eastern edge of the Forest. Divisional Headquarters moved to Grosbeek (on the North-Western outskirts of the Reichswald).

The advance began on the morning of the 11th February. To the North the 6th R.W.F. (160th Brigade) advanced across the road without serious opposition. Slightly further South the 2nd Monmouths passed through the 4th Welch and came up into line with the 6th R.W.F. They met sharp opposition as they crossed the road and sustained some 40 casualties, but succeeded in capturing their objective. At 1.30 P.M. the 4th Welch were ordered to continue the advance, being directed on Dammershof and the Northern part of the large clearing immediately to the East. This they accomplished by 4 P.M. against slight opposition, capturing a few prisoners and one S.P. gun.

Meanwhile further South on the left of the 158th Brigade front the East Lancashires passed through the 7th R.W.F., and on the right the 1/5th Welch advanced towards the road. The going was bad and some opposition was met before both battalions secured their objectives astride the road. At 12.15 P.M. Brigadier Wilsey issued orders for the continuation of the advance, and at 1.45 P.M. the leading Battalions moved off. The East Lancashires were to push on to an angle in the South-East corner of the Forest about 1200 yards north of the Asperden Bridge over the River Niers. On their left the 1/5th Welch were directed on Am Klosterhuf, a small village on the Eastern edge of the Forest. The 7th R.W.F. were to follow the East Lancashires and then turn South to the South-East Corner of the Forest near the Asperden bridge.

Both leading Battalions met stiff opposition. The East Lancashires had several of their supporting tanks knocked out by S.P. guns, but by about 6.30 P.M. the Battalion had reached the Cleve-Asperden road. The 1/5th Welch met their stiffest opposition some 800 yards west of this road and were held up. The 7th R.W.F., moving behind the East

Lancashires, also encountered opposition which had apparently been by-passed by the leading troops.

At 8 p.m. the Divisional Commander ordered both Brigades to halt where they were and plans were made for resuming the advance next day. At about 8.30 p.m. the East Lancashires beat off an Infantry counter attack and throughout the night patrol activity, and minor encounters, continued along the whole front.

The Divisional plan for the 12th February was for both leading Brigades to press forward to the Eastern edge of the Forest, with the 71st Brigade mopping up in rear of the 158th. The latter Brigade was to make every effort to capture the river bridge North of Asperden. At the same time troops of the 51st (Highland) Division were to fight their way east along the Southern edge of the Forest.

The advance was renewed early on the morning of the 12th. On the 158th Brigade front the 7th R.W.F. closed up in rear of the East Lancashires. The 1/5th Welch advanced slowly against stiff opposition, but eventually reached the Cleve-Asperden road. Their further efforts to advance were bitterly opposed and by 12 noon only four tanks of their supporting Squadron were still in action.

Further North the 160th Brigade made progress. At 7.15 a.m. the Monmouthshires passed through the 4th Welch and cleared the North-East corner of the Forest, and later the 6th R.W.F. on the right advanced to positions astride the Cleve-Asperden road.

It was during this phase of operations that the 4th Welch, who had been ordered to push on through the 6th R.W.F., had a very stiff fight. On reaching a track meeting point near the extreme North-East edge of the Forest the leading Company was violently counter-attacked, driven back and its commander killed. The Commanding Officer (Lieut.-Colonel R. G. F. Frisby) rallied the Company and with it, and another, cleared the area and restored the situation. Shortly afterwards the 4th Welch advanced from the Forest and, having captured some 40 prisoners, dug in astride the Cleve-Goch road.

In the early afternoon of this day (12th February) the enemy launched a counter attack in considerable strength. It fell on the right of the

6th R.W.F. (160th Brigade) and on the 1/5th Welch (158th Brigade). This attack was carried out by elements of the 115th *Panzergrenadier* Regiment (of 15th *Panzergrenadier* Division) to the North and by the 104th *Panzergrenadier* Regiment to the South, and was supported by artillery and mortar fire and a number of S.P. guns. The attack was beaten off, partly by well-directed artillery and partly by small arms fire which the defending Infantry withheld until the attackers were within about 300 yards. This caused serious losses to the enemy, who withdrew in disorder.

About the same time small parties of the enemy operating further South attempted to infiltrate into the East Lancashires' positions, but they were mopped up by a platoon from the reserve company and a troop of tanks. Just before dusk some 200 Germans were seen opposite the positions of the same Battalion and it looked as if a counter-attack was about to develop. The enemy was however dispersed by artillery fire and by the unit carriers which were brought up to a position from which fire could be opened "mounted".

That evening on the 160th Brigade front the 2nd Monmouths were ordered forward to the edge of the Forest on the left of the 4th Welch. They met with slight opposition; but by 8 P.M. the Battalion was digging in astride the road facing the village of Niederdamm. On this day the unit took 60 prisoners of war.

We can now turn to the 71st Brigade which had been in rear for the past few days. It passed a wet but quiet night of the 11/12th.

At 12.30 P.M. on the 12th the Divisional Commander held a conference at 71st Brigade Headquarters at which an early advance for the capture of Goch was discussed. However, the enemy's counter attacks later in the day showed that he was still fighting stubbornly in the Reichswald and in consequence the advance on Goch was suspended for the time being. At 3 P.M. the 1st H.L.I. (71st Brigade) were placed under command of the 158th Brigade; but at 8 P.M., when it was known that the enemy counter-attacks had been held, the Battalion reverted to its own Brigade.

By this time the tank strength of the 34th Armoured Brigade had been greatly reduced. The 9th Royal Tank Regiment, which had supported the 160th Brigade with great resolution, was so depleted that it was ordered back to refit and reorganize as soon as anti-tank guns could be got forward to replace it in the anti-tank role. The 147th R.A.C. could only muster two very weak squadrons. The roads and tracks were in a deplorable state, many being only passable to "Weasels". Jeeps, Carriers and other vehicles were bogged by the sides of the tracks, and it was only by heroic efforts by unit Quartermasters, and other administrative personnel, that the forward units were supplied with food, ammunition and other requirements. North of the Reichswald, along the Wyler-Kranenburg road all traffic had to be by "DUKW" (a type of large amphibious vehicle). On the evening of the 12th a further 36 "Weasels" were allotted to the Division. Never were vehicles more welcome: they were practically the only means of evacuating stretcher case casualties.

On the flanks satisfactory progress had been made. To the South troops of the 51st (Highland) Division had reached the Cleve-Hekkens road just within the Forest, and the area north of the River Niers about Kessel.

Meanwhile to the North the 43rd (Wessex) Division were engaged in hard fighting, and experiencing bad going, in their attempt to drive down to the East of the Reichswald. By the evening of the 12th their advanced troops had reached Hau, 2 miles South of Cleve and on the North-East fringe of the Reichswald.

It had now become clear that the enemy – who had apparently doubted the feasibility of an advance through the Forest in the prevailing weather conditions – was now reinforcing. Earlier in the battle he had thrown in a Regiment from each of the 6th and 7th Para Divisions and the 116th Panzer and 15th *Panzergrenadier* Divisions had now been identified in the area. As it seemed likely that the rest of the 6th and 7th Para Divisions would soon become available it was regarded as imperative to maintain the momentum of the advance. Orders were, therefore, issued for the final clearing of the Reichswald on the 13th February.

The plan was for the 71st Brigade with the 1/5th Welch (from the 158th Brigade) to come up in the centre of the Divisional front and advance to the edge of the Forest between Wilhelminenhof to the North and the exit of the Cleve-Asperden road to the South. The 147th R.A.C., which had been in support of the 158th Brigade, was to come under the 71st Brigade for this operation. The 158th Brigade was to swing right to the Southern edge of the Forest, join up with the 51st (Highland) Division on the Niers about Grafenthal and, if possible, capture the Asperden Bridge. C Squadron 53rd Reconnaissance Regiment was placed under command of the 158th Brigade. The 160th Brigade to the North was to hold its positions and mop up within its area.

The 71st Brigade attack began at 10 A.M. on the 13th behind a somewhat hastily prepared barrage fired by the Divisional Artillery and one Medium Regiment. The leading Battalions were the 1st H.L.I. (right) and the 4th R.W.F. (left) with the 1st Oxford and Bucks in reserve. The attack went well from the start, the troops being in fine form at the prospects of getting clear of the Forest. The enemy did not resist as stubbornly as had been expected and by 12 noon both forward Battalions had reached their objectives. About 140 prisoners and two S.P. guns were taken at a cost of 30 casualties – mostly from artillery and mortar fire. After the attack the Oxford and Bucks relieved the 1/5th Welch. A dark and wet night followed with few signs of the enemy, and the Brigade devoted its energies to the pressing problems of maintenance. The tracks were now in an even worse state and many vehicles, including even "Weasels", became bogged and had to be abandoned.

The 158th Brigade's plan was for C Squadron of the 53rd Reconnaissance Regiment to advance to the Southern edge of the Forest followed by the 7th R.W.F. who were to move rapidly on the Asperden bridge. The East Lancashires were to move to a central position, just within the Forest, North of Grafenthal, from where they could operate as required. The Squadron met with no opposition; nor did the 7th R.W.F. until they reached the edge of the wood about 600 yards north of the bridge, when they came under fire from enemy holding the high ground covering the bridge. The enemy troops holding the bridgehead were estimated at about one Company, in a well sited position, dug in and wired. The Battalion deployed and began its attack at 9.30 A.M. After very stubborn fighting, in which the whole resources of the Battalion were used, the attack was finally held up. The Battalion then dug in and spent the night patrolling vigorously to locate the enemy positions.

An explosion during the attack was thought to be the blowing of the bridge, and this was confirmed by air reconnaissance on the following day. No further attacks on the bridge site were made and it was not occupied until the 16th. It is interesting to note that some hand-operated pack flame-throwers, which were used by the R.W.F., proved ineffective as the teams were unable to get near enough to the enemy owing to the fire of some weapons of the "Bazooka" type, a hand-operated anti-tank weapon, about the size of a rifle, which could be operated by two men. The 7th R.W.F. suffered 70 casualties in this action.

During the 14th there was some shelling on the Divisional front, especially along the well-defined edges of the Forest. It was the first good flying day for some time and the Royal Air Force took full advantage of it. No. 84 Group R.A.F. flew 800 sorties on the XXX Corps front on this day.

This ended for the XXX Corps the first stage of the Rhineland Battle, and for the 53rd (Welsh) Division the Battle of the Reichswald Forest. The leading troops had entered the Western edge of the Reichswald on the morning of the 8th February and the Forest had been cleared, although not completely mopped up, by the morning of the 14th – a period of six days. In any previous war an advance on this scale, in the weather conditions which existed would not have been attempted. Mountains and tropical heat have never been obstacles to well trained and properly equipped troops, and in recent times the desert has lost much of its terrors: but a combination of winter rain, mud and flooding had always been regarded as insuperable difficulties. In the past it had been the almost invariable custom for Armies operating in the Low Countries to go into "winter quarters" until conditions became more favourable in the spring. The wisdom of this was confirmed in World War I when in operations, such as the Battle of Passchendaele in 1917, the troops became bogged down in mud, and it proved impossible to maintain the momentum of the advance. In the Rhineland battle conditions became steadily worse from day to day and, if this could have been foreseen in advance, it is likely that the operation would have been postponed. That it was successful was due in large measure to the high standard of training and morale of the troops, and to good organization and staff work; but even so it could hardly have been accomplished without modern devices of very recent production.

The bulldozer, the tracked vehicle (particularly those of amphibious type such as the "Weasel", the "Buffalo" and the "DUKW") and "Movement Light" (used extensively at this time) – these aids just made the difference between what was possible and what was impossible. Nevertheless, it was a close thing and the greatest credit was due to the administrative services who laboured by day and by night to provide the fighting troops with the means to continue their forward move and fight a very determined enemy. The Germans fought with great tenacity in the Rhineland, and on several occasions staged local counter-attacks.

In the case of the 53rd Division the difficulties were increased by operating in a thick forest, which usually made it impossible for vehicles to move off the tracks, and also made it inevitable that many of the enemy were left behind by the forward troops to ambush and harass the rear areas.

It is not an exaggeration to say that the successful attack on the Reichswald Forest, under the weather conditions at the time, was an operation unique in military history and a feat of arms of which the 53rd (Welsh) Division, and their supporting troops, were justly proud.

My father's diary recounts the detail of the struggle:

> *"Two days later, David and I set off in an open Jeep to Embourg. It was absolutely freezing and on the way we saw a queue of G.I.s at a truck on the roadside. It was a P.X. (like our NAAFI). We asked if we could join and the answer was a generous affirmative and we grabbed our mugs from the Jeep. We then saw that the G.I.s all had sticks and mugs. We then watched as each G.I. took his turn, held his stick so that the P.X. lady put ring doughnuts on stick, as many as it would hold. They quickly found us a stick each and there was strictly*

NO CHARGE. This truck would visit them weekly, conditions permitting.

We had been overseas more than six months and in the whole of that time we had seen one NAAFI van from which we had been allowed to PURCHASE one cup of tea and one temporary pack of biscuits.

Embourg was a delightful little village. Our Mess was in a fairly large house on top of a hill. My billet, mainly for sleeping, was in a lovely detached house owned by M. Auguste Liesken. He was a metallurgist in the Steel Works in Liege and having travelled extensively in U.S.A., spoke excellent English. He had two young children and each evening they moved to his parent's house where they slept. This was because this other house had a substantial cellar and although no 'flying bombs' had actually landed in the village, they did occasionally fly overhead. We had about ten days rest in Embourg which was absolute heaven after six months of almost continuous action and sleeping in the open. To stroll into the local Café and order a coffee and aperitif was like being in a new world. Struggling to talk to the locals was an extra bonus.

However, all good things come to an end and so we moved back up North to the Helmond area – at least for a few days. We had left the Ardennes on the 10th Jan and we were about to leave Embourg on the 17th. Two incidents stick in my mind from Embourg. Firstly, Auguste Liesken was able to pass me enough knowledge on his theory that the flying bombs launching pads were limited in number, and had such a small traverse that Embourg did not come within their sphere of operation. We went around the village publicising this fact to such good effect that the elders agreed that it would be safe to hold a dance one night. No one had been out in the dark lately because of the bomb menace. Needless to say, the dance was a tremendous success.

The other event was not a pleasant one. Stuart Shrimpton had been a Captain since the war started. He now had the misfortune to break his ankle in an accident. The rules were such that after 21 days in hospital, he had to revert to the rank of Lieutenant! We were all *disgusted at this but there was nothing we could do. This was the way the Army treated its wounded. Almost unbelievable!!*

After a few fairly quiet days at Helmond, we found that our next target was the Reichwald Forest, a part of the very strong Siegfreid Line. At Helmond we had civilian billets. With one other, I was billeted with a Frau Stockerman and her teenage daughter Loni, this of course being a Dutch family. We explained as well as we could that all we needed was a bedroom which we could share and we would be having all our meals elsewhere. We just couldn't fathom the terrified state in which both the females were.

Fortunately, some of our lads in the next billet were able to tell us that Frau Stockerman was not a widow as we had assumed, but that her husband was actually a German by birth. When the Germans had found out when they invaded, they had taken him for the army, completely against his wishes. I made haste to find a local who could assure the poor females that they were in no danger at all from us and we genuinely sympathised with their position. The atmosphere finally cleared.

The Army now intended attacking the area S.E. of Nijmegen between the rivers Rhine and Maas. This was where the Siegfreid Line was, and the 53rd Div. was given the unenviable task of clearing out the Reichwald Forest. On the 8th Feb the battle started with a tremendous Artillery barrage. More than one thousand guns were said to be engaged in it. The hard frost conditions had broken and conditions underfoot were now very wet and heavy. The troops fought their way in atrocious conditions, but by the next evening, the 9th, all the first objectives had been taken. Ground conditions were so bad that all kinds of vehicles, including tanks, were getting completely bogged down and unable to move. The infantry kept advancing regardless, sometimes against very heavy opposition and also determined counter-attacks.

At times like these the Artillery support was particularly vital. The flooding had created such atrocious conditions that at one time, or so we were told, that of the 72 field guns in the Division, only 12 were capable of giving support fire. Of these, 8 were the guns of 497 Bty!!

At this time poor Dick Potter (who was G.P.O. of E Troop), had a foot blown off by a Schu mine. What made it worse was that an ambulance couldn't get through, so we had to wait for a Weasel (a small tracked vehicle). It was said afterwards that under the prevailing weather conditions the successful attack by the men of the 53rd Welsh Division was an operation unique in military history. By the 17th-18th Feb, enemy resistance, fortunately, was waning and the troops were having a slightly easier time. On the 20th Feb GOCH was captured. (This was the first anniversary of my father's death). But the men had to push further south and again the intensity increased.

On one day I had a memorable diversion. My troop was on the right of the road, opposite; on the left was a Medium Bty. As the day progressed we were aware of dozens of Highland Infantry being placed at something like 10 yard intervals along the length of the road. We soon found out that Winston Churchill was expected and he wanted to fire a shell across the Rhine into the heart of Germany. His car arrived, he stepped out, dressed as a full Colonel and wearing his 'British Warm'. I raced across the road to see it all. The gun was already loaded and aimed. All the great man needed to do was to step forward and pull the lanyard. A young subaltern stepped forward and offered him a set of ear-plugs. With a grand Churchillian gesture the articles were brushed aside. The lanyard was pulled, the gun fired and a great roar of approval rose. As he left, he was within two feet of me and I could clearly see that both ears were absolutely stuffed with cotton wool! The man was quietly smiling to himself. I thought 'What a performance.'

By the 11th March the Div. had completed its tasks and was waiting to withdraw. Between the 8th Feb and the 7th Mar the Div. had suffered 1,229 battle casualties and 3,200 prisoners captured. More than 180,000 rounds of 25-pounder had been fired. The next big task would be to attempt the RHINE CROSSING."

- CHAPTER XI -

THE RHINE CROSSING - OPERATION PLUNDER

*I*t was a disappointment that conditions in the Roer valley had prevented the Ninth American Army launching "Operation Grenade" which had been planned to synchronize with the XXX Corps drive down the Rhineland from the North. The Americans had completed their concentration remarkably quickly, but extensive flooding made the operation impracticable. It was, therefore, necessary for the British and Canadian troops to bear alone for the time being the brunt of the fighting for the Rhineland. Field Marshal Montgomery arranged for the relief of the 52nd (Lowland) Division in the Venlo Sector of the Maas by an American Division, and its transfer, together with the 11th Armoured Division, from the Second British to the First Canadian Army.

With these reinforcements the First Canadian Army ordered the XXX Corps to continue the advance on the two axes: Gennep-Venlo and Goch-Geldern. The II Canadian Corps was to advance further East on Udem and Calcar.

Although the 53rd Division had virtually completed the clearing of the Reichswald Forest it had still a part to play in the Battle for the Rhineland. On the 15th February all the tank "funnies" ("Flails", "Crocodiles", etc.) left the Division, as did the splendid 56th Canadian Anti-Tank Battery (self-propelled) which had served the 160th Brigade so well in the Reichswald.

On the 16th February Brigadier M. Elrington (71st Brigade) took over command of the Division from Major-General R. K. Ross, who went on a period of sick leave. At 12.30 P.M. Brigadier Elrington issued orders at Headquarters 71st Brigade for the next operation. It had been arranged for the 152nd Brigade of the 51st (Highland Division) to attack south of the Niers, their objective being the villages of Asperden and Hervost. This attack was timed to start at 8 P.M. on the 16th. The task of the 53rd Division was to conform to the North of the river by securing a line clear of the South-East corner of the Forest and North-East from near the Asperden Bridge for a distance of about 1500 yards. The operation was to be carried out by the 71st and 158th Brigades – each using one Battalion – and supported by a half-hour preliminary bombardment from five Medium Regiments, followed by a barrage fired by four Field Regiments and three Medium Regiments. This attack was to start at 9 P.M., one hour after that of the Highland Division.

The 158th Brigade on the right employed the 7th R.W.F., whose patrols had been in contact with the enemy since their attack on the bridgehead on the 13th, described in the previous chapter. On the left the 71st Brigade – under Lieut.-Colonel T. McLeod in the absence of Brigadier Elrington who was acting Divisional Commander – decided to use the 1st Oxford and Bucks, who had been holding the edge of the woods to the north.

Both Battalions advanced at 9 P.M. behind the barrage. The Oxford and Bucks met determined resistance from Germans in farm buildings and on the Asperberg feature; but by 10 P.M. success signals were seen on their objectives. However, soon after this some anti-tank guns, and a party of signallers, stretcher bearers and ammunition carriers, leaving the woods to join the forward Companies, were heavily fired on by a party of the enemy in a dug-in position who had been by-passed by the attacking troops. Major G. D. Jephson, who was leading the party, was killed and practically all the remainder were either killed or wounded. Confused fighting followed, small parties of the enemy in isolated buildings round the Asperberg feature fighting with fanatical courage. A party of eight Germans – all armed with Spandaus, which they fired from the hip – made a counter attack: they were all killed. The area was not finally cleared until 7 A.M. on the following morning. Forty Germans dead were counted and 42 taken prisoner, at a cost of 40 casualties to the Battalion.

On the right the 7th R.W.F. had bad luck on the start line, when a few rounds of the barrage fell short and caused casualties. Advancing against moderate opposition, and encountering some mines, the leading troops reached their objective by about 11 P.M. As with the Oxford and Bucks some enemy posts had been left behind and the reserve platoons moving forward came under fire. Mopping up took some time; but was eventually completed in the early hours of the morning with the aid of "wasps" (carrier-borne flame throwers). By 7 A.M. all anti-tank guns had been positioned and the Battalion was firmly established on its objectives. They had suffered 70 odd casualties in the previous attack on the bridgehead and this action cost them another 33. The Battalion was relieved by the 1st East Lancashires during the course of the day (17th February).

On the flanks of the Division good progress was being made, the 51st (Highland) Division capturing Asperden at about midnight on the 16/17th February and the 43rd (Wessex) Division making good progress to the East of the Cleve State Forest towards Goch.

On the 16th Lieut.-Colonel J. M. Hanmer, Commanding the 4th R.W.F. (71st Brigade), sent out a most fruitful patrol. The area of operations was to the East of the Reichswald and South of the Cleve State Forest. The patrol was pinned down by heavy fire in open ground and suffered casualties; but the enemy was induced to bring down his artillery defensive fire. This had the effect of disclosing his disposition and greatly assisted the 43rd Division, whose most westerly elements were operating in the area.

By the 17th the weather had improved slightly and the forward troops of the XXX Corps were reaching country which, although heavily water-logged, was less flooded, and possessed better communications, than the area from which the offensive began and through which it had recently passed. Enemy resistance was waning and it was evident that he had been surprised, and his balance upset, by the speed of the advance. It was felt that with a few more "jabs" our troops would be on the Rhine.

On the morning of the 17th the 160th Brigade with the 2nd Monmouths to the North, and the 4th Welch to the South, cleared the whole area between the Reichswald and the Kleve State Forest. There was no opposition; but a few enemy stragglers were picked up and the operation completed by 12 noon.

In order to conform to the movements of the 43rd (Wessex) Division the Corps Commander ordered that a Brigade of the 53rd Division be sent south to the line of the escarpment to the North of the Niers Valley between Kaiser Alberdekath on the West and south of Pfalzdorf on the East. The 71st Brigade was given this task. The advance began at 2 P.M. on the 18th February with the 1st H.L.I. on the right and the 1st Oxford and Bucks left. The latter Battalion reached its objectives without opposition. The H.L.I. (Commanded by Major C. R. H. Kindersley, in the absence of the Commanding Officer, who was acting Brigade Commander) met with stiff opposition on the left of their front; but this was quickly overcome with the help of a reserve Company and the Battalion secured its objective. In this action the Brigade captured 130 prisoners and that evening a patrol, which went out to the factory area North of Goch, brought in another 30.

On this day the Ninth American Army began its attack across the River Roer.

The 19th February was a quiet day for the whole Division – the first since the Rhineland Battle began. The 158th Brigade moved north out of the Forest and concentrated at Hau, preparatory to moving back into Holland for a few days rest in the Malden-Mook area.

On the same day Main Divisional Headquarters moved to Palandswald, in the large clearing in the North-East of the Reichswald. Here they began at once making arrangements for the Division's next part in the Rhineland Battle – operations leading to the capture of Goch.

The 15th (Scottish) Division had moved south from the Cleve area in order to attack Goch from the North and North-East. The 51st (Highland) Division was attacking from Asperden in a South-Easterly direction. Both Divisions had cleared the anti-tank ditch which surrounded Goch, but the area between the River Niers and the Cleve-Goch road – which lay between the lines of advance of the 15th and 51st Divisions – still contained parties of the enemy. The 4th R.W.F.

(71ˢᵗ Brigade) were ordered to clear this area, which consisted mainly of factories to the North of Goch itself.

Supported by artillery and mortar fire the Battalion advance began at 7.45 A.M. on the 20ᵗʰ. The left Company came under shell fire and the attention of snipers, but with the advance of the 15ᵗʰ Division to the East the situation became much easier and progress was rapid. Two German officers, one of whom was a Battalion Commander and 166 other ranks were captured. They came from the 2ⁿᵈ Para Division and the 190ᵗʰ Fusilier Battalion. During the afternoon the 4ᵗʰ R.W.F., their part in the capture of Goch completed, were ordered back to Pfalzdorf. On the following day the two Scottish Divisions completed the capture of the town.

The 53ʳᵈ (Welsh) Division was now to have a few days rest. The 158ᵗʰ Brigade, as already related, had moved back into Holland and the rest of the Division were to remain in the area of their positions at the end of the fighting and now out of contact with the enemy. On the 20ᵗʰ the 160ᵗʰ Brigade came into Corps reserve at 3 hours' notice with the role of counter attacking in the 15ᵗʰ (Scottish) Division's area should the necessity arise. At the same time the 13ᵗʰ/18ᵗʰ Hussars came under the Command of the 53ʳᵈ Division, followed by the 8ᵗʰ Armoured Brigade on the following day.

On the 21ˢᵗ February the 2ⁿᵈ Monmouths (160ᵗʰ Brigade) moved into the Northern outskirts of Goch in relief of the 6ᵗʰ Bn Royal Scots Fusiliers of the 15ᵗʰ (Scottish) Division.

On the 22ⁿᵈ German aircraft (Me 262s) were active over the Divisional Area, but little damage was done.

During the few days' rest which followed the strenuous days of the Reichswald Battle it was possible to sleep most of the troops in farm buildings and hamlets. For many these were the first nights of shelter since the operation had started a fortnight before. The sun began to shine and the men were able to "dry out" and clean themselves and their clothing. Stores were brought forward and much of the equipment lost in battle was replaced. Nevertheless, the conditions were far from ideal. The 160ᵗʰ Brigade found themselves in the gun area for the operations still being conducted round Goch, and were subjected to continuous noise by day and by night. The area allotted to the 158th Brigade in the Mook area was found to be fully occupied by other troops and they had to move to Nijmegen. This was an irritation which was compensated by the excellent laundry and bath services, and cinema shows, in Nijmegen.

After the fall of Goch the Corps Commander, Lieut.-General Sir Brian Horrocks, sent a message to his Divisions congratulating them on their efforts in the first phase of the operations. At the same time he called for a further effort to complete, with American assistance from the Roer, the conquest of the Rhineland.

Headquarters First Canadian Army's plan was for the Canadian Corps to pierce the German defence system known as the "Hochwald Layback" and advance to the Rhine at Xanten, while the XXX Corps on its right was to fight its way South to Geldern and then wheel eastwards to the Rhine about Wesel. This involved clearing the enemy out of the fortified towns of Weeze, Kevelaer and Geldern. Before the plan could be put into execution a redeployment of the Corps was necessary. This was a most intricate business owing to the paucity of roads behind the front, and was made more difficult owing to the necessity of continuing the momentum of the advance while re-grouping was taking place. It is unnecessary to give the various moves in detail: it will be sufficient to describe those in the immediate area of operations of the 53rd Division.

On the 21st February the 51st (Highland) Division operated to the South West of Goch towards Siebengwald and the 15th (Scottish) Division pushed south from Goch to the East of the Goch-Geldem road. The Highlanders met with heavy opposition, were checked and suffered severe losses. The 15th Division fought their way through thickly wooded country nearly to the bend in the River Niers about 3 miles North-East of Weeze.

To the 53rd (Welsh) Division was assigned the task of capturing Weeze. The plan was to advance South from Goch astride the Goch-Weeze-Geldern road, with heavy Artillery support, assault Weeze and the smaller town of Hees (about one and a half miles to the Southwest) and then exploit to Wemb (another two miles further south). The code name for this was "Operation Leek".

The enemy held positions astride the Goch-Weeze road with about four Battalions between the River Niers and Boeckelt, covering Weeze, and two more Battalions defending Weeze itself. The approach to Weeze from Goch was flat and exposed, except for a few small woods. The town was protected by the Niers and two antitank ditches.

The 8th Armoured Brigade, one Squadron of "Crocodiles" and one of "Flails" were attached to the Division for the operation. A great weight of additional Artillery was to support the advance, including the Divisional Artilleries of the 15th, 51st and 52nd Divisions as well as sixty-four 5.5" guns and six 7.2".

The plan was as follows:

160th Brigade to advance astride the Goch-Weeze railway and secure bridgeheads over the first (and if possible the second) anti-tank ditch. The right flank was to be protected by A. Squadron, 53rd Reconnaissance Regiment (originally it was arranged for the 160th Brigade to advance in "Kangaroos", but this was later cancelled).

The 71st Brigade would then pass through, bridge the second anti-tank ditch if necessary, and capture Weeze.

The 158th Brigade would then go through the 160th and move on Hees to the South-West.

Then, if all had gone well, the 160th Brigade – who were to concentrate and reorganize in the meantime – would exploit towards Wemb.

The preliminary bombardment began at 1 A.M. on the 24th February and at 6 A.M. the 160th Brigade attack began, with the 6th R.W.F. East of the railway and the 2nd Monmouths to the West. The axis of the R.W.F. was the main Goch-Weeze road, and that of the Monmouths a subsidiary road running parallel.

From the outset it was apparent that this was to be a day of stiff fighting. Bitter opposition was encountered from the buildings of Houenhof and Host, and although the reserve Companies of both Battalions were committed, and some progress was made, it became clear that the momentum of the advance could not be maintained.

On the right flank the Squadron of the Reconnaissance Regiment was meeting heavy opposition and continually having to "dismount"; but the situation became easier when they joined up with the 1st Black Watch of the 51st (Highland) Division operating to the West.

In the early afternoon Brigadier Coleman ordered the 4th Welch forward on the right flank to seize the "Starfish" Wood. The whole Brigade would then stand firm.

Meanwhile the Divisional Commander had ordered the 71st Brigade to advance and capture Host, Rottum and the anti-tank ditch.

The 4th Welch passed through the 2nd Monmouths at 4.20 P.M. and in spite of considerable artillery and mortar fire had captured "Starfish" Wood by 6 P.M.

At 7 P.M. the Monmouths put in an attack against some buildings which contained a party of Germans. The attack was only partially successful at the time, but eight prisoners were taken and the enemy later withdrew.

On the left flank the 160th Brigade experienced some trouble from snipers across the river, but these were eventually cleared out by patrols of the 15th (Scottish) Division.

We can now turn to the 71st Brigade. At 5 P.M. the 1st H.L.I. passed through the 6th R.W.F. to attack Host. They were supported by very heavy artillery fire which carried them to the outskirts of the village. Supported by "crocodiles'" they soon shot and flamed their way through the village. At 6.40 P.M., leaving their rear Companies to mop up, the Battalion pushed on to Rottum which they captured by 9 P.M. An enemy counter attack was later broken up by artillery fire. By 9.45 the H.L.I. had three Companies in, or around, Rottum and were within 400 yards of the anti-tank ditch; but were meeting increasing resistance and unable to reach it. One hundred and twenty prisoners had been taken.

At 1 A.M. on the 25th the 4th R.W.F. took over from the two H.L.I. Companies in Host and Rottum. In Host some parties of the enemy fought most bravely and stubbornly, and the village was not finally cleared until daylight.

The advance had been most bitterly opposed, but by the early hours of the 25th the 6th R.W.F. and the 1st H.L.I. between them had broken through two depleted Battalions of the 15th *Panzergrenadier* Regiment between the railway and river, and the H.L.I. had destroyed a company of parachutists placed in Rottum as a second line of defence.

The 71st Brigade had planned that after the capture of Rottum by the H.L.I., the 1st Oxford and Bucks would pass through and capture a small wood from which the anti-tank ditch could be assaulted. The attack began at 9 P.M. but in the darkness, and due to some confusion caused by heavy enemy mortar fire, the wrong wood was attacked. However, a new plan was made and the correct objective was eventually captured. The ground was heavily flooded, which made digging impossible and heavy shell fire caused many casualties – including Lieut. A. F. M. Paget who was mortally wounded. This officer had greatly distinguished himself in the engagement near Asperberg on the 16th and for his action on that day had received an immediate award of the Distinguished Service Order.

The Division was heavily shelled throughout the 25th: two enemy counter attacks against the right of the 2nd Monmouths were broken up by artillery fire. By the evening the total bag of prisoners was 550. Shelling continued all night, but the position on the right was greatly eased by the capture of Hulm by the 51st Division.

At 2 P.M. on the 26th the Divisional Commander issued orders for preliminary moves for a new attack on Weeze. The 71st Brigade was to take over the whole Divisional front and the 160th Brigade to withdraw to Goch. The 12th Kings Royal Rifle Corps – the Motor Battalion of the 8th Armoured Brigade – and B Squadron 53rd Reconnaissance Regiment were placed under command of the 71st Brigade. It was becoming essential to relieve the 1st Oxford and Bucks, who had sustained heavy casualties from shell and mortar fire in their exposed positions. Among their casualties were three field officers – Majors M. A. Ransome, J. H. Busby and D. G. Taylor and three other officers. The 1st H.L.I. took over Rottum from the 4th R.W.F. and the wood occupied by the Oxford and Bucks. The 12th K.R.R.C. took over from the 2nd Monmouths and

4th R.W.F. The Oxford and Bucks then moved back to an area north of the railway.

The night of the 26/27th February was one of active patrolling. A patrol of the 4th R.W.F. on the left got to within a few yards of the anti-tank ditch and was able to give very useful details of its width, depth and general condition. The patrol also reported that the bridge on the Goch-Weeze road had been demolished.

On the afternoon of the 27th Brigadier M. Elrington (Major-General Ross being still on sick leave) gave out orders for the new attack, to be known as "Operation Daffodil". The plan was for the 160th Brigade, with the 13/18th Hussars (less one squadron) and one Squadron 53rd Reconnaissance Regiment attached, to take over the front on the left now held by the 8th Infantry Brigade of the 3rd Division. The 8th Brigade had a small bridgehead over the Muhlen Fleuth – a stream running due east from the River Niers, the junction of the two being about 1 mile North East of Weeze – and it was the intention that the 160th Brigade should enlarge this bridgehead, in order to facilitate a flank operation round the East of the town. This was to take place on the 28th February and on the night of the 28th February / 1st March the 158th Brigade would pass through the bridgehead and secure a crossing place over the Niers opposite, or South of, Weeze. At the same time the Brigade was to send a mobile force under its command – consisting of one Squadron 53rd Reconnaissance Regiment and one Squadron Notts Yeomanry – to the South-East to protect its flank. On the following night the 158th Brigade would cross the Niers and capture Weeze.

No sooner had these orders been issued than a party from the 6th R.W.F., who were to relieve the 2nd Bn The East Yorkshire Regiment in the Muhlen Fleuth bridgehead, set off to make a reconnaissance. Just as they had finished the enemy staged a local counter attack accompanied by heavy artillery fire. This caught the reconnaissance party and inflicted heavy losses. Major E. Hughes, Capt. L. Owen, and Captain G. Griffith were killed and two other officers seriously wounded. The loss of these experienced officers, following so closely the casualties two days before, was a heavy blow to the Battalion.

The 6th R.W.F. crossed the Niers during the early morning of the 28th and went forward under cover of darkness to the Muhlen Fleuth. The relief in the bridgehead was a tricky operation, as the bridge was not a very substantial one, and the forward move was not completed until after daylight. The rear Companies were spotted by the enemy and the area heavily shelled, but the effect of this was to some extent mitigated by the use of smoke to conceal movement. The rest of the 160th Brigade moved into the area during the morning.

Meanwhile the 3rd Division, further to the East, cleared the wooded area up to the Weeze-Udem road. By the night of the 27th/28th February the 52nd (Lowland) Division had completed the relief of the 51st (Highland) Division on the Western flank.

On the night of the 27th/28th the 158th Brigade concentrated in the wooded area about 2 miles north of the Muhlen Fleuth. A daylight attack had been planned, but this was changed later to a night attack.

At 10.30 P.M. on the night of the 28th February / 1st March the 7th R.W.F. began their attack from the bridgehead. The attack made good progress and by 5.40 P.M. on the 1st March the leading elements were within a few hundred yards of the River Niers just North-East of Weeze, but were prevented from reaching the river by three enemy tanks. These withdrew when a troop of British tanks, brought forward under cover of smoke, appeared on the scene. Meanwhile the Eastern flank of the Battalion was protected by a force called "Robinforce", consisting of one Squadron South Riding Yeomanry and one Squadron 53rd Reconnaissance Regiment.

While this was going on the 1st Oxford and Bucks (71st Brigade) were advancing on Weeze from the North, with their left on the Goch-Weeze railway, but were held up short of Weeze – partly by fire and partly by flooding.

This was followed by an attack east of the railway by the 4th R.W.F. supported by a squadron of the 4/7th Dragoon Guards and a troop of "Crocodiles". Attacked by artillery, flame and infantrymen the defenders of the canal to the North of the town gave way. By 3 A.M. the Battalion was established on the South side, a bridge had been built and a troop of tanks sent over. By 6.30 A.M. the anti-tank ditch had been reached, crossed and bridged. At that hour an enemy counter attack was nipped in the bud by artillery fire, but later another attack, in which about 150 infantry supported by tanks took part, succeeded in recapturing the ditch, but failed to reach the canal. By 11 A.M. the position had become stabilized and the 4th R.W.F. were firmly established.

We can now return to the 158th Brigade where we left the 7th R.W.F. in the early morning of the 1st March East of the Niers to the North East of Weeze.

At 9.30 A.M. a revised plan was put into operation. On the right the 71st Brigade was to hold firm until relieved by the 52nd (Lowland) Division. On the 158th Brigade sector every effort was to be made to focus the enemy's attention on the 7th R.W.F., but at the same time the 1st East Lancashires (taking "Robinforce" under command) were to make a left hook and strike the Niers some 1¾ miles South of Weeze.

This was St. David's Day and it is interesting to note that in the early hours of the morning the three Royal Welch Fusilier Battalions were in the van of their respective Brigades. By the mysterious means by which emblems of this kind appear on such occasions, the men of all the Welch Battalions wore leeks in their hats. It is also recorded that many men of the three "adopted" Battalions wore the same emblems.

For the rest of the day and much of the night of the 1st/2nd March the East Lancashires battled their way through the woods. Opposition was not heavy, but it was stubborn in places, and the advance frequently delayed to eject parties of the enemy who opened fire from well concealed positions. The severity of the fighting can be judged by the fact that the Battalion had 69 casualties during the day.

The advance was continued on the morning of the 2nd March, when the Battalion reached the Niers without further opposition, but found the bridge destroyed. By mid-day three Companies had forded the river.

During the night of the 1st/2nd March patrols of the 1st H.L.I. (71st Brigade) had found Weeze clear of the enemy, and on the 2nd March their patrols linked up with those of the East Lancashires at Neuhaus.

In face of the threat to his flank and rear the enemy had withdrawn. The 160th Brigade also sent the 4th Welch – who had relieved the 7th R.W.F. (158th Brigade) – across the Niers in assault boats just East of Weeze, and they cleared up to the main road.

Meanwhile on the flanks of the Division steady progress was being made. On the 1st March the 3rd Division had captured Kervenheim, about 4 miles due East of Weeze, and was exploiting South. On the right the 52nd (Lowland) Division entered Niederhelsum and Heereven.

To the South the Ninth American Army was now only about 20 miles from the Division. They had captured Munchen Gladbach and Roermond and were approaching Neuss and Venlo.

It had been intended that the Division should be relieved by the 49th (West Riding) Division on the 2nd March, but this was cancelled as enemy resistance appeared to be crumbling everywhere and the Corps Commander did not wish to relax pressure by carrying out a major relief.

The 160th Brigade were given the task of clearing up the wooded area North-East and East of Weeze. This they did with the 4th Welch and 2nd Monmouths. The 6th R.W.F. were withdrawn for a brief rest South of Goch, after their struggle to hold the Muhlen Fleuth bridgehead on which the success of the outflanking movement of the East Lancashires had depended.

At 1 P.M. on the 2nd March the 1st Bn Oxford and Bucks and A Squadron 53rd Reconnaissance Regiment were placed under the command of a force from the 8th Armoured Brigade which was to pursue the enemy and capture Kevelaer, about 6 miles South of Weeze. The Armour of this force, which took the lead, was held up by S.P. guns and machine-gun fire from the woods astride the road North of Kevelaer. By this time it was dark and the Oxford and Bucks were called forward to continue the advance. The Battalion dismounted from the "Kangaroos" in which they were being conveyed and by midnight were engaged in an attack on the straggling village of Neuenhof. This was successful after a short Artillery bombardment and Lieut.-Colonel Howard then pushed a patrol forward to the anti-tank ditch covering Kevelaer. They reported no opposition and at 6 A.M. on 3rd March another patrol found the town unoccupied, or at least undefended. The Battalion moved into Kevelaer at 8 A.M. and occupied it. Only 20 prisoners were captured, but the battalion suffered a few casualties from "booby" traps.

On the left the 3rd Division had captured Winnekendonk, two and a half miles East of Kevelaer.

Soon after 8 A.M. the acting Divisional Commander gave orders for the 8th Armoured Brigade force to consolidate Kevelaer and for the 158th Brigade Group to pass through them and occupy Geldern. The 71st and 160th Brigades were to stand fast. The 158th Brigade was to be directly supported by the 4/7th Dragoon Guards, 244th Field Company and one Troop of the A.R.E. Squadron (Assault Squadron Royal Engineers) and was to move on a minimum scale of transport.

The advance began at 1.45 P.M. led by a Squadron of the 4/7th D.Gs. working with a Troop of A Squadron 53rd Reconnaissance Regiment. After meeting slight opposition the leading Squadron reported at 2.50 P.M. that they were in contact with American troops West of Geldern. The 1st East Lancashires, having cleared Veert, reached the outskirts of Geldern where they made contact with the 134th Battalion of the 35th United States Division. The Americans explained that the enemy was holding Geldern and that they were about to clear the place. On receiving this news the 158th Brigade halted and harboured North of Geldern.

Meanwhile on the right A Squadron 53rd Reconnaissance Regiment had cleared Wemb, Twisterden and Lullinger after skirmishes with small parties of the retreating enemy. B Squadron, who had been protecting the left flank had made contact with the 3rd Division across the Niers and reported that all bridges across the river between Kevelaer and Geldern had been destroyed, except one at Wetten.

At 2 P.M. on 3rd March Headquarters 53rd (Welsh) Division, which had been at Goch since the 23rd February, opened at Kevelaer.

At 2.15 P.M. a message was received by Divisional Headquarters ordering the Division to wheel to the North-East and continue the advance on the axis Geldern-Issum-Alpon, whilst the Guards

Armoured Division exploited to the left or northern flank, on the axis Winnekendonk-Kapellen-Bonninghardt.

During the night of 3rd/4th March the 71st Brigade moved down from Weeze to Kevelaer ready to push East through Geldern as soon as this was possible. The 158th Brigade were ordered to secure the town – as the American troops were not fully in possession – and report on the condition of the four bridges over which runs the road to the Rhine at Wesel.

The East Lancashires had already sent a reconnaissance patrol into Geldern and at 4.45 A.M. on the 4th the Battalion moved into the town without opposition. Civilians reported that the Germans had left during the night. Two of the four bridges were intact and by 11 A.M. the Royal Engineers had replaced the other two.

As the enemy seemed to be on the run the projected relief of the 53rd Division by the 49th again postponed.

On this day Mr. Winston Churchill, the Prime Minister, accompanied by the Chief of the Imperial General Staff and others, passed through part of the Divisional area in the course of a visit to the front.

As soon as the bridges in Geldern were ready a force consisting of one Squadron Surrey Yeomanry, the 1st Oxford and Bucks "Kangaroos" and one Squadron of the 53rd Reconnaissance Regiment advanced on Issum which they reached soon after noon. They found the main river bridge at Issum blown, but a secondary one still standing. A patrol of the Oxford and Bucks reported that the bridge over a second stream was also blown and that the far bar was held.

As a result of a meeting between the Divisional Commanding (Brigadier M. Elrington) and the Commander of the 71st Brigade (Lieut.-Colonel J. M. Hanmer), held at Kevelaer at about 2 P.M., the rest of the 71st Brigade was ordered forward to Issum. This move was carried out very quickly on a good and clear road. On arrival they found the troops in Issum held up by the blown bridges. At 4 P.M. the 1st Oxford and Bucks reverted to the 71st Brigade, the Squadron of the 53rd Reconnaissance Regiment also came under its command and the 4th/7th Dragoon Guards moved up in support. Plans were made to attack that night and form a Bridgehead to allow the passage of vehicles over both obstacles – preparatory to an advance on Alpon, some four and a half miles to the North-East.

At 9 P.M. the Oxford and Bucks moved up to the river to provide a firm base for the rest of the Brigade. No opposition was encountered. After a series of Artillery concentrations the attack began at 11 P.M., with the 4th R.W.F. to the North of the main road and the 1st H.L.I. to the South. The stream was crossed without opposition, but soon after progressively stiffer resistance was met by both Battalions. The Commander of A Company of the H.L.I. (Major R. S. Nisbet) was killed and the Company heavily counter-attacked by German Infantry and Tanks; but managed to maintain their positions. The forward move of the supporting tanks was delayed owing to difficulties in getting bridging equipment forward. It was not until 7 A.M. on the 5th that a "scissors" bridge was laid.

North of the road the 4th R.W.F. had similar experiences. At 6.50 A.M. (5th March) the Battalion was counter-attacked, but this position was restored soon after by the timely arrival of some supporting tanks.

At about 8 A.M. further concentrations of the enemy, thought to be preparing another counter attack, were broken up by artillery fire.

Opposition, which had come from the 21st Parachute Regiment, had been unexpectedly stubborn. During daylight the Brigade maintained its positions and during the early hours of the night of the 5th/6th a Company of the Oxford and Bucks and a Squadron of the 53rd Reconnaissance Regiment were sent forward to relieve the 4th R.W.F. who were withdrawn to Issum.

While the 71st Brigade was battling for a bridgehead at Issum during the night of the 4/5th March plans were being made for the rest of the Division. Although the enemy was fighting fiercely on the axis Issum-Alpon there were signs that farther to the north his resistance was crumbling.

The Divisional plan was for the 71st Brigade to push on towards Alpon if possible; the 158th Brigade to concentrate at Issum ready to follow through and complete the capture of Alpon if necessary, and exploit South-East of Millingen and the 160th Brigade to concentrate at Geldern ready for employment as required. However, the unexpected resistance encountered by the 71st Brigade caused this plan to be altered and the 158th Brigade was given the task of attacking on the right of the road against the Western corner of the Die Leucht Forest.

The attack began at 4.30 P.M. when the 1/5th Welch advanced through the H.L.I. and attacked the spur of high ground on the edge of the forest south of the road. This was successful, the Battalion taking more than 100 prisoners, and by 6 P.M. the 7th R.W.F. had started to pass through to continue the advance. Unfortunately at an early stage in the battle their Commanding Officer, Lieut.-Colonel G. F. T. B. Dickson, was seriously wounded, but the Battalion made good progress and by 9 P.M. had secured its objective astride the main road. The prisoners taken brought the Brigade total up to more than 200.

The next stage in the plan was for the East Lancashires, moving South of the road, to pass through the 7th R.W.F. and capture the cross roads about two miles South-West of Alpon. Owing, however, to the quick successes of the other two Battalions it was decided to move the East Lancashires up the main road. The Battalion moved forward at 10 P.M., and the advance went smoothly until the leading Company arrived within about 100 yards of the final objective, when the enemy opened heavy fire from a house by the side of the road. After some very close fighting, supported by extremely accurate artillery fire on the cross roads, the objective was secured. The Battalion then exploited forward to a small hamlet about 400 yards up the road towards Alpon.

Meanwhile the 1/5th Welch had also moved forward up to the edge of the woods, which at this point was only a few hundred yards from the road. At the same time the 555th Field Company were clearing the axis road from Issum towards Alpon. This proved to be a very difficult task as it was heavily mined and cratered; but it was completed by 7 A.M. on the 6th March.

The next task fell to the 160th Brigade which had been resting since the attack on Weeze. It was to clear the Bonninghardt Plateau which overlooks Alpon and the stream which runs roughly North and South through the town. With the 13/18th Hussars and A Squadron of the Reconnaissance Regiment under command the Brigade had completed its concentration at Geldern by 8 P.M. on the 5th March. Stiff opposition was expected on the Bonninghardt Plateau, but it was hoped that assistance would be afforded by the Guards Armoured Division which was operating to the immediate North.

The plan was for the 2nd Monmouths to pass through the 158th Brigade and seize the high ground about three quarters of a mile South-West of Alpon to the South of the road. Advancing through the Monmouths the 4th Welch would then capture the area to the North East and nearer Alpon, whilst the 6th R.W.F. seized the small group of buildings just South of Alpon and the wood to its East.

The 2nd Monmouths debussed about 500 yards East of Issum at 6.30 A.M. on the 6th Supported by tanks of A Squadron 13/18th Hussars the Battalion, with its left on the main road, passed through the East Lancashires at about 8 A.M. Progress was slow as the enemy resisted fiercely and the left flank was fired on by S.P. guns on the edge of the wooded area North of the road. Nevertheless the Battalion pressed forward and by 1 P.M. the objective had been captured and was firmly held; 80 prisoners were taken and about 60 German dead counted. The Battalion suffered 69 casualties in the attack and subsequent shelling of the position. Three tanks of the 13/18th Hussars were knocked out.

At 1.45 P.M. the 4th Welch, supported by a Squadron of the 13th/18th passed through. Resistance was stiff, especially from mortars and S.P. guns, and wireless communications worked very badly – presumably owing to screening in the thick woods. By 4.30 P.M., however, all Companies were on their objectives except C Company on the left, which had lost touch with the rest of the Battalion and of whom there was no news. The enemy was shelling and mortaring the area heavily and casualties were mounting. Majors W. H. Clements and D. I. T. Jones had both been wounded.

At 7.30 P.M. a runner made contact with the left Company near the road. Having taken their objective they had been forced back by S.P. guns firing at very short range. The two Forward Observing Officers of the 133rd Field Regiment had been wounded, and the Company Commander, Company Sergt. Major and all Platoon Commanders and Sergeants – except Lieut. G. Phillips who was now in command – had become casualties. The total Company casualties were 45. Faced with this critical situation on his left flank the Commanding Officer ordered the Carrier Platoon to reinforce C Company in a dismounted role. In this encounter the Battalion captured 63 prisoners of war.

At 5.40 P.M. (before contact with C Company 4th Welch had been established) the 6th R.W.F. passed through the right Company of the Welch. By this time the leading troops of the 35th United States Division were moving up on the East of the Die Leucht and were only about 3,000 yards to the South-East.

On the right the Battalion met some resistance and there was some shelling, but on the whole opposition was light. Supported by three troops of the 13th/18th Hussars the Battalion reached its objective by 6.30 P.M. A small counter attack was beaten off. During the night some enemy parties on the right flank were dealt with satisfactorily by fighting patrols. The ever-pressing problems of supply in the forward areas were greatly eased when three "weasels" arrived during the early hours of the 7th March.

Patrols sent out on the morning of the 7th reported no enemy West of the Alpache Ley, but that any attempts to cross it drew heavy fire.

On the evening of the 6th March orders were received for the relief of the Division by the 52nd (Lowland) Division. The relief was to take two days and begin on the 7th March. At noon on that day the 155th Brigade relieved the 71st which moved back to Holt, where they were joined by the 1st Manchesters who had been relieved by the 7th Manchesters. The relief of the 160th Brigade by the 156th, which took place early on the night of the 7/8th, was a more difficult operation and units of both Brigades suffered casualties from artillery and mortar fire during the relief. The relief of the Division was completed when the 157th Brigade took over from the 158th early on the 8th – except for the 83rd Field Regiment who remained in support of the 52nd Division for their attack on Alpon on the 8th.

On relief the Division concentrated in an area between the Goch-Venlo road and the River Maas. On the 10th March Major-General R. K. Ross resumed command, and on the same day the Division came under the XII Corps, in the Second Army. Harbour parties left for the Brussels area.

On the 11th March, when at Twisterden (5 miles North-West of Geldern) the 1st H.L.I. were attacked by three German aircraft. Three vehicles were destroyed, but there were no casualties among the troops.

The move to the Brussels area look place on the 12th March and by noon on the 13th the Division (less most of its Artillery and Engineers) was located as follows:

Headquarters, 53rd (Welsh) Division – Assche

71st Infantry Brigade – West of Brussels

158th Infantry Brigade

160th Infantry Brigade – South-West of Brussels

53rd Reconnaissance Regiment – North of Brussels

Divisional Administrative Group

Thus, after more than a month's continuous fighting under the most severe conditions, the Welsh Division began a period of rest, refitting, reorganizing and preparation for the next operation – the crossing of the Rhine. It will have been apparent that the Rhineland Battle had been largely a contest against the elements – rain, flood, cold and mud. Nevertheless, there was some very hard fighting against a fanatical enemy defending the frontier of his homeland with the courage of despair. By modern standards the battle casualties in no one engagement had been very heavy – although in several they were by no means insignificant – but there was a continuous drain which amounted to a high total. The Rhineland Battle had resulted in many gaps in almost every unit, and among the casualties were a high proportion of experienced leaders.

Between the 8th of February and the 7th March the Division had suffered approximately 1,229 battle casualties and captured about 3,200 prisoners. More than 180,000 rounds of 25-pounder ammunition had been fired and nearly 350,000 gallons of petrol used.

During the ten days in the Brussels area a great deal of time was naturally spent in replacing and overhauling equipment and general rehabilitation. There were, however, good opportunities for relaxation in Brussels and elsewhere. Some units organized visits to the field of Waterloo; others held belated celebrations of St. David's Day. On the 18th March the 160th Brigade held a ceremonial Church Parade at the Palais de Justice, at which the Divisional Commander took the salute. The Pipe Band of the 1st Highland Light Infantry played retreat in the Grande Place in Brussels.

During this time Lieut.-Colonel K. G. Exham, commanding the 6th Royal Welch Fusiliers, was evacuated sick and was succeeded by Lieut.-Colonel C. F. Hutchinson. Major H. W. Tyler arrived to take over command of the 7th Royal Welch Fusiliers – in consequence of the death from wounds of Lieut.-Colonel G. F. T. B. Dickson.

A number of Decorations and Awards were announced including the Distinguished Service Order to Brigadier J. O. Wilsey (158th Brigade) and a bar to the same decoration to Lieut.-Colonel F. F. E. Allen, commanding the 1st East Lancashire Regiment.

Almost as soon as they arrived in the Brussels area Commanders and Staffs began planning for the next task which was to take the Division to Hamburg and see the end of the war in Europe.

My father begins his account of this phase of the war with a description of the firepower available to the Allied Forces in pressing on through to the Rhine Crossing.

"Perhaps I could explain here that very often when a small number of Infantry were about to engage the enemy, a very large quantity if Artillery could be called upon to give support. This was very often of real significance in reducing casualties. Each Infantry Division contained three Artillery Regts. of Field Gunners, i.e. 25-pounders This gave a total of 72 guns available. However, sometimes, when a single Battalion of Infantry was involved in an attack, it may be deemed necessary to give them the enhanced support of maybe four Divisions' Artillery. For example, the combined firing power of 288 guns. Even this lot may have the power of heavier Artillery added to them.

Around the 12th March, it was envisaged that this enhanced power would be needed. So on that date all the Divisional Infantry began a move to the Brussels area to have a period of rest, refitting and preparation for the next operation. We gunners stayed put and kept on firing.

I must take time now to recount this tale: Some time previously, when we were about to advance through what had once been a hunting country we received orders that on no account were we to attempt to shoot game. It seemed so incongruous that the authorities would see fit to take time to issue such an order in the middle of a War, but issue it they did. On this particular day the guns were situated just in front of a wood. To our left-rear were more trees and one stretch of 'firebreak'. The peace was broken by the sound of a rifle-shot. I rushed out to investigate. One of my gun-sergeants, Bryn Button was waving his rifle in the air and shouting that he had made a mistake and there was no danger. I approached him and he claimed that he had just finished cleaning his rifle and was clearing the chamber when it went off and he had accidentally and very unfortunately killed this poor little deer that happened to be crossing the small open stretch at that time. It wouldn't have done to leave the carcass to rot, so I agreed that Bryn could cut the carcass up and divide it into five shares. One for each of the guns and one share for the Command Post. Now I was the proud possessor of two little paraffin stoves, which were used for odd little feeding jobs. We had acquired a large 'Ali-Baba' jar, which was now almost filled with isinglass in which we preserved our egg stocks. Bryn now quietly approached me and said that he had been able to hold back a few nice venison steaks. The arrangements were quickly made. When he and I were both on night duty, I should start cooking and once things were virtually ready, I would simply pick up the Tannoy and say 'Sergeant Button, to the Command Post immediately please' and Bryn would double across with his plate stuffed inside his blouse!!!

The crossing was to begin on the night 23/24th Mar. We were now very near the Rhine, near Rees and Xanten. We were putting in preparatory fire on targets which had been selected. We saw airborne troops dropping on the far side of the Rhine. One plane had dropped its troops and was hit after turning around for home. The crew bailed out. One was blown across the Rhine and was landing right alongside my Command Post. This fellow landed with his eyes shut tight and shouting 'Kamerad'. He didn't realise that he had blown across to 'our' side, but was convinced that he was about to become a P.O.W.

His relief was unbounded and he insisted that we have some of his surplus items of clothing as gifts. He didn't look a day over 18. It was probably on the 26th that we crossed the Rhine on the Bailey Bridge at Xanten. The Infantry kept advancing and enlarging the bridgehead. After a tremendous battle, the town of Bocholt which had been strongly defended was eventually captured by the evening of the 29th. There were further river crossings ahead and the enemy was managing to blow the bridges as they retired, thus causing our Infantry further delays. By the 31st Mar the town of Vreden was occupied, about 30 miles from the Rhine. On the 2nd April, Gronau was taken.

Things didn't really get easier but things, in some way became looser. For a while, after reaching the Dortmund-Ems Canal in the first week of April, the Division hardly ever acted as a whole and individual Brigades, or even smaller units undertook separate tasks. Continually pressing forward we crossed the Aller and Weser rivers near Verden.

By the 4th April the Brigade had captured the Airfield just West of RHEINE and by the following morning of the following day the Division was established on a line from Gronau-Ochtrup-Salzbergen line, holding the Northern flank as far as the Dortmund-Ems Canal, having advanced about 75 miles since crossing the Rhine. There was considerable resistance by the enemy in the area around IBBENBUREN and the Div. Artillery was used extensively. Elsewhere resistance was patchy, casualties correspondingly lighter and advances quicker.

On the 7th April we were to join 7th Armoured at HOYA. When our troops attempted to cross the Aller at RETHEM, they met tremendous resistance, so the attempt was postponed and attempts would be made *elsewhere. However, within a few days the enemy had, to a large extent; withdrawn so the Aller was crossed at Rethem and Western on the 13th April.*

It was considered that BREMEN would be a tough nut to attack directly, so the 53rd was to push north and capture Verden, then to continue north so as to cut off Bremen from any communication with the East. Verden was captured on the 17th April."

By the middle of March 1945 the United States Ninth Army an Field Marshal Montgomery's 21st Army Group had closed up to the Rhine between Dusseldorf in the South and Emmerich in the North. Further South the United States III Corps (First U.S. Army) had on the 7th March, by taking advantage of a fleeting opportunity established a bridgehead over the Rhine at Remagen and secure intact the bridge there.

The time had now come to cross the great River and advance into the heart of Germany. This, combined with the advance of Russia forces from the east would, it was confidently predicted, bring the German war to an end in a matter of weeks. The main effort from the West – "Operation Plunder" – was to be carried out North of the Ruhr, between Rheinberg and Rees by the U.S. Ninth Army on the right, South of Wesel, and the British Second Army on the left, both under the command of Field Marshal Montgomery. To assist the advance of the Second Army the XVIII Allied Airborne Corps (British 6th and U.S. 17th Airborne Divisions) was to drop east of the Rhine to seize key points in the area North of Wesel. The operation was to be supported by the full weight of the Allied Air forces including, for the initial bombardment, strategic aircraft based in the United Kingdom. The First Canadian Army on the left flank was to guard the Rhine and the Maas West of Emmerich then cross the Rhine and advance into North Holland.

The first few days after the crossing were to be devoted to securing a bridgehead large enough to permit the construction of heavy bridges and allow the passage and concentration of the Armoured Formations, which, with Infantry support, were to break out and over-run the North

German Plain. It was anticipated that after about four days' hard fighting enemy resistance would have weakened sufficiently to allow the break-out. This forecast proved correct.

The actual assault on the Second Army front was to be carried out by the 5th Commando Brigade on the right, who were to capture Wesel; the 15th (Scottish) Division in the centre and the 51st (Highland) Division on the left. The crossing was to begin on the night of the 23/24th March.

On the 23rd March 1945 the 53rd (Welsh) Division began moving from the area around Brussels, where it had been for the past ten days, to the following locations:

Headquarters, 53rd (Welsh) Division

71st Infantry Brigade – In and around Kevalaer

158th Infantry Brigade

160th Infantry Brigade – Weeze

The Division, which was part of Lieut.-General N. M. Ritchie's XII Corps, was to be used to expand the bridgehead and assist in the break out. The provisional plan was that the Division should cross the Rhine and then break out from the bridgehead across the Issel (about 7 miles east of the Rhine) which it was hoped would have already been captured by airborne forces. They were then to advance east and capture the considerable town of Bocholt (4 miles east of the Issel) and then go on a further 10 miles and capture the smaller town of Borken – if the 7th Armoured Division, who were to operate on the same axis, had not already done so. In the event operations did not quite work out like this.

By the evening of the 25th March a substantial bridgehead over the Rhine had been secured and it was becoming clear that the time for the break-out was approaching. At about 5 P.M. orders were received for the 53rd Division to cross the Rhine at 12 noon on the following day, using the bridges opposite Vynen and Xanten. The 26th was a dull day and congestion on the roads slowed up the pace of movement. It was not until about 5 P.M. that the Division began crossing the Rhine – the 158th Brigade by the Class 12 bridge opposite Vynen and the rest of the Division by the Class 40 Bridge at Xanten.

Progress over the bridges, and in the bridgehead, was slow; but by the early hours of the 28th the Division was concentrated North of Wesel, except the 160th Brigade which was further North just West of Hamminkeln. (Between Wesel and Bocholt.)

The 160th Brigade has been in the lead and, on arrival in the concentration area, proceeded to cross the River Issel just West of Ringenberg (which was held by the 15th (Scottish) Division). The Brigade then advanced North along the main road to Bocholt, and by midnight 27/28th March the 6th R.W.F., after a sharp action, had captured Dingden, a village about 5 miles due South of Bocholt.

On the 28th the 158th Brigade pushed North on the West side of the Ringenberg-Bocholt road.

The stage was now set for the Division's next main task – the capture of Bocholt, and orders were issued for this on the evening of the 28th. Bocholt is a town of many narrow streets. It was known to be heavily defended and to be surrounded by a strong mine belt. Many of the approach roads had been blocked with felled trees.

The plan was for the 160th Brigade supported by the 4th Armoured Brigade (less the 44th R.T.R.) to make the main effort by assaulting up the main road from the South and to the right of it. The 158th were to move up through the wooded area to the left of the road to seize the Bocholt-Werth road running due west from Bocholt.

The attack of the 160th Brigade began at 10 P.M. with the 6th R.W.F. on the right and the 2nd Monmouths left. Almost immediately they approached the town the Tanks ran into a minefield and were held up. The Infantry went on unsupported and made good progress until they reached the River Aa which flows through the centre of the town. The far bank was heavily defended, but during the morning of the 29th the 6th R.W.F. managed to secure a crossing – initially in assault boats and later over a partly demolished bridge. At about 11 A.M. the 2nd Monmouths passed through the R.W.F's. bridgehead and, after some sharp fighting, had cleared most of the town by 6 P.M. The Armour then passed through.

Meanwhile on the left the 158th Brigade had advanced steadily. Harks, a village just West of Bocholt, was reached on the early morning of the 29th. The advance was continued to the River Aa where it runs West of Bocholt, and by 9 A.M. the far bank was reported undefended.

It is now necessary to describe another action which had been taking place further east. While the operations at Bocholt, and to the West, had been in progress the 4th R.W.F. (detached from the 71st Brigade) and the 53rd Reconnaissance Regiment had been operating on the right flank in the direction of Krechting and Rhede, in conjunction with units of the 4th Armoured Brigade. The 4th R.W.F. – in "Kangaroos" – had crossed the Rhine on the 27th March at about 8 A.M. By 1 P.M. the Battalion and the 3/4th City of London Yeomanry (C.L.Y.) had passed through the Greys and 2nd King's Royal Rifle Corps, East of the bridge at Ringenberg. Brushing aside minor opposition they advanced north and by dusk had reached a wood East of Dingden. On the night of the 27/28th they attacked and captured another wood some 3 miles further North, both Tanks and Infantry suffering slight casualties. By nightfall on the 28th they had reached the East-West road some 2 miles South-East of Bocholt. Meanwhile the Greys and the 2nd K.R.R.C. passed behind the 4th R.W.F. to clear the woods further to the East.

From dawn on the 28th the 53rd Reconnaissance Regiment was also operating on this flank, with the object of seizing the crossings of the river Aa East of Bocholt, and if possible capturing Rhede. The enemy, however, succeeded in destroying all the bridges, except one just south of Krechting which was seized by a detachment from the Regiment. Unfortunately the bridge over a second stream, slightly north of the first, had been demolished and further progress was delayed.

With the capture of Bocholt the prospects of a complete break out, and a rapid advance east, seemed good. Divisional Headquarters had moved to an area just south of Dingden on the afternoon of the 28th and on the evening of the 29th orders were issued for the regrouping of the Division and plans made for a further advance.

The 4th R.W.F. reverted to command of the 71st Brigade – together with the 3/4th C.L.Y. and half a Squadron of "Crocodiles" – and the 1/5th Welch (158th Brigade) was placed under command of the 160th Brigade.

During the night of the 29/30th March, whilst the 53rd (Welsh) Division was preparing to break out from Bocholt, the formations on the flanks were making satisfactory progress. On the right the 7th Armoured Division had cleared Borken (10 miles East of Bocholt) and were operating on a wide front to the East of the town. On the left the 3rd Division had reached the line of the Aa. Farther to the left the XXX Corps were still meeting strong opposition, but were advancing slowly.

The task given to the 53rd Division was to break out from Bocholt and seize the crossings of the River Dinkel at Gronau, 30 miles to the North East.

The plan was as follows:

71st Infantry Brigade – with the 3/4th C.L.Y. and C Squadron 53rd Reconnaissance Regiment attached – to lead the advance along the axis Winterswijk-Vreden-Gronau.

A Squadron (to the West) and B Squadron (to the East) 53rd Reconnaissance Regiment were to protect the flanks.

Further east the 4th Armoured Brigade, with the 2nd Monmouths from the 160th Brigade under command, was to advance on Gronau via Rhede and Oding, forming a link between the 53rd Division and the 7th Armoured Division.

The first task of the 71st Brigade was to clear the Northern outskirts of Bocholt which were still held by small parties of the enemy. The 1st H.L.I. supported by two troops of "crocodiles", attacked shortly after midnight on Good Friday, the 30th March. Resistance was soon overcome and at first light the 1st Oxford and Bucks, in "Kangaroos", followed the H.L.I. out of the town and then continued to move east of the road. One Squadron of the 3/4th C.L.Y. was supporting the H.L.I. and the rest of the Regiment the Oxford and Bucks.

By 9 A.M. both Battalions had reached a line about 2 miles North-East of Bocholt and were making steady progress. By 10 A.M. the rest of the Brigade Column began to move forward.

The advance proceeded, with the H.L.I. moving up the main road and the Oxford and Bucks to the East of the road and railway. Occasional delays occurred owing to resistance by small parties of parachutists, some with Artillery, and to mines and demolitions. A few prisoners were taken. By 9 P.M. the H.L.I. were within about three and a half miles of Winterswijk having met some stiff opposition South of the town. Resistance was from S.P. guns and Infantry, the former knocking out three vehicles of B Squadron 53rd Reconnaissance Regiment.

By nightfall the Oxford and Bucks, after several sharp brushes with the enemy – during which several "Kangaroos" were knocked out by S.P. guns – had reached a point near the railway about level with the H.L.I. The country was close and the latter part of the advance had been carried out "dismounted".

On the left flank A Squadron of the Reconnaissance Regiment had two or three encounters with parties of the enemy, but finished the day on the line of the Slinger Beek, approximately level with the rest of the Division.

Further to the right the 2nd Monmouths, with the 4th Armoured Brigade, had also progressed well, and by the evening reached a point just South East of Oding.

At 12 noon Divisional Headquarters moved up to Bocholt.

At about 11.30 P.M. on the 30th March the 4th R.W.F. were sent forward through the H.L.I. with the object of capturing Winterswijk. All went well until they reached the Slinger Beek a short distance south of the town. Here they found the bridge blown, but C Company and the men of the Carrier Platoon negotiated the stream and occupied Winterswijk which they found unoccupied. Preparations were then put in hand to construct a new bridge.

During the 30th March the Division captured about 180 prisoners.

At about 2 A.M. 31st March the Oxford and Bucks began moving forward again on the right of the 4th R.W.F., but on approaching the Slinger Beek East of the town they found the bridge there was also blown and the area heavily mined. The Battalion was then ordered to join the rest of the Brigade on the main axis.

The new bridge on the main road was ready for traffic by 12 noon and the 1st H.L.I., with C Squadron 53rd Reconnaissance Regiment under command, passed over and pressed on towards Vreden. The town was occupied without a fight, but the important bridge over the River Berkel, on the south-west fringe, had been destroyed. Whatever shortages the Germans may have been experiencing at this time explosives for blowing bridges was not one of them.

It will be appropriate here to relate a very smart piece of work by C Squadron of the Reconnaissance Regiment. A Squadron (on the left flank) were at this period engaged in a series of skirmishes with small parties of Germans and were not yet abreast of the main column. On reaching the river South-West of Vreden C Squadron Commander immediately appreciated the importance of seizing two other bridges about 1½ miles to the North-West – one over the main river and another over a subsidiary stream. Realizing that A Squadron had been delayed he immediately set off for the left flank. Two troops rushed the first bridge, killing the defenders and removing the detonators just in time. They then pushed on and occupied a bridgehead covering the second bridge without opposition.

By this time A Squadron had overcome the opposition opposed to it and came up to reinforce the bridgehead. This timely action saved the Division the necessity of building a new bridge, or making a detour of some 9 miles.

The H.L.I. pushed on towards Gronau, but at about 6.30 P.M. on the 31st ran into stiff opposition from Infantry and 88 mm. guns at a road junction about 3 miles north of Vreden. The Battalion closed up to the enemy position and dug in. Meanwhile the rest of the 71st Brigade moved forward to Vreden and Divisional Headquarters opened at Winterswijk.

We must now look back a day to the right flank where the 2nd Monmouths were working with the 4th Armoured Brigade.

Early on the 30th March the 6th R.W.F. (160th Brigade) had cleared the Eastern exits of Bocholt and the 4th Armoured Brigade – with the 2nd Monmouths in Troop Carrying Vehicles – moved out, with the Greys leading. Rhede was occupied without opposition but a blown bridge about 2 miles outside the town delayed the Column on the Oding road. The track vehicles found a way round, but the wheeled ones had to wait for No. 82 Assault Squadron A.R.E. to fill the gap. This was completed by 2 P.M. when the Monmouths passed over. Moving towards Oding the Greys made contact with the 8th Hussars and 1st Rifle Brigade (of the 7th Armoured Division) near Gr Burlo – these units having moved north from Borken. As the 8th Hussars were about to attack Oding the 4th Armoured Brigade halted.

On the 31st March, after Oding had been cleared, the brigade advanced through the town and headed north. This movement had only just started, however, when orders came in for them to concentrate around, but not in, Oding. During the 30th and 31st March the only opposition encountered had been "bazooka" teams and other small isolated parties.

On the right the 7th Armoured Division continued the advance on the axis Borken-Ahaus-Nienborg-Rheine. By the afternoon of the 31st they had reached the line Ahaus-Wess'um-Ottenstein, with patrols on the River Dinkel about Nienborg.

We left the 71st Brigade on the evening of the 31st with the 1st H.L.I., in the van, held up about 3 miles North of Vreden. On Easter Day, the 1st April, the 4th R.W.F. went through the H.L.I. with orders to secure Alstatte and then stand fast and allow the 158th Brigade to pass through to Gronau and on to the Dortmund-Ems Canal.

The enemy in front of the H.L.I. had withdrawn and the 4th R.W.F. had no difficulty in occupying Alstatte. Finding the bridge intact they exploited a further 4 miles. Hot on their heels came the 158th Brigade who passed through at mid-day, taking under command the 3/4th City of London Yeomanry and other supporting arms which had been with the 71st Brigade. The 1/5th Welch led the main column up the Gronau road; the 1st East Lancashires headed for Glanerbru (about 2 miles West of Gronau) and B Squadron 53rd Reconnaissance Regiment moved up to take over protection of the left flank.

A few miles North of Alstatte the 1/5th Welch left the main road and took a secondary one leading to Gronau. About 2 and a half miles South West of Gronau the leading tank of the 3/4th C.L.Y. was knocked out by an S.P. gun and from that time opposition stiffened. The Battalion deployed and, with tank and "Crocodile" support, advanced on a cross-roads just South-West of the town. The attack was held up after the leading companies had suffered casualties. The Battalion spent a disturbed night under intermittent shell and mortar fire; but sent out patrols to investigate the defences covering Gronau and the river.

The East Lancashires, who had passed through Alstatte at 5 P.M., advanced against lighter opposition and, although confronted with two S.P. guns, reached the outskirts of Glanerbru at about 7.30 P.M. and were in possession of the place by 9.30 P.M.

Further West B Squadron, 53ʳᵈ Reconnaissance Regiment, patrolled to the Southern and Eastern outskirts of Enschede. Only a few snipers were met and contact was made with the Guards Armoured Division who entered the town during the night of the 1/2ⁿᵈ April.

By the early evening the rest of the 158ᵗʰ Brigade were disposed north of Alstatte.

At midnight on the night of the 1/2ⁿᵈ April Brigadier Wilsey issued orders for the attack on Gronau. The attack began in the early morning and by 6 A.M. the East Lancashires had reached the River Dinkel in the centre of the town without opposition and the 1/5ᵗʰ Welch, about 2 miles South, had established a good bridgehead over the river at Epe. The bridge there had been secured intact and the small garrison mopped up.

In Gronau the East Lancashires met with stiffer opposition, but by 9.15 A.M. had captured the only bridge left standing and had cleared the town. In this action the Brigade accounted for three 88 mm. and one S.P. gun and captured about 50 prisoners plus a hospital containing more than 700 German wounded.

At 8.30 A.M. the 7ᵗʰ R.W.F. (in Troop Carrying Transport) with A Squadron 3/4ᵗʰ C.L.Y. under command, were directed to cross the Epe Bridge and advance along the main East-West road leading to Ochtrup-Rethenberg-Wettringen and Rheine. After minor delays due to enemy action just East of Epe, and to the North-East where the bridge over the Goor stream had been blown, the leading troops were again held up at a strong road block about 2 miles West of Ochtrup. This was a more serious business and at about 6.15 P.M., after the Divisional Commander had visited the Battalion, Lieut.-Colonel Tyler gave out his orders. The essence of these was a right hook by two Companies, supported by a Squadron of tanks and artillery, combined with a still wider right hook by some more tanks. The attack met with shell and mortar fire, but was quickly successful, although the follow up was considerably delayed by mines. Ochtrup was, however, occupied by 2 A.M. on the 3rd and final mopping up completed in daylight.

This successful action had a sad climax when Lieut.-Colonel J. S. Morrison-Jones, the Commanding Officer of the 1/5th Welch, was killed when his jeep was blown up on a mine while he was on reconnaissance near the Ochtrup road block early on the 3rd, Major C. H. Bowker took over command.

Meanwhile the 4th Armoured Brigade (less the 3/4th C.L.Y.) with the 1st H.L.I. under command advanced through Ottenstein and Wessum against negligible opposition. By about 11 P.M. on the 2nd April they had reached Wall (just South of Ochtrup) where they were held up. The H.L.I. were not committed during the advance, but were employed clearing the area South of the railway running West from Wall. On the evening of the 3rd the Battalion concentrated in Ochtrup where it came temporarily under the 158th Brigade.

Divisional Headquarters had moved to Vreden on the morning of the 1st April. The 160th Brigade spent Easter Sunday around Winterswijk – just inside the Dutch border – and were able to hold Church Services before moving on to Vreden. On the night of the 2/3rd April the Brigade made a very sudden move of some 20 miles to the area Wettringen-Welbergen. This was an unpleasant move in the rain and without lights as there were reports of enemy air activity. Just to the South of this area XII Corps Headquarters – moving in the wake of the 7th Armoured Division – had set up their Headquarters. On the evening of the 2nd they received some enemy shells and at the same time an enemy wireless "intercept" indicated that a German counter-attack was likely to be staged in the area. It was inevitable that the troops should connect their sudden move with the unfortunate position in which Corps Head-quarters found themselves!

On the 3rd April the 53rd (Welsh) Division was placed in XII Corps reserve with the task of facing north to protect the left flank of the Corps axis which was now swinging from North-East to the East. The Division was to clear the area up to the boundary with XXX Corps and then take up the following defensive positions:

160th Brigade – right, between the Ems and the Vichte River, with the special task of clearing the enemy from the airfield West of Rheine.

158th Brigade (with 1st H.L.I. under command) – centre, from the Vichte to Ochtrup.

71st Brigade (less 1st H.L.I.) – left, around Gronau

4th Armoured Brigade – to clear the area around Wall and Langenhorst and assist the 160th Brigade into the right sector.

The clearing operation was carried out on the 4th April. No organized resistance was met, except on the Eastern sector assigned to the 160th Brigade. On this day Field Marshal Montgomery visited Divisional Headquarters at Ochtrup.

The 160th Brigade had concentrated in the area Welbergen-Wettringen (a few miles East of Ochtrup) on the morning of the 3rd April. Movement in and out of this area was considerably hindered by the presence of scattered mines. The Brigade's main task was to capture the airfield which lay just West of Rheine.

A Squadron 53rd Reconnaissance Regiment, which was under Brigadier Coleman's command, was ordered to protect the Northern flank and did some fine work. In addition to bringing in a fund of information concerning minefields they discovered a large bomb dump, collected a number of German stragglers, found a hospital containing some 30 Italian wounded and liberated a Sergeant-Pilot of the Royal Air Force.

The advance on the airfield was led by the 6th Royal Welch Fusiliers, who had under command a Squadron of the 5th D.Gs. and a detachment of Medium Machine guns. The Battalion met with some opposition from road blocks and a considerable amount of mine-lifting had to be done; but by the early afternoon of the 4th April the last opposition had been overcome and the airfield occupied. By the 6th April Airfield

Construction Engineers had begun work and the Battalion received a visit from Field Marshal Montgomery.

At about 9.30 A.M. on the 4th April the 160th Brigade was ordered to capture Salzbergen, a scattered village about 5 miles North-West of Rheine, and the bridge over the Ems on its Eastern outskirts. The 2nd Monmouths – with a Squadron of the Greys and A Squadron of the Reconnaissance Regiment attached – were given this task. The Battalion left Neuenkirchen at 12 noon and approached the Southern outskirts of Salzbergen at about 4 P.M. A road block, which had been previously probed by A Squadron 53rd Reconnaissance Regiment (who had been operating with the 6th R.W.F. around the airfield) was captured by 5 P.M. Some 40 minutes later the Germans blew the Ems river bridge. Another road block was encountered which proved to be a more difficult proposition than the first. This and other opposition, including mines, resulted in fighting throughout the night; but by about 4.45 A.M. the bridge had been reached and by 6.30 A.M. the village had been cleared.

The total captures in this operation were 40 prisoners, and seven 20-mm guns. Losses were 1 killed and 14 wounded. The 2nd Monmouths remained in defensive positions around Salzbergen until the 8th April.

By the morning of the 5th April the 53rd Division had completed its task of clearing the Northern flank and was established on the general line Salzbergen Ochtrup-Gronau. At noon on the 4th the 1st H.L.I. had reverted to command of the 71st Brigade, and at midnight 4/5th April the 4th Armoured Brigade left the Division to join the 52nd (Lowland) Division. The 3/4th City of London Yeomanry, however, remained with the 53rd.

The defensive role was about to end and the 53rd (Welsh) Division to begin a new phase in the final stage of the war against Germany.

- CHAPTER XII -
THE FINAL PUSH

*O*n reaching the Dortmund-Ems Canal during the first week in April the whole of the British Second Army changed its North-Easterly course and began a marked swing to the East.

The 11th Armoured Division of the VIII Corps advancing from the South had cleared Osnabruck and secured a bridgehead over the Zweigken-Osnabruck Canal at Halen, and also won a bridgehead over the Dortmund-Ems Canal South of Ibbenburen. On the 3rd April the 7th Armoured Division had begun taking over these bridgeheads for the use of the XII Corps, as the VIII Corps was to swing east from Osnabruck. On the same day the 52nd (Lowland) Division took over the Rheine sector from the 7th Armoured Division and on the next day had won a bridgehead over the Dortmund-Ems Canal at Altenrheine. On release from the Rheine Sector the 7th Armoured Division took over the Ibbenburen bridgehead, but had met increasing resistance in their attempts to enlarge it.

The next stage was to be the release of the 7th Armoured Division from its commitments in the Ibbenburen area to permit an armoured drive east from Halen to the River Weser. This was due to start on the 5th April. The Rheine and Ibbenburen bridgeheads, and subsequent attacks from them to the North, were part of the plan to protect the left flank of this armoured drive, and it was precisely in this sector that the enemy was to offer the stiffest resistance with the best of his remaining troops. The troops in the area, from North to South, were: the 8th Para Division, the 7th Para Division, 15th *Panzergrenadier* Division, *Großdeutschland* Brigade (opposite Rheine) and an improvised formation consisting of two Officer Cadet Training Units and a Non-Commissioned Officers School (in the Ibbenburen area). Whereas in some places the advance into Germany was reminiscent of the drive across France and Belgium the previous year, in this sector the enemy fought with great determination. Moreover, the weather for the past few days had not been good and in consequence air support had been restricted.

The new role of the Division was to relieve the 131st Brigade of the 7th Armoured Division, and later the 155th Brigade of the 52nd (Lowland) Division, in the Ibbenburen bridgehead, leaving one Brigade – the 160th – to operate under the 52nd Division in the Rheine Sector. The Division was then to advance north and clear the enemy from the South of the Ems-Weser Canal in order to protect the XII Corps axis, and subsequently to follow in the wake of the 7th Armoured Division.

The 7th Armoured Division – with the 155th Brigade (52nd Division) coming under command as soon as possible – was to advance to the River Weser leaving its own units to protect the left flank of the Halen bridgehead.

Plans for the 53rd Division were changed very frequently on the 4th as the situation was extremely fluid, and it was not until 2.30 A.M. on the 5th that the Divisional Operation Order was issued. The 71st Brigade was to proceed to the Divisional concentration area – the area Emsdetten-Mesum-Burgsteinfurt – South of the Ibbenburen bridgehead, and then move into the bridgehead to relieve the garrison as early on the 5th April as possible. The rest of the Division (except the 160th Brigade which was under the 52nd Division) would follow into the concentration area.

The 7th Armoured Division had secured the high ground between the Canal and the town of Ibbenburen; but the enemy, although short of supporting weapons, was fighting well.

At 3 P.M. the 71st Brigade moved up to the Canal. The attack was to begin at 9 P.M., directed from South to North astride the main road, with the 1st H.L.I. on the right and the 4th R.W.F. on the left. The objective was the railway which runs through the Northern outskirts of the town. The 1st Oxford and Bucks were to be ready to pass through and secure the high ground north of the town over which the Rheine-Osnabruck road runs. The attack was to be supported by the Divisional Artillery, two Medium Regiments and a half Squadron of "Crocodiles" of the 7th Royal Tank Regiment.

The attack began according to plan and met with little resistance until it reached the Ahe Stream just South of the town. Here both road bridges were found to have been destroyed, but the stream was not a formidable obstacle and soon after midnight the Sappers, assisted by Infantry, had made crossing places. The "Crocodiles" managed to cross by the bridge in the H.L.I. sector. When these came into action resistance weakened, and by about 3.15 A.M. both Battalions had reached their objectives. With daylight much mopping up had to be done and it took all day to clear the town of the last snipers.

At 4.15 P.M. the Oxford and Bucks, who had moved forward behind the attacking Battalion, passed into the town. Houses were burning fiercely and there was a great deal of indiscriminate fire from the enemy on the flanks. However, the Battalion moved forward with only light casualties. An experienced officer remarked that he had never known so much noise and firing with so little damage. By daylight the Battalion had crossed the Rheine-Osnabruck road immediately North of the town and soon afterwards occupied the spur 300 yards further North.

This completed the immediate task. Casualties had been light and prisoners numerous. The H.L.I. captured over 200 for the loss of 17 men; the 4th R.W.F. about 100 for a casualty list of 11 and the Oxford and Bucks 70 with only 5 casualties.

On the completion of this operation Divisional Headquarters moved forward to Elte, a few miles South-East of Rheine, and arrangements were made for the 158th Brigade to continue the advance. The plan was as follows:

The 158th Brigade to pass through the 71st and clear the country north of the railway and bounded on the west and north by the Ems-Weser Canal and on the East by a line running due North from Ibbenburen, and if possible seize one bridge across the Canal leading to the North.

One Squadron 53rd Reconnaissance Regiment to clear the area west of the Ibbenburen and South of the railway and if possible seize the bridge at Gravenhorst.

The remainder of the 53rd Reconnaissance Regiment to clear the area East of Ibbenburen.

71st Brigade to be prepared to send one Battalion to assist the Reconnaissance Regiment if required.

The 155th Brigade (52nd Division) was to concentrate and rejoin the 7th Armoured Division as soon as possible. The 7th Armoured Division reported that opposition East of Ibbenburen was either negligible or very disorganized.

The forward move of the 158th Brigade was considerably delayed by traffic congestion and it was not until about 10.45 A.M. that the East Lancashires, who were leading, passed through the Oxford and Bucks position North of Ibbenburen and moved west. Considerable opposition was encountered, but with the support artillery and with the aid of some "Crocodiles" (which had been taken over from the 71st Brigade) the advance continued. Some enemy artillery fire was encountered and the leading Company of the East Lancashires beat off a small counter attack which came in from the North-East. On reaching the Munster State Forest, the Battalion moved North in the direction of the Canal bridge at Kampmen and to the West of it.

Meanwhile the 1/5th Welch, who had been moving behind the East Lancashires, directed their advance North West and by 8 P.M. reached the Canal. Opposition had been light except in the final approach to the Canal where it was severe, but both bridges were found to have been blown.

Further South the 7th R.W.F. reached the Canal without opposition at 7.30 P.M., but here again the bridges had been destroyed.

South of the Railway C Squadron of the Reconnaissance Regiment met only light opposition, but found the bridge at Gravenhorst destroyed.

To the East the 53rd Reconnaissance Regiment (less C Squadron) cleared the "Star" Route (the main road coming up through Ibbenburen and then going East through Osnabruck) and the country to the North of it. This was to be XII Corps main axis and line of supply. On the 7th the Reconnaissance Regiment captured a whole Company of Officer Cadets in the wooded area a few miles North-West of Osnabruck.

By mid-day on the 7th April the whole area had been cleared and C

Squadron 53rd Reconnaissance Regiment took over the entire front of the 158th Brigade along the Ems-Weser Canal. The Brigade concentrated in the area just North-West of Ibbenburen.

Divisional Headquarters moved to Westerkapeln (6 miles North-West of Osnabruck).

At 10 P.M. the H.L.I. (71st Brigade) were ordered to move to the area South of Bramsche, some 10 miles North of Osnabruck – to prevent the enemy crossing the Canal there. The rest of the 71st Brigade followed the next day with the task of guarding the Canal crossings in the area and clearing the country to the East and South-East of any stragglers left behind by the 7th Armoured Division. These tasks were accomplished without difficulty.

On the 5th April the 52nd Division had extended its bridgehead across the Dortmund-Ems Canal and had captured Dreirwalde. The immediate object of the Division was to advance some 5 miles North-West, capture Hopsten and a bridge over the Hopsten Aa, whilst at the same time securing the left flank.

The 160th Brigade Group was located west of the River Ems, although patrols of the 2nd Monmouths had operated across the river. Its task was to protect that part of the left flank that lay west of the Ems until the progress of the Guards Armoured Division made this no longer necessary.

On the morning of the 6th April the 4th Welch relieved the 5th Kings Own Scottish Borderers in the bridgehead to free them for operations with the 4th Armoured Brigade North of Dreirwalde. The advance of the 52nd Division on Hopsten made good progress, but the 4th Armoured Brigade met stiff opposition. Consequently on the morning of the 7th the 6th R.W.F. (with one Squadron 3/4th C.L.Y. attached) was ordered to cross the Canal, move north to the area of the 4th Armoured Brigade, and relieve the 5th K.O.S.Bs.

At noon on the 7th April the 2nd Monmouths crossed the Canal in relief of the 5th H.L.I. (157th Brigade) and with the task of clearing the area East of Dreirwalde. This operation was uneventful, as there were only a few stragglers in the area.

Headquarters 160th Brigade then crossed the Ems and set up in the South-Eastern corner of Rheine. During the evening of the 7th April orders were received for the Brigade to move East on the following day and rejoin the 53rd Division. This order was amended at 1.30 P.M. on the 8th and the Brigade ordered to join the 7th Armoured Division at Hoya, on the Weser some 23 miles South of Bremen.

Whilst the 52nd (Lowland) Division had been operating to secure the left flank of the XII Corps, the 7th Armoured Division on the 5th April broke out from the Dortmund-Weser Canal bridgehead in a vigorous North Easterly drive directed to the Weser South-East of Bremen. Little opposition was encountered at first and on the 7th April the towns of Hoya, Riede and Syke – to the South of Bremen – were cleared of enemy. At this stage resistance stiffened and it was then that the 160th Brigade was ordered forward from the Ems to come under command of the 7th Armoured Division. German resistance continued especially on the left towards the great City of Bremen – which was in XXX Corps area.

When Brigadier Coleman received orders to move forward the situation on the Weser was fluid and somewhat obscure. He therefore visited Major-General Ross at 53rd Division Headquarters at Westerkapeln at about 7.30 A.M. on the 8th in order to get the latest information. The Brigade was to close up to the Weser at Hoya with one Battalion on the loop of the river at the town and one on either flank of the loop. Reconnaissance of the river to the South was to be carried out by B Squadron of the 53rd Reconnaissance Regiment which was to join the Brigade as it passed through Westercapeln. Any undestroyed bridges were to be seized, and failing this reconnaissance and plans for an assault crossing of the river were to be made. The object of these operations was to pave the way for the further advance of the 7th Armoured Division to the Elbe. It was anticipated that the rest of the 53rd Division would follow the 160th Brigade very soon. To assist in its task the 160th Brigade was to be joined by the 282nd Field Company with 45 Assault boats.

By daylight on the 8th the Brigade Column had begun its 85 mile move, enlivened by the streams of liberated prisoners and Displaced

Persons of many nationalities – all moving west. These were exciting times, as it was becoming apparent to all that the war in the West was drawing to its close.

Brigade Headquarters was at Gehlbergen. B Squadron, 53rd Reconnaissance Regiment, operating to the South was much hampered by the many minor water obstacles in the area; but reported Drakenburg, on the East bank of the river, occupied by the enemy.

The assault boats and bridging equipment of the 282nd Field Company were assembled at Duddenhausen, less than 3 miles from Hoya.

Early investigations confirmed that, apart from a few stragglers, there were no enemy troops on the Western bank; but the Eastern bank appeared to be strongly held. The 4th Welch sent a patrol of 1 officer and 12 other ranks across during the night: their boats were shot up and 9 other ranks failed to return.

At 9.45 A.M. on the 9th April the 6th R.W.F. made an assault crossing at Hoya assisted by smoke provided by the 7th Armoured Division. This attack was successful and casualties were light. Bridging began soon after noon and by 11.30 P.M. that night a Class 40 Bailey bridge had been constructed.

During the day the rest of the 53rd Division moved forward and at 4 P.M. the 160th Brigade reverted to Major-General Ross's command. The next stage in operations was for the 158th Brigade to pass through the 160th at Hoya and seize a crossing over the River Aller about 7 miles to the East.

At 11.30 P.M. the leading Battalion – the 7th R.W.F. – began crossing the bridge on foot, and quickly occupied Hassel. By 4 A.M. the 4th Welch (from the 160th Brigade) were in possession of Eystrup to the South. The 1/5th Welch crossed the bridge at 3.30 A.M. followed at once by the 83rd Field Regiment and Brigade Headquarters.

The enemy opposing the advance was the 5th Marine Garrison Regiment, but in the early stages they offered only slight opposition, The advance of the 1/5th Welch continued until resistance was met about 2,000 yards West of the Aller at Rethem. An attack round the Northern flank to capture the town met with initial success, but was eventually held up in very open country. Meanwhile a "coup-de-main" force of a Section of Carriers and two "Wasps" (flame-throwing carriers), under Sergeant Moses, M.M., was sent down the road in an attempt to seize the bridge. It forced a way through part of the town, but failed to reach the river. After an exciting experience in the town, during which it destroyed two S.P. guns and their crews, the detachment returned having lost one "wasp" and its crew and had three other men wounded. Unfortunately no tank support was available at this time.

Meanwhile the East Lancashires had occupied Hohenholz and Hamelhausen in rear of the 1/5th Welch, but a party of enemy cut the road behind them killing the D.A.A. and Q.M.G. of the Brigade, Major A. K. Lemon. Eventually the situation was restored and communications opened.

At 3.45 P.M. Brigadier Wilsey ordered the 1/5th Welch, supported by two Field and one Medium Regiment, to attack Rethem. At 4.15 P.M. the Battalion repelled an enemy counter attack. The Battalion's attack met with heavy fire almost immediately after crossing the start line and the Commanding Officer then ordered defensive dispositions to be taken up.

During the night of the 9/10th April the 7th R.W.F. cleared Hulsen in order to protect the left flank of the Brigade. The 1/5th Welch also made another attack on Rethem which, although it made good progress at first, was unsuccessful. The forward Companies suffered heavily in the subsequent withdrawal from a very exposed position. Some 60 men were killed or missing and about 20 wounded.

It was apparent that the crossing of the Aller would be a tougher proposition than the Weser and the attempt to cross at Rethem was abandoned for the time being. It was to be another 48 hours before a bridgehead was established on the East bank of the river.

On the 10th April the 4th Welch (160th Brigade) were ordered to occupy Stedorf and Westen and by 9 P.M. both places had been cleared. Opposition was slight on the following morning when patrols were sent into the villages North of Westen, but later in the day they were cleared by a small force of Infantry and Tanks sent from Westen.

On the evening of the 11th the 4th Welch were ordered to establish a small bridgehead across the river at Westen that night, with a view to a possible crossing in strength on the following day. One platoon was sent and met with no opposition; but reported that the current was very strong and boating a somewhat perilous operation.

Meanwhile the 2nd Monmouths (160th Brigade), who had been at Nienburg on the Weser, where they had been relieved by the 4th R.W.F. (71st Brigade), moved to a concentration area just west of Rethem, preparatory to another attack on that place.

The operation began at 3 p.m. on the 11th April when 24 typhoons attacked Rethem very effectively. The advance progressed well to start with, but was held up by heavy Spandau and S.P. fire some 200 yards South of the railway. The attack was renewed, but the Monmouths could make no headway. The village was now burning fiercely, but the enemy (2nd Battalion of the 5th Marine Regiment) could not be dislodged. It was therefore decided to discontinue the attack and Brigadier Coleman issued orders to that effect. The German garrison had put up a most stubborn and gallant resistance.

Rethem, with its good road communications and the river bridge there, was essential to the further advance of the XII Corps; but it was now decided to cross the Aller elsewhere and outflank the place.

Plans were therefore made to establish a bridgehead opposite Westen and for the 71st Brigade to pass through, move south and cut off the enemy from the North and East. The 160th Brigade would then make another assault on the town. However, these plans were overtaken by events. A tank reconnaissance on the 13th April indicated that the enemy had abandoned Rethem and at mid-day the 2nd Monmouths moved in. There was some opposition, but it was slight and the Battalion collected about 120 prisoners.

Before these events – in the early hours of the 12th the East Lancashire's (158th Brigade) had begun an assault crossing at Westen. An officer and 12 other ranks were drowned in the swift current when a boat overturned, but by 8 a.m. a bridgehead had been gained. The enemy consisted of Hungarian troops who were only too pleased to surrender to the British. With some difficulty a bridge was constructed and by the late afternoon the whole Brigade was across the Aller. Meanwhile the 4th Welch (160th Brigade), with tank assistance, cleared the villages to the west of the Aller and north of Westen.

The 71st Brigade was now given the task of crossing the river and opening the road Rethem-Walsrode, the latter a town about 10 miles to the East. Led by A Squadron 53rd Reconnaissance Regiment, the Brigade crossed the river in the order 1st Oxford and Bucks, 1st H.L.I., 4th R.W.F., and moved along the road leading South-East.

By 2 A.M. on the 13th the Oxford and Bucks had captured Gross Hauslingen and the H.L.I. Kl. Hauslingen. At 7.30 A.M. the 4th R.W.F. passed through to attack Altenwahlingen, but met with considerable opposition which delayed the advance for some time, and it was not until 11.15 P.M. that the Battalion had secured its objective. The country was open and intersected with water obstacles, and the enemy opposing all three Battalions put up a very creditable resistance. By 1.30 A.M. on the 14th the 1st H.L.I. had moved forward and established themselves on the high ground astride the road on the left of the R.W.F.

At about 10.30 P.M. on the 13th the enemy, in about Battalion strength, counter-attacked on the 158th Brigade front. The attack fell mostly on C Squadron of the Reconnaissance Regiment and the 7th R.W.F. and was repulsed after sharp, and somewhat confused, fighting.

At first light on the 14th – shortly after the H.L.I. had moved forward – another enemy counter-attack, directed from the North-East, was put in against the 71st Brigade. This was a more serious affair and for some three hours a confused battle raged along the Otersen-Altenwahlingen road. The Headquarters of both the H.L.I. and Oxford and Bucks came under close range small arms fire and Brigadier Elrington, who was in Gross Hauslingen with the Oxford and Bucks, was cut off for a time until rescued by some Armoured Cars of the Reconnaissance Regiment. By 9 A.M. the enemy had been overcome; 129 Germans were killed, 79 wounded and 163 taken prisoner – mostly from the 1st and 2nd Battalions of the Marine Regiment.

It will be as well here to explain the plans prepared by Lieut.-General Ritchie for the further advance of the XII Corps.

By about the evening of the 10th April it had become apparent that the capture of Bremen would be a tough job, and not one suited to an Armoured Division. It was, therefore, decided to bring the 3rd Division into the XII Corps to relieve the 7th Armoured Division South of Bremen. The task of outflanking the City from the East would be assigned to the 3rd and 52nd (Lowland) Divisions, whilst the 7th Armoured Division concentrated around Nienburg preparatory to taking part in an armoured drive to Harburg on the Elbe, just South of Hamburg. The 53rd (Welsh) Division, with the 4th Armoured Brigade was to push north and capture Verden (on the Aller, just south of the junction of the Aller and Weser). It was then to move north to cut Bremen's communications with the east.

During the period 14th to 17th April the 6th R.W.F. (160th Brigade), mounted in "Kangaroos", were under the 4th Armoured Brigade in a clearing operation beginning at Rethem in the South and moving North to Scharnhorst about 3 miles North-East of Verden. This was an exhilarating experience in what the Battalion described as "Swanning with the Greys". They had a hand in the capture of Kirchboitzen, Vethem, Bendingbostel, Scharnhorst and other villages. Many prisoners were taken.

By the 16th the whole Division was moving north, and on the 17th the 71st Brigade captured Verden – the day on which The Greys and 6th R.W.F. entered Scharnhorst. Meanwhile the 156th Brigade, of the 52nd (Lowland) Division, had come under command and at about 4 P.M. orders for the following day were issued. These were as follows:

4th Armoured Brigade to advance on Rotenburg.

The 71st Brigade to clear north of Verden so as to allow the 156th Brigade to pass through towards Achim on the road to Bremen. The 158th to move on Rotenburg in the wake of the 4th Armoured Brigade in order to free the latter for operations against Bremen after the capture of Rotenburg. The 160th Brigade to be prepared to move east to the Soltau pocket under command of the 7th Armoured Division – the 6th R.W.F. returning to the 160th from the 4th Armoured Brigade.

Operations on the 18th April went as planned.

The 1st Oxford and Bucks (71st Brigade) captured Dauelson against slight resistance and by 10 A.M. the 156th Brigade had passed through along the main road North of the Weser towards Bremen.

On the 19th the 4th Armoured Brigade (less the 3/4th C.L.Y. which came under the 158th Brigade) passed to command of the 52nd (Lowland) Division as did its 156th Brigade – for the assault on Bremen. The 158th Brigade took over the area south of Rotenburg. On the same day the 160th Brigade left to join the 7th Armoured Division.

Meanwhile the Guards Armoured Division (now under XII Corps) who had penetrated to an area east of the 53rd Division had been heavily counter attacked on Visselhovede and it was decided to clear that area. On the 20th April the 158th Brigade advanced from the west on Visselhovede and reached the villages of Jeddingen and Witture – a few miles to the west of the town. Resistance was stiff at times. On the same morning the 71st Brigade was switched to take over from the 32nd Guards Brigade in the Visselhovede area. Patrolling west they linked up with troops of the 158th Brigade that evening.

At this stage it will be well to pause in the narrative of the 53rd Division to give a brief summary of the general situation, as it was on the 19th April 1945 – taking the Western front from south to north.

The French First Army (De Lattre de Tassigny) had occupied Kehl and Stuttgart. The Seventh U.S. Army (Patch) was moving on the Upper Danube, via Wingburg. The Third U.S. Army (Patton) was driving on Dresden, where it was expected to join up with Russian troops under Koniev. The First U.S. Army (Hodges) had surrounded Leipzig. The Ninth U.S. Army (Simpson) had won a passage over the Elbe South of Magdeburg. The Second British Army (Dempsey), as already described, was closing in on Bremen and advancing to the Elbe and Hamburg. The First, Canadian Army (Crerar) was moving on Amsterdam in the process of clearing all Holland.

To the east the Russians had cleared East Prussia and Pomerania, captured Vienna and were beginning their final thrust to the middle Oder and Berlin.

The German armies were crumbling everywhere. There was now no coordinated defence; but improvised battle groups, varying in strength from a Brigade to a Platoon, were fighting with skill and courage and, as we have seen, they were still capable of staging well-coordinated and determined counter attacks.

Hitler, from his underground Headquarters in Berlin, was spending his last days (News of Hitler's death was received on the 2nd May. Mussolini was assassinated on the 28th April) in issuing directions to Armies which had already disintegrated, in a vain effort to stem the Allied advances from east and west.

British troops were in great heart, and operating at a high tempo, in what all realized were the closing days of the war.

In the XII Corps area operations were extremely fluid and units were collecting prisoners, sometimes complete units, sometimes mere stragglers, in increasing numbers. Nevertheless, resistance was still being offered and the garrisons of some of the larger villages and towns often fought with great courage. It was never safe to rely on an easy victory.

These were the conditions in which operations were carried out during the last fortnight of the war in the West.

The 21st April was spent in clearing and mopping up the area between the XXX Corps on the left and the Guards Armoured Division on the right, in other words the area roughly between Rotenburg in the North and Visselhovede in the South. By nightfall the task was virtually completed and some 700 prisoners had been taken.

The next operation planned by XII Corps was an advance by the 53rd (Welsh) Division on the left and the Guards Armoured Division on the right in a North-Westerly direction to cut the autobahn between Hamburg and Bremen at a point about Elsdorf. The Divisional task was given to the 71st Brigade and the 53rd Reconnaissance Regiment, while the 158th Brigade took over from the 71st in the Rotenburg area.

The advance began on the 23rd with the Reconnaissance Regiment leading and the Brigade behind deployed on a three Battalion front. Progress was slow but steady. There were large groups of enemy, supported by artillery in the woods North-West of Rotenburg who shelled the Brigade very accurately as it advanced. It was whilst directing these operations that Brigadier Elrington's jeep was blown up by a mine. He died shortly afterwards, mourned by the whole Division and not least by the fighting soldiers of the 71st Brigade who knew him so well. He was one of many senior officers in the Division, and in other Divisions, who met their death in this way, and those who did not fight in Europe in 1944-45 may well ask why there were so many casualties of this kind. The explanation is to be found in the very fluid nature of operations against an enemy who laid mines lavishly during his retreat. Senior commanders made a practice of pushing well forward to reconnoitre the country ahead. This necessitated passing columns on the move and often drove them on to the verges of main roads which had not been properly cleared of mines, or tempted them to make diversions up side roads, or across country, where undetected minefields existed. As they usually travelled in jeeps, or similar light vehicles, accidents of this sort nearly always proved fatal.

Lieut.-Colonel J. M. Hanmer, 4th R.W.F., took over command of the Brigade pending the arrival of Brigadier C. L. Firbank, D.S.O., from the 3rd Division, on the following day.

On the 24th April the 160th Brigade, who had been operating with the 7th Armoured Division in the Soltau area, again came under command of the Division. There they had been engaged in mopping up parties of the enemy in the woods uncomfortably near Tactical Headquarters of 21st Army Group and Second Army which had moved to Saltau. During these operations the Brigade took about 5,000 prisoners at very small cost.

On the 25th the 71st Brigade made good progress, reaching the Hamburg-Bremen autobahn and, with the help of "Typhoon" air support, captured the villages of Gyhum, Bockel and Wehldorf.

The 160th Brigade, who had come up on the right of the 158th on their return to the Division, met with stiffer opposition. The 2nd Monmouths fought their way through the woods North-West of Rotenburg but by daylight on the 26th the enemy, holding the line of the waterway North West of the town, had withdrawn. The 4th Welch then crossed by a damaged bridge, swung west and occupied the villages of Betersen and Waffensen.

At about mid-day on the 26th orders were issued for a final drive due West towards Bremen by the 53rd (Welsh) Division (left) and the Guards Armoured Division (right), whilst the 52nd (Lowland) Division assaulted the city.

On this day the 2nd Bn. The South Wales Borderers joined the Division (158th Brigade) from the 49th Division and the 7th R.W.F. left to take their place in the 49th. However good the reasons for changes of this kind may be they are rarely popular with the units concerned. For the Welsh Division it was sad to lose the 7th Royal Welch Fusiliers who had fought so gallantly since the early days in the Normandy beachhead.

German resistance in Bremen collapsed before the move West had got going and then at 6 A.M. on the 27th April the Division was ordered to halt and stand its ground.

By the 28th the 51st (Highland) Division had passed across the Divisional front en route for the Elbe. With the fall of Bremen operations west of the Elbe virtually ceased, except for mopping up isolated parties offering resistance and the collection of stragglers who had ceased to fight.

The Division was now to move piecemeal to the Elbe. On the night of the 29/30th April the 160th Brigade relieved part of the 11th Armoured Division on the Elbe about Winsen.

The 15th (Scottish) Division had carried out an assault crossing of the Elbe on the 29th April and on the 2nd May the Division began passing through the bridgehead. On the 3rd the Germans surrendered Hamburg and declared it an open city. The population had been ordered to remain indoors. The 7th Armoured Division had already entered Hamburg and the 53rd (Welsh) Division was ordered to relieve it and assume responsibility for the town.

At dawn on the 4th May 1945 the 53rd (Welsh) Division began to enter Germany's largest Port and second city. The entry and occupation were without incident and by breakfast time troops of the Division were on the bridge over the Alster in the heart of the city. The heavily-bombed town presented a gaunt appearance. The only Germans to be seen were the civil police who were posted at intervals of about 100 yards on either side of the road.

This was the end.

Hitler and Mussolini were dead.

On the 1st May troops of the British 21st Army Group had joined up with Russian troops between Lubeck and Rostock.

On the 2nd May Marshal Zhukov's Second White Russian Army Group entered Berlin, and on the same day all German forces in Italy surrendered to Field Marshal Sir Harold Alexander.

On the 4th May all enemy forces in North Germany were surrendered to Field Marshal Sir Bernard Montgomery at his Tactical Headquarters on Luneburg Heath.

On the 7th May 1945 all German Forces by sea, land and air surrendered unconditionally to the Allies.

The great German war machine, which a few years before seemed so formidable, had disintegrated and Hitler's Germany was in ruins. Except for a few territories in Asia and some islands in the Pacific, still held by a tottering Japan, the Allies were now undisputed masters of the World.

The 53rd (Welsh) Division could look back on the war years with satisfaction and pride. They had to wait nearly five years before going into action; but the long and thorough training in the United Kingdom was not wasted time. Its value was seen in a series of battles and engagements which, in a period of ten months of almost continuous fighting, carried them from Normandy to the Elbe.

My father's diary ends with these words:

"We spent the next week or so operating in the Soltau area. On the 24th we were to advance to try an attack and cut the Bremen-Hamburg autobahn at a point near Elsdorf. For a while we met stiff opposition, and then we were to turn West and advance on Bremen. However, resistance in Bremen collapsed, so we halted. On the night of 29th/30th April, the Brigade relieved 11th Armoured on the Elbe

near Winsen. On the 2ⁿᵈ May, we began passing through a bridgehead created across the Elbe by the 15ᵗʰ Scottish Div. The Division began to enter at dawn on the 4ᵗʰ May. Our particular billet area was in HARBURG which was a suburb of Hamburg, situated on the South of the Elbe.

On the 4ᵗʰ May 1945, all enemy forces in North Germany were surrendered to Field Marshal Sir Bernard Montgomery on Luneburg Heath!!!!

The Welsh Division enjoyed a series of uninterrupted successes. They never lost a battle or failed in any major task entrusted to them."

APPENDIX I

The following extract is taken from the Daily Herald, 12th March 1945. Article written by Victor Thompson.

They Fought Non-Stop for a Month

They are sitting in the ruins of a German village trying to bask in the reluctant March sunshine. They are shaved and their boots are clean. They have a large hot meal inside them, a great content in their minds.

They come from the Fifty-Third (Welsh) Division. If you have not heard of it and its notable deeds, that is entirely because security has cautiously hidden its identity much longer than I think is necessary.

Out here, however the Fifty-Third is spoken of with deep respect, especially by the German paratroopers, the cream of the German Army, who it has recently beaten.

Glory and Death

And today, the ban being lifted, I can at last reveal that of all the tough fighting on the British and Canadian sector between the Maas and the Rhine, the most sustained was endured by the Fifty-Third Welsh.

And if we are to get the matter quite straight it must be said that English Regiments are well represented in that division.

Other divisions were put in and did their task and were pulled out. There was plenty of glory – and of pain and death – for all. But the Welsh went in on the first day and stayed until the last, and from what I saw of them during that terrible month I know that no troops fought more gamely anywhere.

They went into action on the grey morning of February 8th with their ears deafened by our mighty barrage. They went straight into the grim

Reichswald forest, and they knew already that the armour which might have made their task easier was bogged down, and that the aircraft which would have made it easier still were grounded in the mists.

Forty men were wounded in the first clash. Men of the Field Ambulance hand-carried the wounded, because the only available road was Chewing Gum Alley, a clinging morass that all of us who ever trod it will ever remember with loathing.

Meanwhile, the men of the 53rd were plunging ever deeper into the fortified forest – into the mud, into the enemy – and the Sappers kept a way to them open through the mud bath. Amphibious ducks and weasels were aiding them by taking up supplies and taking out the wounded through the floods to the north, and the front-liners slogged ahead deeper and deeper into the enemy's forest defences, fighting sometimes from tree to tree, halted often, but going back never.

Corporals as C.O.s

Sometimes battalions were temporarily out of touch, sometimes corporals became commanding officers because all the officers were killed or wounded.

The artillery thunder by day and night was such as to make sleep impossible. Even when the Welsh finally burst out of the woods into the daylight again and had their first brief rest of less than a day, they were only 100 yards away from where the shells were dropping.

They went on to Goch and finished the task that others had begun. I saw them there and although the paratroop opposition was still tough they were almost elated because they were out of the forest, out of Chewing Gum Alley. They said to me "Don't call us the Fifty-Third Welsh any more, call us the Fifty-Third Woodland."

Here is what Private A. Williams of Ynysybwl, South Wales, told of the capture of a German Colonel and his men:

'As I came up to search him for weapons', he said, 'he must have thought I looked threatening, because he said, "Are you an English gentleman?" I said, – of course I am – and a Welsh one too!'

Those Road Mines

There, too, Lieutenant A. Cowan of 16 Scotsman Road, Toller-lane, Bradford talked of the huge problems facing the Sappers.

In one stretch of two miles, he said, Jerry had blown the road in seven places. The craters were huge, and there were more prepared charges which had failed to explode and which we gingerly had to remove.

These charges were comprised of a hundred pounds of TNT, six feet underground, with a layer of shells on top of that and a layer of mines on top of that again. Still we managed to get the road open and keep it working.

They were still at it on St. David's Day, the day for the Welsh. Some of them found leeks and wore them and went into action and died. The Scots alongside them saluted their comrades' day with bagpipes.

There were house-to-house fighting and counter-attacks. The paratroopers fought frantically, but they had always finally to give best to the hard fighting 53rd.

One German soldier came in to surrender, and said if we would let him go back he would bring 200 of his comrades. We took a chance. He returned with 20 others. He was told that was not enough. He went back again and came back with another 40.

Not many Germans surrendered however. Most of them fought in a way which we should describe as heroic if it had been on our side, but which, since it happened against us, is usually described as fanatical. Anyway, it was fierce – almost as fierce as the way the Welsh fought.

40 Miles of It

They made the first contact with the American spearhead probing up from the Ninth Army Front, and it was right that they should have that honour. They had certainly paid for it with many dead and wounded.

They went on and on and it is only now, with the Rhine's left bank secured at last, that they are out of the battle.

They have foot-slogged 40 miles in a month. Fighting for every yard. They have fired 1,000,000 rounds of machine-gun ammunition alone. They have had the longest, bitterest sustained fighting of the war, and they are today very, very tired.

And yet, as they sit here in the ruins, drinking interminable mugs of tea, they seem, apart from their weariness, entirely unaffected by their experiences.

Man, it seems, can get used to anything, and always endure a little more. If there is any maximum of endurance, however, then the men of the 53rd who fought in Normandy and in the Ardennes and at 's-Hertogenbosch have surely set it in the Rhineland.

APPENDIX II

*T*he following extract is taken from the final chapter of 'History of the South Wales Borderers and the Monmouthshire Regiment, Part III, The Second Battalion The Monmouthshire Regiment', by Lt. Col. G. A. Brett, DSO, OBE, MC.

The Gunners

No story of the 2nd Monmouths would be complete without a tribute to the gunners who supported them in every action. 497 Battery (Panteg) of 133rd Field Regiment, Royal Artillery, was affiliated to the Battalion, and training in Ireland and England had brought the units into the closest companionship, which was cemented by their acting together in nearly forty engagements, great and small. Throughout all these actions the speed and accuracy with which any call for fire was answered bred in the infantry complete confidence that, whatever happened, "the Gunners would compete". And compete they did: often firing concentrations 100 yards in front of the forward platoons, sometimes beating off counter-attacks by skillful and timely defensive fire, and always ready to give the utmost support at any time and in any conditions.

The men serving the guns and bringing the ammunition were in the nature of things not known to the Battalion, but it is due to the Royal Regiment to give the names of those whom the 2nd Monmouths constantly saw in action. With Major R. Hughes, MC, the Battery Commander (known familiarly as "One-five Charlie") were Bdr. Harris, L/Bdr. McNally, Fetter and Wheater and Gnr. Young. With Captain D. Thomson, later relieved by Capt. D. Bishop, DCM were Bdr. Jopling and Gnr. McGeoch. Others were Sgt. Passmore, Bdr. Rush, Sgt. Simpson, Gnr. Lister and Bdr. Dickson who was killed in action near Goch. To all of them and to those at the guns, the battalion now says: "Thank You."

A letter from Major H. J. Jourdain, MC, commander of "B" Company sent to Major R. Hughes MC on May 8th 1945 reads as follows:

"To: Officer Commanding 497 Battery, 133 Field Regiment RA.
From: O.C. B Coy. 2nd Bn. The Monmouthshire Regiment.

Now that happier times have come I would like to send you on behalf of the officers, N.C.O.s and men of my Coy. our heartfelt thanks for the Artillery support which we have had from 497 Battery through this long campaign. Whenever or wherever we have asked for fire support, it has been forthcoming, and more than that, it has been provided before we dreamt we should need it.

Normandy, Voorheide, the Ardennes, the Reichswald, Rethem and others are names which recall so much to us all. In all of them the faithful 497 backed us up until our "Artillery Support" became taken for granted. We know what hard work was entailed and are profoundly grateful for it.

You will no doubt receive many tributes of congratulation. This is one from a Rifle Company, which has had cause to need your support so often. I am sure that no unit has ever had such efficient backing as we have had.

Good luck to you all in the future, and thank you.

Harburg
8th May 1945
(Signed H. J. Jourdain, Major)
VE Day
O.C. B Coy. 2nd Bn. Mons Regiment

53rd (Welsh) Division Honours and Awards	
V.C.	1
D.S.O.s	28
M.C.s	124
D.C.M.s	24
M.M.s	175

Total Ammunition Issues			
Small Arms		Mortars	
Mk. VIIIZ	6,179,400	3-in. mortar H.E.	176,854
.303 Ctn.	3,786,656	4.2-in. mortar H.E.	96,250
.303 Bdr.	3,582,992	2-in. mortar H.E.	52,494
9 mm Sten	2,935,700	2-in. mortar SMK	37,278
.303 Tracer	712,620	3-in. mortar SMK	18,596
.303 Incendiary	289,536	3-in. mortar Ill.	18,216
P.I.A.T. H.E.	20,340	2-in. mortar Ill.	18,126
		4.2-in. mortar SMK	3,416

Guns		Mines and Grenades	
25-pdr. H.E.	1,318,793	36 grenades	45,012
25-pdr. SMK	94,629	75 grenades	36,492
25-pdr. super carts	59,743	77 grenades	26,778
40 mm	49,168	Mines, A./Tank, Mk. V	11,455
6-pdr. A.P.C.B.C	10,088		
6-pdr. S.A.B.O.T.	3,906		
17-pdr. A.P.C.B.C.	3,154		

XXI Army Group fired over 1.3 million rounds of 25 pdr. shells during Operation Overlord.

53rd (Welsh) Division, Summary of Casualties during Operation "Overlord"

Period	Killed		Wounded		Missing		Missing / Rejoined	
	Officers	O.R.	Officers	O.R.	Officers	O.R.	Officers	O.R.
29 June – 12 July	12	89	24	496	4	28	-	18
13 July – 26 July	20	180	51	830	13	332	-	124
27 July – 9 Aug	6	75	19	350	–	23	1	44
10 Aug – 23 Aug	12	178	43	821	3	86	1	50
24 Aug – 6 Sep	2	37	9	83	1	21	-	–
7 Sep – 20 Sep	6	18	22	480	3	116	–	24
21 Sep – 4 Oct	4	30	8	248	–	62	–	25
5 Oct – 18 Oct	5	65	14	510	–	14	–	5
19 Oct – 1 Nov	3	45	20	250	2	73	–	5
2 Nov – 15 Nov	3	33	3	178	2	14	–	10
16 Nov – 29 Nov	–	16	4	98	–	6	–	4
30 Nov – 13 Dec	1	5	3	48	–	3	–	1
14 Dec – 27 Dec	4	7	7	70	–	4	–	1
28 Dec – 10 Jan	3	35	16	154	–	15	–	78
11 Jan – 24 Jan	–	1	–	–	–	-	–	3
25 Jan – 7 Feb	5	130	31	661	–	83	–	50
8 Feb – 21 Feb	10	146	36	660	–	70	–	24
22 Feb – 7 Mar	2	60	10	201	–	34	–	24
8 Mar – 21 Mar	1	48	14	180	–	45	–	10
22 Mar – 4 Apr	7	132	34	591	5	202	1	27
5 Apr – 18 Apr	3	33	9	150	–	11	–	11
19 Apr – 4 May	4	33	10	162	–	13	–	15
Totals	**113**	**1396**	**387**	**7221**	**33**	**1255**	**3**	**553**

Total casualties (killed, wounded and missing) in XXI Army Group during operation Overlord was 143,984.